The
Grief Club

The Grief Club

The Secret to Getting Through All Kinds of Change

MELODY BEATTIE

Hazelden
Center City, Minnesota 55012-0176

1-800-328-0094
1-651-213-4590 (Fax)
www.hazelden.org

ISBN-13: 978-1-59285-349-6
ISBN-10: 1-59285-349-8

Editor's note

This book includes the author's personal accounts of dealing with loss and grief, as well as others' true stories. All personal stories that appear in this book have been used with permission. In some cases, names, dates, and circumstances have been changed to protect anonymity, but many individuals have requested that their real names be used.

This book is for educational purposes. It is not intended to replace medical advice. This publication is intended to provide authoritative and accurate information, and it is up-to-date and timely as of its date of publication; however, it is not meant to replace the services of a trained professional, physician, support group, or recovery group. This book is sold with the understanding that the publisher and author are not rendering individual psychological or medical services, or individual services of any kind, to the reader. Should such services be necessary, please consult an appropriate professional.

26 25 24 23 22   9 10 11 12 13

Cover design by David Spohn
Interior design by David Spohn
Typesetting by Tursso Companies

This book is for *Us*.

Contents

Acknowledgments

For your help, support, and guidance I acknowledge and thank:

God; Shane, Nichole, Michael, and the boys (Julian and Maceo); Michael Bodine (for continually keeping me in contact with the True Storytellers); John, Jeanette, and family (Brandon and Courtney); Jeanne, Bob, and family; brother Jimmy, Pam, and family; Mom, Dad, Joanne, and all the family and ancestors including Great-Grandma Annie; David Zempel and Patty (thanks for being back in my life); Dr. Forest Tennant (for making normal life possible); Dr. Hank Golden, whose dedication to healing has brought me back one more time; Dr. Randy Harris; Dr. Willem Zeegers and the Alpha Klink (for a new spine); Dr. William O'Brien and Dr. Ron Benbassot; Lloyd Wright; Christopher Pierce; Mark Mintzer and Global Patient Network; Isaac Shachory; Faith Heinemann (for generously sharing her experience); Becky (for the patience of several saints); Lori Yearwood (for research and her story) and her dad, Vernon; Andy Delk; Howard Wills; Stephanie and family; Ginny and Chuck Miller; May; Tom Greenly; Kate Somerville; David Beattie; Steve and Scott; Peg; all the people who anonymously shared their stories with me—you know who you are, and I am deeply grateful for your generosity; Dr. Frank Ryan (lots of docs keeping this body going); Marcie New and Josh; Stacey Peasley and her dad, John; Dr. Jennifer Schneider; Ruth Anderson—my first counselor who believed there was a human being underneath the addictions when nobody else in the world did; the judge who had enough sense to send me to treatment in 1973; Lorraine and Pat (Gramps) Teel; Chuck Beattie and Allison; Dan Cain, R. S. Eden, the old Eden House, and the Board of Directors; Hazelden staff; Sonja Ray; Sharon Koukkarin, M.S.L.P.; Steph and God's Remedy; Bradley Quick; Cindy, Sharon, and Erica—who keep my life intact when I crawl in a cave and write; C. J.; all the Twelve Step programs, because when I needed help I didn't have any money, and they're free; and all the seen and unseen angels in my life. Many of you are living people. If I've overlooked or forgotten anyone, know you're not forgotten in my heart—nothing is accomplished alone. I deliberately left out the names of many people to protect their anonymity. You know who you are and how much I love and respect you.

Welcome to the Club

The doctors walk into the room, a room quiet except for the whoosh-ing sound coming from the machines forcing air into my twelve-year-old son's lungs. "It's an illusion," a doctor says. "He's not alive. His brain died days ago. Your son is gone."

"There's hope," I say.

"No, there isn't," the doctors say back.

You're wrong, I think. *There's always hope—isn't there?* At least there was until now.

"You've got until one o'clock this morning to say your good-byes," another doctor, a woman, says. "Then we're shutting down the machines."

Conversation over. No options are offered to me. I go into the fam-ily room created for the people doing vigil with my daughter, my ex-husband, and me. I pick up the Bible. *I'll read where the pages open,* I think. *I'll get a sign. I've gotten messages that way before.* The pages fall open in my hands. I read under my thumb. It's the story of how Jesus brings Lazarus back from the dead. Even if I won't admit it, I know the truth. This isn't a sign. It might mean something, but I don't know what it is.

I go back into the intensive-care room. People filter in to tell Shane good-bye. When they finish, I hold Shane in my arms. He's covered with bandages, hooked up to tubes. A nurse turns off the machines. The whooshing noise stops. I hear one faint sound. It's Shane exhaling his last breath. A nurse rests her hand on my shoulder. "It's going to take a long time. Eight years at least," she said. "It's going to be hard, but you'll get through it. I know. My daughter died when she was nine."

All I can think is, *I don't want to be like her—have a dead child. I don't want to go through this. Somebody made a mistake.*

It takes years to understand the meaning of that brief conversation: I had been welcomed to the club.

It wasn't the first club I unwillingly joined.

The man is tall, gaunt with a long, thin face. He used to drink too much. That's why his wife left, he lost his job, his car broke down, and his dog bit him. Then he joined AA (Alcoholics Anonymous). When he stopped drinking, his wife came home, he found a different job, bought a new car. His dog stopped biting him and licked his hand instead. With all the differences between this gaunt man and me, the first time I heard him tell his story, I found something we had in common. He never liked himself, didn't feel like he belonged. That's why he started drinking too much—alcohol eased the pain of being alive. Then his buddy alcohol turned on him. It destroyed his life. When he tried to quit drinking, he couldn't stop. The AA program and a Higher Power did for him what he couldn't do for himself. Now he stands by the door when I walk into the sparsely furnished room—twenty metal folding chairs piled around three chipped Formica tables. "Welcome," he says. "I'm glad you're here."

I'm not glad I'm there, but I don't have anywhere else to go. The gratitude comes later, when the program changes my life.

Fast-forward eight years. I walk into another room. This one is filled mostly with women. I see only two men. A long table is spread with cookies, lemon bars, steaming pots of coffee, hot water for tea. A perky woman runs up to me. "Welcome to Al-Anon," she says. I step backward.

"I'm not an Al-Anon," I say. "I'm a recovering addict."

"Oh, that's great!" she gushes. "You're in AA *and* Al-Anon. You're a double winner."

I don't feel like I've won anything, much less two things. My husband drinks. I've been clean and sober our entire marriage and I'm the one who has to go to meetings and get help? Go figure. I sit down at the table. I listen to people tell stories about how much being married to an alcoholic hurts, how crazy we get when we love someone who drinks, and what we can do to help ourselves instead of obsessively trying to fix the alcoholic and letting him make us insane. I've been avoiding feelings for so long I forgot I had any. Now emotions flood me. Yeah, it really does hurt to watch alcohol destroy our love. That's all I wanted—a family. A husband and kids. Was that asking too much? For the first time in years, I cry. Crying is the miracle that begins my healing. I feel my own feelings instead of trying to fix, help, blame, control, or wish I was dead.

Al-Anon didn't save my marriage. It saved me.

Most of us find ourselves joining clubs whether we want to or not. Someone dies and we join the *You Weren't Supposed to Go Away and My Heart Is Broken* Club. Or the phone rings and we're thrust into the *Why Do I Have Cancer?* Club. Or we call our mom and she doesn't recognize our voice. When we say our name, she becomes more confused. "*Who is this?*" she asks. At first we joke about it, say things like, "I'd tell you to make a list so you don't forget, but you'd probably forget where you put the list." Then we realize it's not funny. The person we love is in there someplace, but we can't find her anymore. A stranger has taken over. We belong to the *Somebody I Love Has Alzheimer's Disease and We're Saying a Long Good-Bye* Club.

Then comes the day we look in the mirror or someone shows us a picture of ourselves, and we reel in shock. Do we really look like that? We're members of the *I Still Feel Young but I'm Getting Old* Club. We're not sure if we should get a face-lift, have a noninvasive procedure, or let ourselves wrinkle up. Sometimes the clubs sneak up on us. One day we realize we're spending more time in doctors' offices than we are hanging out with friends. Somewhere along the way, we've joined the *I've Got a Chronic Illness* Club. There are the *I'm a Financially Broken Man (or Woman)* and the *Empty Nester* clubs. The list goes on. Then there's the last club we'll join, the *My Time Is Running Out and I'm Going to Die*

Club. The lucky ones are the ones who've consciously joined clubs before then. We know how it goes: initiation, transition, then we're changed. The luckiest ones know death isn't an ending; it's a transformation too.

Some of the clubs are formal. Some aren't. We meet people one at a time going through the same experience as we are. When a problem first appears, we think we're the only one who has it. We feel alone. Before long, it looks like there's an epidemic going on. We wait for life to be like it was, then one day we get it: Life as we know it is gone. It's never going to be the same again.

After my son died, I sat in my office surrounded by books about grief. Some were books people had given me because they wanted to help. Other books I bought. I'd open a book, start to read it, then either put it on my library shelf or hurl it across the room. It's not that the books aren't good. Many are important and well written. The books didn't help me. Not one book led me to believe that this process I was in was a mysterious, transformational one. I couldn't find anyone to tell me each minute, whatever I experience is a valid, beautiful moment—however tragic it is. That's what I needed to hear: *Grief is a sacred time in our lives, and an important one.*

What helped me most were two things. One was reading stories about life after death, because that gave me the feeling that my son was okay. When you love somebody, it's important to know where and how that person is.

The second thing that helped was stories—hearing honest accounts about how people felt, what they went through, and what helped them, not contrived stories saying how they thought they were supposed to feel and what they thought they should do. I promised myself then that if I ever came out the other end of this tunnel, I'd write a book about grief that I wouldn't have tossed across the room. At the time of writing this book, it's been more than fifteen years since Shane died. Only recently have I felt I have anything valuable to say.

This is a book of stories about people going through many different losses. Writing this book held several surprises. I was *amazed* at how eager people were to share their stories with me. I thought people would be reluctant to talk about painful parts of their lives. Early on I saw that wasn't true. People wanted to talk, and they wanted me to listen. They wanted to know their pain counts and what they went through can do some good. Telling our story to people who listen and care is a powerful, healing thing to do.

Something else that surprised me is that many people insisted I use their names. I disguised some people's identities to protect their privacy. No stories are composites. I've changed names, ages, places of residence, and certain details so you can't recognize some people. Even if you think you know the people I've disguised, you don't. No experiences have been exaggerated. I haven't altered important facts. If anything has been changed, it's similar to what it replaced. My name is on the book's cover, but to all the people who shared their stories goes a warm thank-you. This book belongs to us.

I chose common loss experiences, a different one for each chapter. In each chapter, I also include secrets or milestones that apply to *anyone* and to *any* kind of loss. So even if the loss in a chapter doesn't have anything to do with your life, the secrets in the chapter are universal and likely will apply to whatever changes you're going through. You can search out the chapter that has a loss like yours, but don't miss the milestones in the other stories too.

I'm not approaching grief from the classic five stages of denial, anger, bargaining, sadness, and acceptance. Elisabeth Kübler-Ross has written books about that. These stages are valid and worked into the stories. I'm looking at grief as a transformational process. The book is about getting through the time that starts when something happens that turns our world upside down and we lose our old normal, until the new normal begins.

Some people think I'm an expert on codependency, but if I'm an expert at anything, it's how to take care of ourselves when we're going through grief. I'm not writing this book to tell you to do it my way. If you're going through pain, you either already are or soon will be an expert too. My hope is that this book will help you find comfort in your life and the circumstances taking place right now. I want to give you confidence that you'll be guided, led, and able to figure out what to do.

At the end of each chapter, I've included activities. Some have to do with the loss covered in that chapter. Some have to do with the secrets I've touched on in the story. You'll probably find activities in each chapter that apply to you even if you aren't going through that chapter's loss. Some activities are basic, such as teaching how to write comfort letters to people going through grief or how to be more nurturing to people in pain (including ourselves). You don't need to do all the activities for each chapter; that would be too much. I've given enough different activities for each chapter that you're likely to find at least one that works for you. I do suggest that you do the first activity in this book—the Master List of Losses. Another important activity is the list of What's Left. It's the third activity in chapter 12, "Facing Change." Other than those two activities, use your judgment about which ones to do. Sometimes the activity that might be most helpful is the one that makes us groan when we read it. We think, *Oh, I don't want to do that*, but often what we resist is what we need most. Other times we'll be drawn to an activity. We'll look at it and think, *That would be interesting*. Anyway, you choose.

You don't have to be in raw grief to benefit from this book. The stories and activities will work on old loss too. I've included statistics and information at the end of each chapter about aspects of that story. Some of these statistics may surprise you; some stunned me. I've included references: national phone numbers and Web site addresses for information, help, and support. I can't guarantee how long they'll be accurate. I don't include footnotes, but the thinking in this book is based on and backed up by other books, experts, and authorities. I've either attributed sources within the text or listed references in the bibliography.

Choosing which losses to cover was difficult. We encounter so many problems. Everyone and everything we have will eventually pass away. There are enough losses and problems to write volumes. I hope the secrets, tips, and activities will help you whether I've touched on your loss or not.

Of the thirteen books I've written, I expected this to be the most painful yet. Surprised again. Of all the books I've written, this one brought me the most joy. The people, the stories, the work have given and taught me so much. I'll miss the writing when it's done.

On a radio show, the host asked me to tell the guru story I wrote at the end of the introduction to *Codependent No More*. It's one of my favorite stories. I'll tell it again.

Once upon a time, a woman seeking enlightenment traveled to the mountains in a land far away and found a guru to teach her. "I want to learn everything there is to know," she told him. "I'm not leaving until I do."

The guru led her to a cave, then left her with a stack of books. Each day he returned to check on her. With his walking stick in hand, he hobbled into the cave and asked, "Have you learned everything there is to know?"

"No," she'd say.

When she said that, the guru raised his stick and whacked her on the head.

This scenario repeated itself for years. Each day it was the same. Then one day the guru entered the cave, asked the same question, heard the same answer. But this time, when the guru raised his cane, the woman reached up and grabbed the stick. She stopped his assault in midair.

She expected to be scolded. This was her turn to be surprised. The guru smiled. "Congratulations," he said. "You've graduated. You've learned everything you *need* to know. You've learned you'll never learn all there is to know and you've learned how to stop the pain."

One of my teachers told me this story. One of his teachers taught it to him. It summed up the theme of *Codependent No More—stop controlling other people and start taking care of ourselves*. Although I've written many books since then, this book picks up where that one left off. But this is more than a follow-up or upgrade.

A woman I barely knew was talking to me about the pain I experienced after my son's death. I was telling her that the first year hurt, the second year hurt more, and year three hurt too. She listened to my story, then tried to explain away my feelings.

"Isn't that codependency, this prolonged grief thing you're in?" she said. "Aren't you just feeling sorry for yourself? Maybe you need to read your own books? Let go?"

I wanted to bite off her head. I bit my tongue instead. I know—and most of the time remember—not to expect people to understand what someone is going through unless they belong to the same club.

"No," I said. "It's more than that."

"Then which stage of grief do you think it is?" she asked.

"It's more than that too," I said.

The more time that passes since writing *Codependent No More*, the more I've come to believe that grief plays a much larger part in co-dependency than I used to think it did. The low self-esteem, the pinched face giving off the miseries, the bitterness that comes from all that pain and guilt. The repression, depression, denial, the whirlwind of chaos we create trying to stop the losses heading our way when we're involved with someone who's in trouble with alcohol, drugs, rage—they all come with codependency, but they also come with grief. So does not wanting people we love to leave.

We can't always put life, people, and our behaviors in a tidy box.

And no matter what the guru in the cave said, sometimes we can't stop the pain.

If you're living the Great American Dream or if you have a problem that you can easily solve and your life soon returns to normal, maybe this book isn't for you. It's not a book about overcoming. In many ways it's not a classic how-to. It's for people in transition, people going through change and loss. It's for people in pain, people who are numb, and people who aren't sure what they're feeling. It's for people who are broken; it's about trusting God and life to put us back together again. It's about radical faith, enough faith to eventually turn to the same God who allowed the disaster to happen—whether a disaster is personal or global—and ask for help finding and fighting our way back to life. It's about knowing that when we're too confused or angry to ask for help, God is guiding us then too.

"I met death and it transformed me," said Maggie, who you will meet later in this book. "It was dark, ugly, and I was alone. I spent two years driving around looking for a building tall enough to jump from and die. I was doing everything people suggested—going to therapy, doing the right things. But nothing helped. Life didn't have meaning anymore," she said. "I lost all hope."

"What happened that triggered all that pain?" I asked. "Was it one thing? Several things happening at once?"

"It was an avalanche," she said.

This isn't a book with a no-pain no-gain theme. It's about that time in our life when what was familiar disappears, we're not who we were, and we're not yet who we're becoming. Our instinctive reaction during times of loss is to try to control things around us. It's normal. We're scared. We don't want any more pain. We want to cut our losses, and we think control keeps us safe. But when we get tired of controlling, there are other things we can do. The stories in this book will show what others have done when their lives got turned upside down. My hope is that you'll be able to see some of yourself in them.

I ended the introduction to *Codependent No More* with the guru story. It seems right to end this introduction with a story like that too. This is a version of a story about a woman who went to a Buddha for help. (I don't know who first told the story. I've read different versions in many books but can't find a source to attribute it to.) Unlike the woman in the guru story, this woman wasn't seeking enlightenment. She wanted help stopping her pain.

"My son died," the woman said to the Buddha. "Please bring him back to life."

The Buddha said yes, he would do that. At the thought of having her son back, the woman's pain began to lift. "But there's something you have to do first," the Buddha said. "Bring me three rocks. Each must come from a person or family who hasn't experienced loss."

The woman went in search of three people who qualified to give her the stones. A long time passed before she returned to the Buddha. When she did, she held out empty hands. "I couldn't find people who could give me the rocks," she said.

"What did you learn?" the Buddha asked.

"I learned we all suffer and lose someone or something we love."

After a loss happens, this journey of learning begins. We learn we're part of—one with—this universal club. We're unique but not as different from others as we think. Coincidentally (or maybe not) it's the path to enlightenment too.

One secret to going through change and grief is this: It's all done with mirrors. If we're alone, we can't see who we are. When we join the club, other people become the mirror. We see ourselves when we look at them. Slowly we accept who we are. By being honest about who we are and how we feel, we'll be a mirror for them too. Seeing us will help them love and accept themselves.

The day will come when we'll welcome others to the club and we'll know we're making peace. I was at the drop zone one day (the place where skydivers jump out of planes). I saw a woman who had just lost her thirty-five-year-old son. He was a skilled skydiver and a Hollywood stuntman. He'd fallen off a ladder and fatally injured his head. I put my hand on her arm. "It's going to take a long time. It's going to be hard. But you'll get through this," I said. "I know. My son died when he was twelve."

One of the darkest places is that place where we don't *get* or understand ourselves, and we think nobody else gets us either. We feel lost and alone. We lose touch with the connection we have to ourselves and each other. It's this connection that keeps us in Grace. When someone *gets* us, when they understand us, we understand ourselves. Then somehow the unacceptable becomes okay. We might not be happy about it—whatever *it* is—but we'll find peace. It's not a clinical description of the process, but what we're talking about here isn't a clinical thing.

It's part of the mystery we'll explore in this book.

I was talking with a new friend I made when I began writing *The Grief Club*. I felt comfortable with him the minute we met. I told him about the struggle I'd been going through ever since the phone rang and the doctor told me I had hepatitis C. "I've spent so much of my life feeling unlovable and untouchable," I said. "Now I'm riddled with this disease? I've worked hard the past two years to learn how to take care of my liver and health. But I've been waiting for this time to be done so I can start living my life. I've been frantically trying to control this, make it go away. I've been obsessed. I horrify myself with visions of dying a torturous death.

"But lately I've been remembering what I learned in the past," I said. "I asked myself, what is my problem? What's the matter? I'm healthy. My liver is in good shape. The hepatitis virus is almost gone. I'm the same person I've always been. This thing about trying to make the problem go away so I can begin living my *real* life is crazy. There hasn't been one single thing that's happened to me that isn't an important part of my path. I'm not dying from hepatitis; I'm living with it. I don't have to wait for anything to happen to be whole. I'm already complete."

"Tell me about it," my friend said. "I went through that whole thing twelve years ago when they told me I had HIV."

That's why I feel so comfortable with him, I thought. *We belong to similar clubs.*

Later that day I was talking to another friend. He asked how I was.

"Great," I said and meant it. "Now that I've finally surrendered to having hepatitis C."

My friend smiled and said (you guessed it), "Welcome to the club."

CHAPTER 1

Initiating Change:
When a Child or Someone We Deeply Love Dies

The man sitting in the reception room at the doctor's office looked so forlorn, staring at the floor. I don't usually talk to strangers, but there was something about this guy. I deliberately moved and sat next to him. "What's your name?" I asked. "What's wrong?"

"I have migraines," he said. "Bad ones. They really hurt." Then his face scrunched and he started to cry. "My daughter died," he said.

That's what's wrong, I thought. The Tibetan monks say there are temples hidden in every city around the world. These temples are in plain view—the best place to hide anything. But only awakened people see them; the temples are hidden to everyone else. That's what I saw in this man: the Temple of Grief.

I touched his arm. "I don't know how you feel, but I know how I felt when my twelve-year-old son died," I said. "It's the worst."

He looked up and into my eyes for the first time in our conversation. "Then you know what it's like," he said, sounding relieved. I know the feeling. He finally found someone who belongs to the *My Child Died and My Heart Is Broken and Nobody Gets It* Club.

I wanted him to know I'm wasn't a "Lookie Lou," someone who gushes and says, "I know how you feel because last year my cat died too." "People generalize," said a bereaved mother. "They compare losing a child to losing a parent. It's not the same."

I asked about his daughter, what happened, how old she was, how long it has been. You don't need to ask how long it has been because when you lose your child, it happened yesterday even if it's been ten years. But there's a difference in stages. Year one—stunned, numb, disbelief. You don't want to be here going through this. Year two—worse. You want to be here even less. Years three, four, and five—you still don't want to be here, but you keep waking up alive. Five through ten—gradually getting better each day. You've learned you can live with a hole in your heart and missing your child so much you think you'll explode. You start wanting to live again. You're on the mend. Besides, someday you'll see your child again. After everything you've been through, you can wait. Also, you've noticed you're happier than most people. Something inside you has changed.

A certain freedom comes with going through the worst. You're not expecting life to make you happy now. Your hand isn't outstretched anymore. You know there's no brass ring. There's only now and that's enough. You make peace with that, with what is. Surprise, surprise. You came out the other end. What began as coping turned into thriving. You found a new way to live.

The man at the doctor's office told me his daughter died in a car accident a year ago, when she was twenty-one. He dug through his wallet and showed me her picture. I say how beautiful she is (because she is), then I listen while he talks. Like him, the first words out of my mouth for years when I met anyone were "My son died." People who haven't lost a child get afraid when we say we lost a child. They change the subject quickly, thinking it's too hard on us to talk, harder for them to listen. What they don't know is that we need to tell our story again even if we've already told it one hundred times before. It makes the unthinkable real. It gives us a sense of control. Telling our story is important, whether we're telling the story of how our marriage went bad, how we stopped drinking, or how our wife or daughter died. It helps if people listen *and* care.

We don't just lose someone we love. We lose a piece of ourselves—sometimes more.

"I feel so lost," the man said. "That's the hardest thing. The feeling has lasted so long. Is it normal to feel as lost as I do?"

I felt lost other times—when I graduated from high school, when I finished treatment for chemical dependency, when I divorced. But I'd never felt as lost as the week my daughter and I stayed at a hotel in downtown St. Paul, Minnesota, the week of my son's birthday. That year it became the week of his death.

Sometimes we get a clue, a hint about what life is really like. We all know a family whose daughter-in-law got cancer, then died a lingering death. She was only twenty-five. Or the family whose son died in a motorcycle accident when he was twenty-three. We tell ourselves, *It's the exception. Happily ever after is the rule. Those horrible things happen to other people but not to us.* We don't want to hear these stories. We don't want to get too close. We can handle hearing about financial troubles or alcoholism. Those kinds of problems are okay. But this angel of death who rips families apart? No thank you. Take your story and get away.

A month or so before Shane died, Nichole came bounding into the house after school. "Guess what we learned today?" she asks. "Did you know that before the end of the year one child we know will die?"

I didn't know that. I also didn't know the child who died would be mine.

Or did I? Sometimes I think part of us knows what's coming—has known for a long time.

I'm standing on the sidewalk, staring up at the roof of our three-story Victorian house on Pleasant Avenue in Minneapolis, Minnesota. "My God, Shane, be careful," I scream. "How did that boy get up on the roof?" I ask my daughter, who's standing next to me.

"He climbed the tree next to the house and swung across on a branch," Nichole explains. "He told me he could do it. He saw it on TV."

"Shane, stand still. Don't move!" I scream. "Just keep looking at me. The firemen will be here soon!" He's not scared. It's an adventure to him. I'm petrified. The fire engine screams to a stop. I don't take a deep breath until my son is safely down.

"Mom, can we have a swimming pool in the backyard—just a little one?" my daughter asks.

A wave of terror jolts through me when I hear the words. "No way," I say. "It's too dangerous with your brother. Something could go wrong."

"Mom, why are you taking the four-wheeler away?" Shane whines. He pleads with me to give it back. "You're not careful enough," I say. You'll drive through electric wires or do something careless and hurt yourself. The answer is no."

There was this feeling about him from the day he was born. The first year, I held him all the time. I wouldn't share him with anyone else. He was a good baby. Then he started to walk. His feet hit the ground running. He didn't stop until he died.

We're at the movies on a Sunday afternoon. Shane puts his feet on the back of the seat in front of him. I start to nag, then stop. *Make every moment count.* It's as if someone spoke the words in my ear.

You don't have to tell me that. Since Shane was born, I know how important each moment is. What I want to know is, do they still count after he's gone?

We're at a restaurant: Shane (about to turn twelve), Nichole (fourteen), and a few of their friends. We're there to celebrate Shane's birthday. I hold up my water glass. "Here's to the next year. May it be the best yet. May you have everything you want!" Clink. Clink. Clink.

"I don't have money to buy you a present, but how would you like to come skiing this weekend with me and my friends instead?" Nichole asks her brother.

Shane's eyes light. He says, "Yes!"

"Just promise me this," I say to both children. "No matter where we are on our birthdays, we'll always get together."

Nichole instantly says yes. Shane hesitates, then agrees.

Two days later, on Saturday morning, Shane, Nichole, and her friend Joey leave for skiing. Their sitter Chrissie drives them. Joey's mom will drive them home. "I love you. Be careful. Be home by six."

"Love you too. See ya!" Shane says.

At eight o'clock the phone rings. A man's voice tells me Shane's hurt. We do a vigil at the hospital. Family and friends pile into the room. The machine pumps air into Shane's small lungs but it's too late. He's already dead. He slipped on an icy patch—a mogul. It knocked his brain stem loose when he hit his head.

Nichole and I stay at a hotel in downtown St. Paul. I can't go back to our house, see Shane's vacant room. Not yet. I'm wandering the hotel hallways looking at my key. I can't find the room. The numbers blur. I walk and walk. The numbers on the doors don't match my key. I sit down on the floor and wait. Someone will find me, help me. Lost? I've never been this lost in my life.

We all have plans about where our life is going. The night before Shane's death, I closed the deal on a new house. We were moving into a mansion in the city to celebrate our last years living together as a family. I was going to work, write books. The kids would go to college, get married, have children of their own. Isn't that how life goes? Your children grow up and leave home, then the parents get old and die first?

After Shane dies, I can't work, can't write for years. You can't write when you have nothing to say. "Thank you so much for your work," a reader writes me in a letter. "Your books helped so much. I'm finally happy after so many miserable years." I'm glad she's happy. I'm not. Why are other people's children alive and Shane is gone? Something I did must have really ticked God off.

People are kind, but they don't get it. They tire of waiting for me to be myself. I run into an acquaintance at the mall the week before the first Christmas after Shane's death. He asks what's wrong. "Shane's dead," I said. He steps back. "Aren't you over that yet?" he asks. I'm furious at him for saying that. Why should I be mad at him? It's the same thing I tell myself.

"Be patient with yourself," a friend says. "Your son died. You're grieving. You didn't just lose your son. He took a few things with him on his way out."

Yeah, I think. *Like my ability to write. My desire to live. My belief in life and myself. Shane, if you have to go, could you at least give me those things back?*

The day before the accident, Shane opens my jewelry drawer and points to a cross. "Can I have that?" he asks. Before skiing he shows me the cross. It's hanging around his neck. "God is with me now," he says.

That's good. He's not with me. What was God thinking anyway? Does God ever make mistakes?

"I feel numb. Or I cry. Or I sit and stare. I listen to the same songs over and over. I can't work," I tell the therapist. "I can't get on with my life."

What's her advice? "If you feel sad, cry. If you feel numb, feel that. Ninety-five dollars, please."

It's the best money I ever spent, but it takes time to understand. You don't eat an elephant all at once. You eat it bite by bite. *I don't want to eat an elephant.* I know, but there's one on your plate. Break life into tiny pieces. *A day at a time?* No! Smaller than that. *I don't have to accept Shane's death? Accept what I'm feeling now? I hate it that he's gone. I can't stand my life. I don't want to be here.* Those are the feelings you need to accept. *It hurts.* Resistance hurts worse. Don't complicate grief. It's not abnormal. There isn't a right way to grieve. Becoming aware of a feeling neutralizes that emotion. That feeling disappears and another one takes its place. Some losses don't have an ending. We have feelings as long as we live. We still miss the person, but we go on with life.

There's more. Stop working for the prize. Stop dating to get married. Stop dressing to control what people think. It's all about control. Control doesn't keep us safe, even though we think it does. People die in their houses walking down their steps. Do each thing for itself. Be there while you're doing it. Stop being someplace else. Let life be what it is. Stop looking for Big. The magic happens when you stay small. Ninety-five dollars bought more than the secret to grief. It paid for the secret to life.

Whatever we don't have isn't the missing piece. The moments we live for their own sake turn to moments of joy. Something way more profound and lasting than happiness is peace.

Nichole and I move the night she graduates from high school. I need the California sun and surf. In Minnesota, everything I look at reminds me of what I lost. Besides, Minnesota no longer feels like home. California does. We live at the beach. The waves are the only thing louder than the sounds in my head. The waves never stop, but sometimes you don't hear their sound. They're like the waves of grief. None are the same. Some are big and angry. Some small. Each one washes a speck of pain away, and no matter how many waves there are, there'll be more. Don't kid yourself. The ocean never stops, and if it does, watch out. The only time there are no waves is ten minutes before the tsunami comes.

"Be still and know I'm God."

"I know that. But look what You've done."

Ten years later, I'm in another therapist's office. She deals with trauma using EMDR (Eye Movement Desensitization and Reprocessing). You blink your eyes, look in the direction she points, talk about what happened, and your trauma emerges, shrinks, then disappears. EMDR neutralizes disturbing thoughts. "Trauma keeps you locked into what you were doing the moment you got slammed with the traumatic event," the therapist says. "You're frozen in time, and your body stores the trauma inside."

I'm like a snapshot of myself when Shane died?

She asks me to show her where on my body the trauma is.

"I walk to the emergency-room door. The nurse is waiting for me. I get hit right here," I say, placing my hand on my heart. I'm reliving the event for her, but I don't know if I can go back there and feel what I felt then. Sometimes I travel back there emotionally, but that happens when I'm not trying. I don't know if I can do it at will. Pain has a life and a mind of its own. I blink, look where she points, and instantly time-travel back thirteen years. It's like I'm right there at St. Paul–Ramsey Medical Center. In her office I'm sobbing, the heaving sobs that shake your belly and make your eyelids puff for days. "An arrow came out of the nurse's eyes when she looked at me and asked if I had someone to call. It hit me here, in my heart. I had to hold my diaphragm tight," I explained to the therapist. I wondered if she'd understand. It barely made sense to me. "My heart was so shattered I had to use my diaphragm to hold my heart in place. If I didn't, my heart was so broken it would have fallen out."

"Put your hand on your diaphragm and breathe into it," she says. "It's okay to relax it now."

I don't have to hold my heart together anymore? The break lines mended? My heart won't fall apart?

"The way you want to feel again is the way you'd feel if it never happened," the therapist says. "Trauma keeps you locked in, stops you from doing what you were going to do when you got hit with the traumatic event."

Oh, yeah, I remember what I was doing that night the ski patrol called. I was having a life. Then the doctors said "no hope," and everything I have disappears. I'm broken inside. My daughter knows. "Mom, everyone thinks you're fine. I'm the only one who knows you're not," she says. She's right. How do I get past that?

"How did you?" the therapist asks. "You tell me."

I point to the spider plant hanging from the ceiling. "Like the baby plant on the tip of the leaves. I moved to California and grew a new one of myself. I left the other me behind. She hurt too much," I say. "She wasn't any fun. She was dark. Unhappy. Always crying and sad. She spoiled everything for everyone. I had to leave her behind. She ruined Minnesota for me. She would have wrecked California too."

"Do you think you could come and get her now?" she asks. "Take her with you?"

"Only if she'll behave and stop crying all the time."

Surrender to everything, even being traumatized. It's paradoxical. Surrendering means we lose control, but it gives us control too. It restores our connection to ourselves, God, life. We become aligned. Judith Acosta and Judith Simon Prager wrote *The Worst Is Over*, a book about the power of words to heal. "When you sit down with someone who has been traumatized," they write, "know that you are entering a hallowed space."

Here's a short course in what to say and what not to say if you want your words to help:

"Melody, did you know that in my religion we consider it an honor to be chosen by God to be the mother of a child who dies?" Pin a badge of honor on someone's chest. Someone loved me enough to do that for me about hepatitis C. Instead of telling me that it was my fault from shooting drugs and that I deserved to be sick, my friend says, "It's a badge of honor. It means you went through the sixties; you really lived."

"You and Shane were close, really bonded," another friend says. "Anyone could see that. When you lost him, you lost a big piece of yourself."

"Mrs. Beattie, did you know that Shane read to me during lunch hour at school every day? My daddy was away at the Gulf War, my grandma got sick, and my mommy was sad. She stayed in bed and cried all the time. But every day Shane made me laugh." The little girl with the big brown eyes and glasses had been standing in line at a book signing for over half an hour to tell me that. She wipes her eyes. "I'm sad," she says. "Mrs. Beattie, I miss Shane too."

"It's really hard, the hardest thing you'll ever go through. But you're going to be okay. You'll get through this. I know you will," a friend says. "I believe you can."

"Grief is a selfish thing. It doesn't help your son. You're only feeling sorry for yourself when you cry," snips a colleague in the self-help field.

"If you really believed in God and life after death, you wouldn't be crying. You'd be happy for your son," a metaphysical relative says.

"Well, at least your daughter's still alive," a healer says.

"Shane's happier, better off now," the minister says.

"Don't waste time feeling sad. There's no such thing as death. I had a near-death experience. I saw the light," another friend says.

"God didn't do this to your son. The devil did," a reader writes.

"Oh, he was just a spoiled brat anyway," a friend says to another friend about my son. "What's the big deal?"

Which statements heal? You tell me. Better yet, use the words that heal to help a friend who hurts.

"How'd you get through it?" a friend asks. "Did you pray?"

I'm too angry to talk to God at first. Then I realize I've joined an elite club. Mary, mother of Jesus, went through the same thing. You can't tell me she didn't miss her son. Besides I'm in a double bind. I know

God is real. I need Him, even if He allowed this horrible thing to happen. Maybe God didn't do it. Maybe it was natural law. You hit your head a certain way and you die. But God didn't stop it, and I know He could have. That means it was meant to be. Another not-helpful thing to say. Let us say that to ourselves—please.

My friend Marge calls big loss—the stuff that changes us and our lives forever—*initiation*. Initiation into fraternities and clubs are tests you go through to prove you're worthy. That's not what she's talking about. She's talking about the spiritual lessons we go through as we work our way back to God. The illusion is that we're separate. Our oneness is what's real. Initiations wake us up to that.

Loss and change can be sacred turning points. "The same events that cause pain trigger enlightenment," Mark Epstein wrote in *Thoughts Without a Thinker*. At first we shut down, become bitter. Later we open our hearts. Gethsemane is the garden of grief. Jesus wept there. I did. Have you? Eventually each of us walks the Via Dolorosa, the Path of Sorrow, writes Max Heindel in *Ancient and Modern Initiation*. We have a cross to bear, a burden. Maybe some people get let off the hook, but most of us have to carry some big weight through life. We lose someone or something important. Then our job is to feel close to God, love other people, and be happy anyway. We learn to live carrying the weight of that loss.

Elisabeth Haich went deeper than that in her book *Initiation*. I couldn't tell if the book was fiction or real. But at the end, where Haich writes that all the trials and tensions of the world take us back behind our ego where the Divine Self is waiting, that part I know is truth. We aren't the God of the Western world, but each of us is a piece of the Divine. Pain and loss initiate us to our oneness with each other, God, and life. Nothing can separate us from God, no matter how alone we feel.

One day I receive a call from a stranger. He read the book I wrote about Shane's death, *Lessons of Love*. His daughter died in a ski accident too. He became involved with The Compassionate Friends (TCF), a group that supports parents and other family members after the death of a child. The man organizes sessions with George Anderson for members of TCF groups.

I watched a special about George on television. George is a medium who sees and talks to dead children. Even skeptics say George is for real; he's not a phony or charlatan. I tried to make an appointment to see him but gave up after a year because his line was busy all the time. A lot of people are standing in line waiting to talk to people they love who died.

"I've got one session with George available," the man said. Did I want it? Yes! Nichole and David (Nichole and Shane's father) went with me to see George. At his last birthday dinner, Shane promised we'd get together on our birthdays no matter where we were. He kept the promise he made. The date we got together, the only available appointment, was Nichole's eighteenth birthday. That's when we talked to Shane.

Shane said he loves and misses us too. He added that being our guardian angel is more than a full-time job. George said, "That kid is a pistol, a handful." I said, "Yes, he is."

Our lost loved ones aren't really lost, even though we can't see them. They're living in another place. Susan Apollon, author of *Touched by the Extraordinary*, says there are many different ways for our loved ones to make contact. They may communicate telepathically, in visions or dreams. Sometimes we sense their presence. Flickering lights or the smell of cologne might be *hello* from the other side. Although many people feel a contact, some don't. Their love is still real.

Whenever I miss Shane too much, I spend time with him in my dreams.

I'm standing at the door of the plane. My skydiving instructor gives me the count. Ready. Set. Falling through the air. I watch the altimeter on my wrist. At five thousand feet, I pull. My parachute pops opens. God, I love that sound. I realize that if I don't stop living in the past, I'll miss the rest of my life. Jumping out of the plane teaches me to be here now. There are some beautiful, interesting things going on in my life even though Shane is gone.

I'm climbing a mountain in a village in China, step by step. At the top is a temple. Nothing is forever. Everything comes to pass. Impermanence is the truth. It hurts to learn that at first. Then it sets us free. There's this thing that moves us through life, a Force. Life happens through us, but not by thinking about it. It happens more naturally than that.

En route from California to Minnesota, what I see is so stunning I have to stop the car and pull to the side of the road. The red spires in the Utah desert take my breath away. At least God did some things right. When did I start feeling happy again? I didn't notice. Each moment and feeling became the next. There's not that much difference between feeling happy and feeling sad. They're all temporary feelings, moments in time.

At the doctor's office, the nurse calls the man's name. It's his turn to see the doctor. "So it's normal to feel lost when your child dies?" the man asks. He's visibly torn. I see he wants to keep talking now that he's finally met one of his own.

"It's so normal to feel lost," I say. "You have no idea how normal it is. Like a friend of mine says, 'When we're most lost is when we're most guided.' Don't worry if you don't know what to do next. You'll find your way."

My daughter brings her friend to my house a week after her friend's best friend dies. My daughter's friend tells me the story of her friend's death. It was a motorcycle accident. She describes what her friend was like, what they did the last time she saw him, everything he said. She realizes now he was really saying good-bye. Suddenly she pulls her sweatshirt hood over her head, then down covering her face. I hear her crying softly underneath.

"She's embarrassed," my daughter explained. "She doesn't want any-one to see her cry."

"I understand. I used to feel that way too," I said. "Once I cried for eight years."

About 2,500,000 people die annually in the United States. Children and young adults under age 25 account for between 45,000 to 50,000 of these deaths.

Source: National vital statistics reports

ACTIVITIES

1. Make a Master List of Losses—a loss inventory. Some people lead charmed lives. They don't experience much loss until later, when they begin aging, friends die, and their bodies begin to fail. For others, life is a series of losses. It feels like (and they are) losing something or someone all the time. Some losses are expected changes that most people experience. Other losses are sudden and unexpected, but they may not be as rare as we first think. At the end of this book, you'll find a Master Loss Checklist, a list of most possible losses, changes, and passages that people experience as they journey through life. Review the list and mark your losses. Be thorough. Activities in other chapters will refer back to this list.

2. Have you lost someone you love? Could you use some support? The Compassionate Friends is an excellent resource for parents, grandparents, and siblings of a child who died. TCF groups have chapters in most cities around the world. It is also an excellent clearinghouse for trustworthy grief support resources for other kinds of losses. Contact TCF at www.compassionatefriends.org or by calling 877-969-0010 (toll-free) or 630-990-0010.

3. Keep a diary of any dreams or contacts with a deceased loved one. Jot a few notes about the content of the dream or describe the contact.

Maybe you sensed your loved one's presence or heard a song that had meaning for you. All that matters is that the connection meant something to you. Write about it. As the years pass, I've come to believe that I didn't lose my relationship with my son; the relationship changed its form.

4. Engage in rituals that honor your loss. It helps me to write a letter or card when I start really missing Shane. On Shane's birthday and death day, I like to make a memorial with his picture, a burning candle, fresh flowers, and a cake. One bereaved mother likes to send her deceased daughter's picture to friends on her daughter's birthday. It helps her remember the good times instead of just dwelling on what she lost. A friend suggests making a scrapbook. She says working on the scrapbook gives her a safe place to grieve and gives her some control over the pain. What rituals help you honor your grief?

5. Remember the best. A friend, a bereaved parent, told me that in therapy her counselor advised her to remember the good moments instead of only dwelling on the painful last months while her daughter died. This is valuable advice. It's important to honor our grief and all our feelings about someone we love who's gone. But pain doesn't have to be the sole focus of our memories and the only way we recall the person we love who's gone. As you go through the grieving process and heal your heart—and when and if you feel ready—how about creating a book of memories of the good times you had? Devote this book to writing about fun, memorable events. Include things you learned, things you or the person said or did, places you visited, trips and activities you both enjoyed. Get creative. Paste photos or other souvenirs in your book. This is a project to work on when you're missing your loved one that will allow you to spend time with him or her in your mind and heart. (This is a variation of a scrapbook activity suggested by a friend.) Honor how important your loved one was and still is in your life.

CHAPTER 2

Remembering Changes:
Facing Alzheimer's Disease

An elderly husband and wife walk out of the airport. Suddenly, the wife, a round-faced woman with frizzy hair, begins beating on the man. She's swearing at him and calling him names. He patiently waits for her to stop. He doesn't hit back; his only gesture is to shield his face from her blows. When she settles down, he looks around, wondering who saw. It's been three years since his wife was diagnosed with Alzheimer's disease (AD). She's getting worse. It's difficult when her outbursts happen at home, embarrassing when they occur in public. He doesn't have enough money to hire a caregiver all the time. His choices are to bring his wife with him and risk a scene or to put her in a nursing home. He wants to postpone that as long as he can.

Once, when his wife started screaming in a restaurant, the waitress thought he was abusing her. He explained that his wife had AD, then quickly paid the bill and left. He thought it would be nice to take his wife out to eat, but it wasn't worth it anymore.

The most common form of dementia, AD can mimic other diseases. Brain tumors, depression, other neurological diseases (some treatable), nutritional deficiencies, drug reactions, and thyroid conditions need to be ruled out, writes Faith Heinemann, Ph.D., in *A Different Reality: An Alzheimer's Love Story*. She started an Alzheimer's support group when her husband got sick because she realized how important support is. Faith describes those years before her husband died as a tragically beautiful time in their marriage. That's when life taught her about unconditional love.

Faith and Claudia met while walking on the beach. They used to walk alone. Now they enjoy walking together soon after the sun comes up. They both like the sounds of the waves crashing and the crying gulls. The dolphins swim by, and some days, a pod lingers to play. It's like a personal show nature puts on for them.

Claudia isn't big on coincidences or magical thinking. Her family comes from the old country. She's grounded in her approach to life; things are what they are, and what you see is what you get. But it did strike her as comfortingly odd when she met Faith for the first time. They started talking one day when they were both walking alone on the beach. Only days before, Claudia had crossed that line—the one most people get pushed over—from thinking her mom was forgetful to admitting that her mom was sick. Alzheimer's disease was corroding Claudia's mom's mind.

Faith is the person who welcomed Claudia to the *Someone I Love Has Alzheimer's* Club. At first when her mom was diagnosed with AD, Claudia felt singled out, alone in her dilemma. Then it changed, and it seemed like everyone Claudia met had a family member with the disease. Was there an epidemic going on?

Faith gave Claudia a copy of the book she'd written and invited Claudia to attend her AD support group. "No, thank you," Claudia said at first. Claudia preferred to keep family problems at home, where they belonged. How would going to a group help? Besides, Claudia already had enough to do. Sitting around listening to other people complain wouldn't change a thing. At the end of the day, whether she went to a group or not, Claudia's mom would still be sick. Attending the group wouldn't make her mother's illness or Claudia's pain go away.

Most people have an average of eight years to live after being diagnosed with AD, although some people live for another twenty. It's a disease that can't be cured, although there are medications, techniques, and nutritional supplements that may slow the disease's progression and ease discomfort. AD is diagnosed by carefully monitoring symptoms and ruling out other possible causes. The clumps of plaque and tangled fibers that corrode thinking and positively indicate AD can be visibly detected in the brain only when an autopsy is performed.

Red flags signaling Alzheimer's are forgetfulness, disorientation, personality changes, impaired judgment, and loss of ability to perform routine tasks (like brushing teeth or writing checks). People with the disease might ask the same question repeatedly, forgetting that it was asked and answered minutes ago. They'll tell you the same story over and over because they don't remember they already told it. Then symptoms worsen. It hurts when someone you love can't remember who you are. It's even worse when they act like you're a stranger and scream at you to *go away*. Soon they can't find their way to familiar places. They can no longer drive, cook, take care of themselves. It's unsafe to leave them alone. They could start a fire, get lost, injure someone else or themselves. Some people with AD get lost in their neighborhood or in their own home. It's a marker that the end is near when they no longer recognize themselves in the mirror. The day comes when they can't remember how to chew or swallow. Eventually AD ends in death. Some forms of dementia can be reversed, but the dementia from Alzheimer's only gets worse.

"It's a disease that affects the people who love the person with AD more than it hurts the person who has it," Faith says. The person with AD usually doesn't have the consciousness to recognize what's going wrong. Memory fades so much they forget what life was like and how they were before the illness began.

"I'm one of the lucky ones," Claudia says. "My mom doesn't become angry or violent. It's easy to care for her. She's like a sweet, innocent child."

Claudia's mother wasn't that ill with AD until the family got the news about Claudia's brother, John. Claudia and her sister were close, but John was the family favorite. He had some troubles. He went overboard with drinking and had a marriage that ended in divorce. Then he went to an alcoholism treatment center and became clean and sober. He was always lovable, but he was the greatest after that. He became a model father to his children and a good ex-husband to his ex-wife. Lately, he had been overly attentive to everyone in the family and his friends. Now Claudia understands why. John was saying good-bye.

He went over a speed bump on his motorcycle. How could anyone die going twenty miles an hour? His helmet didn't protect him; he knocked his brain stem loose. Losing John broke his mother's heart. When Claudia's mom attended John's funeral, she understood clearly what happened. Her only son was dead. Then Claudia's mother went downhill fast. That's when Claudia joined the support group. It wasn't that Claudia couldn't handle it on her own anymore. Just like she enjoys her walks on the beach with Faith, Claudia wants to go on her journey through her mother's AD with understanding people at her side.

We is more powerful than *I* or *me*. Groups, especially well-functioning, sane ones, aren't about people complaining, being victims, and groveling in misery. Groups are a safe place to say how we feel, a place to give and receive support. Something beyond mere support takes place in a group. Together, we are more than you or I am alone.

I saw the power of the group illustrated most clearly when I was climbing Emei Shan, a mountain in China. Mountain climbing in China sometimes means climbing up hundreds of thousands of steps. It can take days to get to the top of the taller mountains. Many times I became so tired I had to stop and take a break. Other times I'd push myself to keep going. One day something happened on Mount Emei that showed me another way to gain strength when I was tired. I was flagging, about to collapse on the steps from sheer exhaustion, an aching back, and hurting feet, when a group of women appeared from the rear. These Chinese women were strangers to me, as I was to them. They didn't speak English; I didn't speak Chinese. But we instantly bonded by our mutual desire to climb to the top. We belonged to the same club. They could see I was wearing out. Anyone could see that. One woman grabbed hold of my left hand; another woman tightly clasped my right hand. Two ladies got in front of us. A few settled in behind. As a group we climbed step after step. My fatigue disappeared. I felt renewed energy to carry on. There is a pronounced and noticeable strength that comes from being part of a group, whether we're climbing a mountain in China or climbing one in our lives. Are you caring for a loved one with Alzheimer's, dealing with the death of a child, recovering from an addiction, healing from cancer, or dealing with a chronically ill spouse? Reach out and let someone take your hand. Help each other get to the top. Together, you will have more strength than any of you have alone.

That's the power Claudia discovered when she attended the AD support group. "My mother got so much worse after my brother died," Claudia said. "She went downhill rapidly. I was having a terrible time myself. I love my brother and missed him so much. I still do. I can't remember ever crying that hard for that long in my life. I didn't know people could feel that much pain. Being in that much grief was a place I didn't know existed until then.

"This sounds strange, but after my brother died, I was grateful that my mom had Alzheimer's disease," Claudia said. "It was a blessing because she forgot John died. She doesn't talk about him often, but once in a while, she still mentions his name. 'I haven't seen John,' she'll say. 'Have you heard from him?' I'll tell her I talked to him and he's fine. At least Mom doesn't have to spend the last years of her life grieving the loss of her son.

"I hear people whine and complain who don't have a serious problem, and I want to shake them," Claudia said. "They don't know what real emotional pain is. Then there's that group of people who have never experienced major loss. Those are the ones who don't get it, who don't understand at all what I'm going through. I'm happy for them, that they haven't had any serious loss yet. But I want to warn them, tell them nobody is immune from this big, deep pain in life. Sooner or later, it's coming for everyone, and one day it's going to be their turn. I don't mean that in a spiteful way," Claudia explained. "But eventually loss is part of everyone's life."

Claudia didn't just lose her brother to death and her mother to Alzheimer's. Claudia lost her innocence. There's a dark tunnel that many of us go through when we lose our innocence and see what life is *really* like. We can lose faith, become cynical, and feel disappointed in our lives. Something else, something deeper is simultaneously taking place. We're being introduced to radical faith.

Radical faith is different from the simple faith many of us had, the faith that says, *If I do good things, then only good things will happen to me. If I'm a good person, people I love won't die. God will protect and take care of me and the people I love.* Radical faith is bold. It's not squeamish, fundamentalist, judgmental, or blaming. It's courageous. It says, *I can be a good, loving, decent human being and still be vulnerable to tragedy. My world can be shattered in a moment. Life can be viciously cruel, but it's still worth caring about. Disasters happen to other people and they can happen to me, and it's nobody's fault.* When we surrender our defenses, our innocence becomes restored. Faith then becomes a matter of will, something we declare. *I will have faith in life,* we say. We laugh again. Our hearts are stronger than we think.

Claudia still enjoys walking on the beach with her friend Faith. She enjoys attending the support group too. People who have Alzheimer's have constantly changing needs. As the disease progresses, more loss appears. It helps to talk about the situation. People learn from each other. We might think that talking about feelings won't change a thing, but emotional validation is a healing technique. When how we feel is validated, we move out of resistance and into balance. We acknowledge the emotion. Confusion lifts. We know what to do next. Groups help people stay present and real.

The local Alzheimer's support group meets in a back room at the Catholic church in the town where Faith and Claudia live. Once a month on Saturday morning, people begin filing into the room. Some bring chips or homemade cookies. The smell of brewing coffee and the sounds of people talking fill the room. The people attending are a diverse group, middle-aged or older. Many look tired. The meeting begins.

"It finally happened," Claudia announces. "The selfish jerk left." The jerk is her stepfather. He's been with her mother for thirty years. Unlike Faith, who used the opportunity of her husband's illness to learn unconditional love, Claudia's stepfather chose to leave. "We've been expecting it," Claudia says. *We* means Claudia and her sister. They take turns spending the weekends with their mom. "I'm glad he left," Claudia said. "We had to hire full-time nursing care anyway because he wouldn't do anything during the week. I get so angry at him," Claudia said. "He had the nerve to say to Mom, 'You're getting to be a bit much, aren't you?' I wanted to physically harm him when he said that. Now we don't have to look at his face every weekend when we're there. Mom doesn't know he's gone. She doesn't remember being married to him."

One woman in the group says she feels irritated, drained, and annoyed. Her relatives are squabbling over money and inheritance issues. She talks about how money can bring out the worst in people instead of letting the illness bring out love. Other group members agree. One woman looks tired. All she wants to do is listen today.

Faith started the group when she was taking care of her husband, Al. He began displaying symptoms of AD in 1993. In 1995 he was diagnosed. Faith took care of him at home through the days when he looked at her and didn't recognize her until his death. A respected therapist in Los Angeles, Faith is still committed to the group even though she no longer lives with AD. She says helping other people helps her feel good.

Giving away what we want to keep is one of the oldest feel-good tricks in the book. Sharing the growth we've experienced makes our growth real. The more hope we give away, the more we have.

Faith tells her favorite story about the day she left her husband at home with a nurse's aide while she went to do errands. After Faith left, her husband tried to leave the house. He made it as far as the garage. He was hiding there, waiting for his chance to escape, when Faith pulled into the driveway and pressed the remote button to open the garage door. His opportunity arrived! The door opened. Al darted out of the garage. He pressed the remote button on the way out to lower the garage door to block the aide, who was in hot pursuit. Faith instantly pushed the button to open the door. She didn't want the door slamming down on her husband or the aide. Her husband pushed the button to close the door. The door went up, down, up, down. Finally, Faith captured her husband and brought him into the house. By then the three of them—

Faith, Al, and the aide—were tired. They were worn out from laughing about the slapstick comedy that had just taken place.

"It's crucial to maintain a sense of humor," Faith tells the group. "You've got to look at the lighter side. You have to laugh to survive."

Something biochemical happens when we laugh, whether it's a chuckle or laughter that comes from the belly. Doctors agree that laughing changes body chemistry. Laughter heals. Daily or PRN (as needed) tee-hee. Think it's irreverent to laugh or that our dilemma is too solemn for jokes? It's not. Whatever situation we find ourselves in, the law of humor applies to us.

A grief specialist attends the group whenever he can. This Saturday he passes out an article written by Darryl Potyk, M.D., announcing that the number of people with AD is expected to quadruple over the next fifty years.

"Why?" group members ask.

"Because we're living longer," the grief specialist says. The one thing that puts people at risk for getting Alzheimer's is getting old, and more of us are doing that because we've become so skilled at prolonging life.

Claudia shares happy news. Most of the time her mom doesn't remember who Claudia is anymore. But last weekend her mom put her hand on Claudia's cheek. "Oh, I know you," her mom said. "You're my beautiful Claudia." The moments of remembering are precious. They're becoming rare.

Alzheimer's disease is an ambiguous loss. We're losing someone we love, but when do we say good-bye? The losses from AD change and increase over time. It's a situation where the people who do best are people willing to surrender control. Some people associate powerlessness with admitting that they can't control their use of alcohol and drugs, but many life situations are out of our hands. Peace comes when we acknowledge that. By surrendering to each moment, we see what we need to do to care for the other person and ourselves. Surrendering is a powerful technique. It's different from coolly detaching, compliance, resignation, or shrugging our shoulders and saying, "I don't care." When we surrender, we step into active partnership with life.

Faith, an elegant and stunning lady with long, silvery hair, tells a story about looking in the mirror one day and feeling shocked at how old she looked. Suddenly, she felt grateful because at least her husband didn't have to watch her getting wrinkled and old. She says his illness had spared him and her ego that. Then Faith says it's likely Al would have seen her through eyes of unconditional love too.

Claudia talks about her lingering sadness over her brother's death.

"My brother recently died too," another woman in the group says. She looks at Claudia and me, then starts crying. "My only question is when does this stop?" she says. She's pointing to the tears on her cheeks.

"I'm not dealing with Alzheimer's, but I know about loss," I said. "It's been fifteen years since my son died, and the waves of grief haven't stopped yet. It gets easier, though. And maybe the waves aren't all bad."

I was watching a movie, and in it a little boy referred to scars on our body as "zippers" because of the way scars resemble zigzag zipper lines on the skin. Maybe the scars from losing someone we love are like zippers on our hearts. We can't stay open and crying all the time. That would hurt too much, and we wouldn't get anything else done. So we shut off the pain. But these emotional zippers keep us from closing our hearts too much or too long. The waves of grief keep us open. They let other people in and let our feelings out.

Five million people in the United States suffer from Alzheimer's. Without a cure, this number will increase to 16 million by 2050.

At age 60, 1 in every 10,000 people develop AD.

By age 85, 1 in every 3 people are demented (most from AD).

Worldwide, the population of people 60 years and older will double over the next 50 years, and for the first time in history, the elderly will outnumber the young.

More than 50 million Americans are caring for a chronically ill, aged, or disabled loved one.

Sources: Institute for Neurodegenerative Diseases and National Family Caregivers Association

---

ACTIVITIES

1. Write your memoirs. You don't have to wait until you're old. Make this an ongoing project. Start while you're young. Write about events in your life that are funny or sad—the events that have meaning for you. You're not writing this for publication; write it for your family and yourself. You can include pictures too—anything you want. Start taking a walk down memory lane now. It's a kind thing to do for yourself and for following generations. My mother undertook this project when she was seventy-five. It's hard for her to remember many events from her life now, but she has everything that was important written in her book.

2. Does someone you love have Alzheimer's? Do you know someone who has a spouse or relative with AD? You don't have to go through it alone. Contact the Alzheimer's Disease Education and Referral Center at www.alzheimers.org or 800-438-4380; the Alzheimer's Association at www.alz.org or 800-272-3900; or the Alzheimer's Foundation of America at www.alzfdn.org or 866-232-8484. For support for caregivers, contact the above numbers or the National Family Caregivers Association at www.thefamilycaregiver.org or 800-896-3650.

3. Could you use some group support for whatever problem you're experiencing? Look in the yellow pages, call your county hospital, or search on the Internet. Support groups are easy to find, and many are free or low cost. You don't have to do it—whatever *it* is—alone.

4. Buy your favorite comedy movies. Watch them over and over. Hang

out with friends who have a sense of humor, and develop your own sense of humor too. After my son died, my daughter's teachers were discussing her behavior with me at a school conference. "How can she be grieving?" one teacher asked. "We see her laughing in the hallways. It doesn't look like she's sad." I had to explain that being in grief doesn't mean that people cry all the time. It's important to find humor wherever and whenever we can. Look for the lighter side of life.

5. Don't ingest aluminum. While the Alzheimer's Association and medical science has not documented any clear role for aluminum causing or contributing to Alzheimer's, many holistic and alternative medicine practitioners believe there may be a connection. Holistic sources suggest that aluminum can easily be avoided by not using deodorants and antiperspirants containing aluminum (health-food stores contain many effective and beautifully scented alternative choices); not cooking in aluminum cookware or cracked nonstick cookware; not using food or beverages stored in aluminum cans; not using antacids containing aluminum (Tums and Rolaids are pure calcium and contain no aluminum). Aluminum absorbed from any of those four sources has no dietary or nutritional benefit and won't be missed. Why take a chance?

CHAPTER 3

Touch That Changes:
When We Don't Feel Blessed

"I used to feel blessed when something good happened, when God reached down and touched my life in a way I could see and feel," I said to a friend. "Now I think I'm lucky when tragedy doesn't strike or a horrible situation doesn't get worse."

"I know what you mean," he said. "I miss those days too, when God felt so close."

We reminisced about those times when we could feel God's hand reaching down and moving us and our lives around. *A God thing* was always happening in someone's life. We knew we could trust God, and if we forgot, one of our friends was there to remind us. Blessings flowed like water—silly little miracles and great big miracles. Something was always happening that had meaning for someone. Then the miracles seemed to disappear. "What happened?" I asked.

For a long time he was quiet. "I don't know," he said.

I used to feel special to God. Before I turned five, I thought God was the greatest. The next seven years pounded that out of me. Family problems. Dad left. My half-brother and half-sisters left, including Jeanne, the sister who loved me most. Mom was openly burdened by me. I felt sad that she had to be strapped with me when she wanted to be free. There was abuse, an abduction, molestations. A lot of tough things happened for everyone

in that house. I spent two years home from school confined to bed rest—
no tutors, no friends, no sitter, no family. Just me, my books, and TV.
When I was walking to church one Sunday morning—I was about
twelve—I started thinking. *"God Is Love" signs are plastered all over
church. If God is love, why isn't there any love for me?*

I looked up at the sky. "You must not love me," I said. Step Three in
Twelve Step programs says we make a decision to turn our lives and wills
over to the care of God as we understand Him. I did the opposite that
day. I consciously took my life and will back into my own hands. From
then on, instead of going to church on Sundays, I hung out at the corner
and smoked cigarettes. When I got home, I lied about where I'd been.

I figured I could do at least as good as God had done, maybe better,
with my life. The next twelve years went by fast. By age twenty-four I
was an addict. I'd been on a six-month drugstore robbing spree with my
boyfriend. We were both facing felony charges. He was already in jail.
The sixties were sex, drugs, and the Rolling Stones. We felt entitled to
get high. It was an exciting time. Then the seventies came along. Society
was on the cusp of learning that anyone could be an addict or alcoholic.
We weren't disposable. If you sobered us up, you'd find a human being
inside. When we got clean, we could do things other people couldn't—
like help other addicts and alkies get sober. We could be as good as we'd
been bad. We were useful; there was a place for us in the world. It had
been fun to get high, but it was even more exciting to get sober. We
believed in recovery. We believed in people. We believed in life, and we
believed in God. There was a revolution going on. "For a while it was
Camelot," a friend said.

A wise, kind judge once gave me an option: jail or chemical dependency treatment at a state hospital for as long as it takes. I chose treatment, but the first few months there, I continued to use drugs. I didn't
know how to stop. Early one morning, my probation officer came to
visit. I'd been up all night wired on methamphetamine—cheap, nasty
speed. I didn't mean to do that. That's the thing with addicts. We don't
intend to drink or use drugs. Usually the times we most shouldn't drink
or use is when we end up drinking and using the most. Loss of control

is the identifying stamp and seal of addiction. We lose control of when we use, what we use, how much we use, and what we do when we're drunk or stoned. But it's not that simple, because all the while we're losing control we tell ourselves we're choosing. Any illusion I had about choosing to use disappeared that night. For the first time, I saw that I was out of control. I didn't want to use, but I couldn't help it. Coincidentally, that's the First Step of Twelve Step programs—we admit we're powerless over alcohol and our lives have become unmanageable. *I see!* I thought. *I get it! My probation officer will be here in two hours, and I'm stoned out of my mind, and that will give him the right to put me in prison for five years. That means I'm not choosing. I'm insane.* I was worried about the timing of my insight. Was it too late?

My probation officer arrived. We talked. He didn't notice that I was stoned, and thank God he didn't demand a urinalysis. I got by, but I didn't feel relieved. I felt guilty and scared, and both were new feelings. Where did a conscience come from? I hadn't had one in years. After my probation officer left, I sat on my bed and looked at the ceiling. "God, I don't know if You're there and if You care, but if You are and You do, and there's a program that will help me get sober, please help me get it," I said.

Nothing happened. A few days later, I was sitting on the sprawling hospital grounds smoking a joint. I laid back to watch the clouds. It was a hippie, stoned thing to do. But when I stared at the clouds, something happened. The clouds and sky turned an ethereal purplish color. I knew everything was connected, and I knew I had no right to keep using drugs. I wasn't entitled anymore. *If I put half as much effort into doing the right thing as I had into doing what's wrong, there isn't anything I can't do*, I thought. I took one more hit off the joint, then my recovery began. I vowed to do everything I could to stay sober the rest of my life by staying clean for the next twenty-four hours.

This God I prayed to had blessed me with an inner transformation. It started inside and spread outward until it touched every part of my life. It made me a different person. I didn't change my behaviors. Something inside changed, then my behaviors changed too. I knew God is real. God heard my prayer. God loved me. God cared, and not imper-sonally, like, "Oh, God cares about *everyone*." God knew my name. God knew where I lived. I didn't tell anyone about this experience for years. I was already in an institution. If I told anyone the sky turned purple and I talked to God, I might never get out. But that feeling of being spe-cial to God stayed with me for most of the next eighteen years. For a while during my codependent days, I thought God abandoned me. Then I learned the problem wasn't God. I was the one not doing my job. God would take care of me, but He needed my help. He needed me to stop obsessing about other people and take care of—*take responsibility for*—myself. Once I got clear on that and reconnected with myself, I reunited with God. It was just like old times—God and me again.

Then Shane died.

You think a lot of things—you feel a lot of things—when someone you love that much dies. You think and feel more things than, say, when a parent or friend dies. They call the death of a child the worst loss there is. I'm not playing the *my pain is bigger than your pain* game, but this loss is big. I never felt special to God again.

We all like to feel special to someone. We want to be a parent's favorite child or the teacher's pet. I'd never felt like anyone's favorite until God and I got back together again when I was in treatment in 1973. In many ways it might have been easier if I'd never felt special to God because then I wouldn't have known what I lost.

"God didn't take Shane away from you," people said when I told them how I felt. God might not have done it, but I know this: God is so omnipotent, so powerful, and so almighty that God could have stopped Shane's accident from happening if that's what God wanted, and nothing anyone can say will ever change my mind about that. It's not that I doubted God's existence. I know God is real. I questioned how God felt about me.

I didn't feel blessed anymore. The blessed ones are the ones who walk away from accidents. They're the ones who almost get killed, but don't. They're the ones who get sick, then recover. That's what we're taught. That's how being blessed feels.

I missed feeling special to God.

One of the first things to go when we experience loss is that feeling of being blessed. People feel blessed when they escape the jaws of death because they swerved in the nick of time and missed getting hit by the bus. They feel blessed when someone they love flatlines, but CPR brings them back from the other side with miraculous gifts of healing and prophecy and a hair-raising story that becomes a best-selling book. People feel blessed when they almost lose their home, but the day before foreclosure a $25,000 check arrives, and there is enough money left over to pay taxes and buy a dining-room table too. It's not as easy to feel blessed when the accident happens and you become a quadriplegic. Or you declare bankruptcy and lose the house. Or the person dies and there's no story to tell, at least not one that anyone wants to hear.

It's hard to call those things the loving hand of God.

This is a story for anybody in the *I Used to Feel Close to God, but I Wonder if He Knows Where I Live Now* Club. It's a story about *a God thing*, the kind we used to tell.

Isaac and I live in the same condo building. I own the left side, upstairs and downstairs. Isaac lives downstairs next door. Isaac's family emigrated from Israel. After a stint in the Israeli army, Isaac joined his family here when he was nineteen. He's been married and divorced twice, has children. "Nobody in California throws anything away," Isaac says, "so I started a self-storage business." Isaac's done well for himself. Now he's older. He enjoys life at the beach.

Living at the beach is a blessing I almost missed. For years I drove past the same stretch of road by the ocean, thinking, *that's where I want to live*. I knew I couldn't afford a house there so I didn't bother looking. One day a woman approached a mutual friend. She had to sell her condo. She needed money fast. The condo was on the street where I wanted to live. "No way," I said when I heard the price. "It's too good to be true." When something's too good to be true, we don't call it *a God thing* anymore. Now we call it a scam. After I bought the condo, I almost sold it. "Don't you get it?" a friend said, trying to pound some sense into me. "That house is a gift from God." I stopped trying to give the condo back; now I call it home.

Sometimes we do goofy things when we're grieving. One of those things is called magical thinking. Because I closed on the deal for a house the night before Shane died, part of me connected buying a house with his death. I'd been a homeowner most of my adult life, but after Shane died, I rented for years. When I signed the paperwork closing the condo deal, my hand started shaking. My eyes got teary. *What's going on?* I thought. That's when I realized I'd been afraid to buy a home all those years because I thought I'd lose someone else.

I was pounding a mezuzah into my door frame the day I moved into the condo. A mezuzah is a portion of the Holy Torah written on a small scroll, inserted into a decorative cover, and placed by the door to signify blessings on a Jewish home. I'm not Jewish, but I needed the luck. A tall, skinny man wearing a flimsy bathrobe walked over. I could see his shorts hanging out underneath.

"I'm Isaac," he said. "I live next door. I'm glad you live here now. Welcome home."

Isaac and I had our little routine. I'd stare at my computer screen—frustrated and stuck, trying to write. Isaac would walk by my window. "Are you busy?" he'd yell through the glass. "Yes," I'd say. "I need to talk," he'd insist. Then he'd go to my door and rap until I let him in. We became neighborly friends. There's only three of us living in the building; it's an informal co-op association. Isaac used to manage it, but he asked me to take over. It was a goodwill thing; I agreed. It wasn't that much work.

One day when my housekeeper and I were cleaning the garage, we found a box of hardcover copies of *Lessons of Love*, the first book I wrote after my son's death. I had bought them from the publisher for a dollar each after the paperback version was released. It was a hard book to write, harder to read. It made people cry. I told the publisher that when I wrote it. "Nobody wants to read about the death of a child," I told him. "Write it anyway," he said.

"What do you want to do with these books?" my housekeeper asked.

"Do whatever you want," I said. "They're yours."

Before this year, Isaac thought that the year he was diagnosed with cancer and his last wife divorced him was as bad as it could get. This year was making that year look easy. First his liver failed from the cancer. But he got on the transplant list. Then the doctors put someone else's liver in him. The operation was a success; Isaac's new-used liver worked. But now he had to take more than fifty pills a day so his body wouldn't reject the liver. And the transplant surgery was hard. He had tubes running into him, tubes leading out of him. After the surgery, Isaac caught pneumonia. The medicine they gave him to cure that made him go deaf. It took him a year to learn to read lips. Things he didn't even think about when he could do them looked like miracles now. They were the little things—like being able to sit on the toilet and go to the bathroom instead of wearing a bag—that he'd give anything to have back. He didn't have the front of his stomach anymore. A see-through plastic tarp covered his intestines instead of the skin that he used to have there. The doctors said they could do another surgery; they could cover his stomach so his insides didn't show. But that meant another surgery, more time in the hospital, then a long recovery at home. Isaac had been so sick when they did the transplant, he didn't have time to think about it. This time he had more time to worry. The idea of another surgery scared him. He knew what he was in for. A lot could go wrong.

Now Isaac spent most of his life in bed, flat on his back. Recently, the doctors implanted a device in his head. It helps him hear basic sound vibrations. He can almost hear the waves hitting the shore. Combined with his memory of how the ocean sounds, the little he hears is like listening to a symphony. When he was in the hospital all those months, he started writing poetry. He wrote poems about feeling grateful for his children. He wrote poems about his life. He considers himself only part of the man he used to be, but still a lucky man. "Sometimes I forget I've got someone else's liver," he says. "Sometimes I forget about all the tubes and bags. And as crazy as it sounds," Isaac says, "sometimes I forget I'm deaf." Isaac connected with the part of himself that's real, the part of ourselves we can't lose.

Isaac was fighting hard to stay alive and to come back from each thing that knocked him down. His children were grown, but they wanted him around. Besides, it wasn't in his nature to give up. All his life, even as a child in Israel, Isaac was a fighter. Surviving, coming out ahead of the game, was what he did best. But he'd give anything to have his old body back. What he really wanted was to walk a mile or even a block. Hell, he'd be happy to get up and walk around his house.

His housekeeper gave him a book to read. She got it from the housekeeper who worked for the lady next door. He finished it that day. He was trying to fall asleep that night, but he couldn't get the story out of his mind. He'd been through a lot, but suddenly he felt blessed.

I'd been lying on my couch, bedridden for months. Something had gone terribly wrong with my back. I didn't know it yet, but I would soon be on my way to an operating room in Germany, where doctors would gut me like a deer and insert two artificial discs into my spine. These discs would be my only chance to lead a normal life. I thought about my neighbor Isaac and everything that's happened to him: a liver transplant, almost a year in the hospital, all those tubes and bags. Then to top it off, he lost his hearing too. I admired his will to live, his determination. I visited Isaac when he came home from the hospital. He showed me the poems he wrote while he was sick. Isaac writing poems? I read them. They're good. They came from his soul. He told me he'd walk again someday. I wasn't so sure. On Christmas for me, Hanukkah for him, I sent him a card. "You're an inspiration," I wrote. "You give me courage and strength." Isaac was genuinely happy to be alive.

Whenever I started feeling sorry for myself, thinking about Isaac usually snapped me out of the blues, but it wasn't helping much now. I hurt. I'd been in pain for months. I'd been going to the best doctors, seeing my holistic people too. Nobody had been able to fix me. Nothing worked. To make it worse, it was *that time of the year:* Shane's birthday and the anniversary of his death. Time does strange things when it comes to loss. It had been fourteen years, but it felt like Shane died last night.

I was sitting on the couch looking at Shane's pictures. In one he's kneeling, wearing his green football jersey posed with a football in his hand. Why didn't I go to more of his games? I would have, if I'd known he was going to die. There was the picture he'd given me the last Mother's Day he was alive. The Compassionate Friends turned it into one of those picture buttons you pin on your jacket. I had candles burning by a bouquet of fresh flowers. It's how I celebrate his birthday and honor his death. Some years his birthday and the anniversary week isn't that hard. One year I was having so much fun I almost forgot. Then I felt guilty. We think we're being disloyal when we laugh. Shane hated it when I cried. He'd want me to be happy; I know he would.

Lately, all my losses were piling up. The minute I got on top of one loss, something or someone else disappeared. First there was finding out I had hepatitis C. It took two years to get strong and healthy, two years of being angry and resisting before I was able to surrender to having that. It was only four days after I surrendered, realized I was stronger and healthier than I'd ever been, that the problem started with my back. I had four days without having a huge problem dominating my life! If life was trying to break me, it was doing a good job.

Sometimes I felt so angry at God. There didn't seem to be any way to get a break, get some relief. It wasn't just the losses. It was that feeling of being abandoned, separate from God and all alone in the world. That's what was getting to me now. I'd been stuck on this couch so long from the physical pain that I lost the sense of being connected to God or anyone in the world. I needed to feel God's touch. "Can't You give me some kind of sign?" I said. "Give me something to let me know You're still in my life? You're giving me all this hard stuff. Has it ever occurred to You that once in a while people need to feel love? Are You even there anymore? Do You care?" I was having a temper tantrum. But sometimes we need to stop controlling what we feel and let it out, scream it—even if nobody hears.

Rap, rap, rap.

My eyes were red and swollen from crying, my face was a wet mess of tears and snot when I heard knocking on the door. I didn't want anybody to see me this way. I wiped my face with my sleeve. Couldn't I grieve in peace?

The knocking continued. I opened the door. Isaac! There he stood, wobbling and shaking with his tubes and bags and his cotton bathrobe and his shorts hanging out. "You walked!" I yelled into his face so he could read my lips. "That's so good," I said.

He was proud of himself. He told me he'd walk again, but I didn't know that meant *to my house*. I guided him into my living room. I didn't know what to do with him and all his tubes and bags. Was this his first time walking? Would he be okay? He talked loudly, the way people do when they can't hear how they sound.

"My housekeeper gave me a book," he said. "Your housekeeper gave it to her. I just finished reading it. I couldn't fall asleep. I didn't know you lost your son. I'm so sorry." Isaac was standing there, wobbling, with tears running down his cheeks. "I've been through a lot," he said. "But to lose your child? My children are alive. I couldn't go to sleep. I had to come over here and give you a hug."

With all his tubes and bags and his robe flapping, Isaac wrapped his skinny arms around me in a gentle embrace. It's the best hug I ever had. I pointed to Shane's pictures. "Today is his birthday," I said.

I yell at God that I need to feel His touch, and He sends Isaac? Sometimes all it takes is a hug. When it's God's touch, it makes a broken heart whole. If Isaac can get up and walk, it's time for me to wake up my warrior spirit. We deserve to be at peace, no matter what we're going through.

A woman approached me, a friend of a friend. She sought me out because she knew I'd lost my son. "My religion believes that it's a special honor and blessing to be chosen by God to be the parent of a child who dies," she said. "I feel like it's important that I tell you that."

"I didn't know that," I said. I thanked her for caring enough to say that. With one sentence, she started me on the road to feeling blessed again.

We need a national campaign to redefine what it means to be blessed. The problem with not feeling blessed is when we don't feel blessed, we don't see how blessed we are.

The first successful liver transplant was performed in 1967 by Dr. Thomas Starzl at the University of Colorado Health Sciences Center in Denver, Colorado.

On May 30, 2006:
  92,308 people were waiting for organ transplants in the United States
  66,788 were waiting for kidneys
  1,736 were waiting for a pancreas
  2,486 were waiting for a kidney/pancreas transplant
  17,215 were waiting for livers
  215 were waiting for intestines
  2,973 were waiting for hearts
  3,010 were waiting for lungs
  146 were waiting for a heart/lung transplant

More than 9 out of 10 Americans believe in God.

Sources: Organ Procurement and Transplantation Network and Fox News Poll

ACTIVITIES

1. Keep a God book that's just for you. Have your losses affected your relationship with God? Review your Master List of Losses. Which losses have tested or challenged your faith the most? How? Consider keeping a journal on this subject. We need one place where we can say what we think and how we feel, including being angry at God, without feeling judged. An acquaintance was upset with me at Shane's funeral. I told her I was angry with God. She told me that it wasn't okay for me to feel that

way, and I'd better stop feeling that way now. When she scolded me, I disconnected from my feelings. Later, I had to go back and uncover how I felt. People don't mean to interfere with our grief, but some don't understand. It can be detrimental to repress *any* feelings we have. Underneath the anger, I felt hurt. God can handle our anger, our hurt, even our rage. Look at the conversations Job had with God. Tell God how you feel. Tell Him you need to feel His touch again. Then record your stories in your God book. Consider sharing some of them with a friend. It can be as helpful to others as it is to us to hear stories about how God knows where we live. Remember, all it takes to make it a God story is that it holds meaning for us.

2. Write about your grief. Write a story—a movie, an article, a book, poems, a play. In her book *Transcending Loss*, author Ashley Prend (quoting R. Benyamin Cirlin, a bereavement specialist) writes about how important it is to express our grief interpersonally or artistically. She suggests writing a letter to our deceased loved ones, or writing a letter to, or even from, our grief. Tell our grief how much we hate it, she says, or see what our grief has to say to us. We can use any artistic medium to tell the story of our loss—singing, music, dance, drawing, sculpting— whatever form we choose. Tell our story as many ways and as many times as we need to express what's in our heart.

3. Become a TLC person—talking, listening, and caring. Do you want to be a comforting, nurturing person? Many people are frightened of people going through pain, sickness, and loss. Throughout this book I'll mention how some things people said negatively affected people (including me) going through grief. I'll also write about the things people said and did that helped. *The less said, the better* is a good rule of thumb. My hope is that writing about what's helpful and what's not will help validate how you felt or feel when people say these things to you, and it will help all of us learn how to get better at comforting people who hurt.

We need more compassionate people in our world. Lecturing, nagging, judging, intellectualizing, and scolding isn't comforting, and it doesn't heal or help. When someone dies, it doesn't help to tell the survivors that the person who died is happier now and in a better place. It's not comforting to tell a person to buck up, because a death or painful loss or sickness is God's will. A comforting person will let people discover that for themselves. It's also not helpful to ask people why they're not over that (their grief) yet, or say that their grief is prolonged and that they're wallowing in self-pity and feeling sorry for themselves. Let people talk. Listen. Care about what you hear. Let people tell their story over and over again, if that's what they need. Don't judge them. Don't try to talk them out of their feelings. Trying to change how others feel is a way of trying to make ourselves feel better—not them.

Don't vaguely mention that someone should call you if he or she wants something. If you want to help, think of something concrete and tangible you can do to help, then do it. Once a week, make a casserole and bring it to your friend's home. Don't stay unless you're invited. Your friend may want company or may want to be alone. Your job is to comfort and help your friend—not entertain yourself. Invite your friend to a movie. Or bring a stack of your friend's favorite movies to him or her. If you don't know what your friend likes to watch, ask. Go to the movie store, pick up the movies, drop them off, and when they're due, pick them up and take them back. That's a practical gift to do for someone in grief. Or bring a bag of this person's favorite tea. Or help him or her with grocery shopping once in a while. In the early stages of my grief, I was so traumatized that it was hard to go to the grocery store. It helped to have someone do that for or with me. There were times when the simplest tasks felt impossible to do. Paying bills was monumental—almost impossible. My brain didn't work from the trauma.

It's tempting to avoid people who are sick or going through grief. Emotional pain isn't contagious. You won't *catch* disaster from them. If your friend is sick (unless it's a virus), it's not contagious; otherwise your friend would be in an isolation ward. If you know someone who's sick—going through chemotherapy or radiation or suffering with any chronic or even fatal illness—make it your plan to call this person once a week. Be sure to ask if he or she is up to talking when you call. Then listen to the answer. Make it a goal to become a nurturing person. We might need a lot from God, but that's one thing God needs from us. He can't come down here and get movies, go grocery shopping, or give people hugs. If you don't know anyone to practice your comforting and nurturing techniques on, practice on yourself.

4. For information about organ donation or transplantation, contact the United Network for Organ Sharing at 888-894-6361 or www.unos.org.

CHAPTER 4

Changing Bad into Betterment:
When We Lose Our Health

Have you ever had a problem sneak up on you, sneak up on you so subtly and insidiously that you honestly did not see until months or even years after the problem started that it was ruling, dominating, and ruining your life? Not only your life—the problem was affecting your entire family, and you didn't see that either? How can that happen? Easy. Perhaps you wake up each day thinking, *Today is the day I'm going to feel better.* Or, *Today is the day I'm going to the doctor, and he's going to cure me. He'll solve this problem, and I'll get my life back, just like it used to be.* Only you don't. You wake up, and day after day, then month after month, you find yourself living in pain. The pain gets worse. You explore one option after another until the lights finally go on and you see—*I haven't been myself, had a pain-free day, for months or years! Where did my life go, and how did this happen?* You look around and see other people living their lives and going merrily on their way, and you're not. You may be confined to your home, bed, couch, or wheelchair. Maybe you're still out there trying to live your life, but it's not easy.

While this may not be much comfort, you aren't alone. Please listen. You may feel frustrated—even outraged—but you aren't being punished by God. There is within you a still, small voice that you can trust. It will guide you through this. You can trust what you're going through even if it looks and feels like you can't.

Most of us have heard about the wounded healer theory. We get a horrible problem. We don't know why it's happening to us and not to some jerk that deserves it (not us). Then we struggle through the problem and find some answers, and just as subtly as the problem sneaked up and ruined our lives, we find ourselves being organically used by life to help others, and we're able to give this help *because* we had the problem. While it looked like we were being (unjustly) tortured, we were actually in school. Life was preparing us to be of service in ways that we couldn't imagine when we were lying on our couch, begging God to take us out if He couldn't or wouldn't heal us.

Years ago, I attended a weekend writer's conference. It was only two days (and only during daytime hours) that I was entrusting the care of my children to their father. I worried the entire time. Was he drinking? Was he actually taking care of them? Well, at least they were old enough to fend for themselves. And he was a chemical dependency counselor! Me? I couldn't get a job as a counselor. He was being written up in the newspapers, being bowed to and revered, and the man was a great counselor. He just couldn't stop drinking.

While I'm at this writing workshop, the teacher is telling us to write what we know, and I'm obsessing—I cannot stop thinking about my husband and his drinking. I'm scrawling in my notebook that *I can't stand this. Is he drinking? I cannot take this marriage any longer. God what am I supposed to do?* Simultaneously, I was wondering what the instructor was talking about when he said, "Write what you know." I was too close—the proverbial so close to the trees I could not see the forest. I was so close to this mess of a life I was living that I couldn't see the story in it, see the value in it, or see that I would come out the other end and this bad thing I was going through would someday not only be resolved, it would be used for the betterment of humankind. Maybe it was good that I couldn't see that. When we know or even think we know an outcome, we start controlling, trying to make it happen. Then we botch things. We start thinking we have to make the success of our work happen or that we made it happen in the first place instead of realizing that life is doing its work through us, and all we need to do is relax, be present, keep our intentions pure, get out of the way, let life have its way with us, and things will work out fine.

Some of us may use our pain to help others vocationally, some as unpaid service workers. Some of us may be used as unsuspecting examples. After my son died, I watched people open their hearts and value the moments they had with their children so much more because they realized what gifts these moments are. I've also run into people who aren't out of the woods with their problem yet and are proclaiming how they've got to write a book or write a movie and they know it's God's will, and usually that's when life doesn't unfold the way people expect. It's usually the unsuspecting culprits who get sucker-punched by life—who barely know what hit them—who find themselves, to their surprise and the astonishment of families and friends, not only coming through the problem but having the problem turned into their new vocation—one that genuinely helps other people who are where they've been. We become paid or voluntary workers who welcome people to the club, show them they're not alone, calm their fears, and help them find their way around this new terrain.

That's what this story is about.

You can tell a lot about someone by the pictures in his home. A walk through Mark's house shows a six-foot, two-and-a-half-inch man free-falling from a hot-air balloon, arms outstretched, with a huge smile on his face. Mark skydived. He played basketball, tennis, volleyball, and soccer. He rock climbed. He ran a computer consulting business that made him as much as twelve grand a month and allowed his wife, Diane, to be a stay-at-home mom for eighteen years. Mark wasn't smiling only because he was exhilarated from jumping out of a hot-air balloon on a gorgeous day in California's Temecula Valley. He smiled because he had a loving wife, had three wonderful children, and was living life the way it should be lived—to the fullest.

Occasionally he'd be slowed by being "twisted up." Many people have a favorite phrase to describe a back problem. "My back went out," they might say. It's not technical, but it describes how it feels. In the early eighties, Mark might have been twisted up after Sunday volleyball, but he'd be standing tall by Tuesday tennis. By the late eighties, he didn't untwist as quickly. He went to a doctor and got bad news. Two discs in his lower back had moderate bulges. "No more sports," the doctor said. "Give it all up."

What Mark heard was, "Life in prison with no possibility of parole." So Mark did what any passionate skydiving, rock-climbing, soccer- and basketball-playing enthusiast would. He fired his doctor. Then he hired another doctor, an orthopedic surgeon, who skydived. "You can stop doing everything, and your discs will still go bad," his orthopedic surgeon said. "Go live your life, but be smart. If what you're doing is causing problems, stop. Stay fit. Enjoy life. None of us knows what the future will bring, so go live!"

Jumping sports like basketball and volleyball hurt, so Mark eliminated them. For the next ten years, he lived smart. Until the day he was exiting the 405. Until the day the two underinsured kids in the Acura didn't know that the cars in the right lane on the exit ramp weren't moving and came roaring around blindly from the left at forty miles per hour—ramming into the back of Mark's BMW and slamming him into the car in front of him. Mark got out and assessed the damage. *Minimal*, he thought. His back felt stiff. The dented left fender scraped the tire, but he could still drive away from the accident scene. What Mark didn't understand until three body shops and two back surgeries later was that the frame on his car had been irreparably damaged, and so had his back. Many days fade unnoticed, but some we remember. The day Mark (Mr. Active) Mintzer remembers is August 19, 1997—the day the accident he thought was minor totaled his car and his life.

Mark went from taking an occasional pain pill to being a full-time pain-management patient. He went from being twisted up a few times a year to having his tall frame contorted like the grotesquely twisted purple monster figure in the kids' toy chest. He stopped working. His income dropped to a $1,100 a month disability check. Sunday soccer with the children eventually disappeared. Mark tried skydiving twice after the accident, but it hurt so much he stopped. Mark thought he was doing right by playing soccer whenever he could. It was the only activity he could do at least sometimes without pain. What he didn't know was that following the advice to live smart and stay active would be partially why Mark lost hundreds of thousands of dollars in his accident lawsuit.

The judge awarded Mark $25,000, enough to pay attorney's fees but not enough to touch medical bills or compensate for lost income. A picture of Mark playing soccer with the children—doesn't that prove he's not in pain? Testimony that Mark was a skydiver—can those crazy skydivers be trusted? A form where Mark listed a neighbor as an emergency contact was even twisted to present Mark as a crazy skydiver who would do anything for a thrill including have an affair with a neighbor. At arbitration Mark testified for thirty minutes. The insurance company's attorney grilled Mark for six hours, warping his testimony and presenting lies as fact. Mark thought he'd have a chance to set the record straight when his attorney examined him, but Mark's attorney responded by asking Mark only one question. *That's it?* Mark thought. "Why didn't you do something?" Mark demanded on the way out the door. "Why didn't you make sure the judge understood my case?" His attorney responded, "Not enough time. I've got to be in court first thing tomorrow. Got a ton of work to do. Bye."

Mark simmered, even wrote a letter to the judge, but the judge didn't respond. *Nothing's fair.* Easy to say to someone else. It feels different when it happens to us.

Over the years following the accident, a problem Mark thought was minor gradually dominated his life. As Mark became housebound, his wife, Diane, dusted off her nursing degree and went back to work. Years later, when Mark discovered a letter Diane wrote to their sixteen-year-old daughter, he learned how frightened his brave wife really felt. She had reached her breaking point and didn't know how much more she could take. Mark wasn't the only one in pain. His entire family was suffering too.

"I'm burned out and tired," Diane wrote. "It's not easy to take care of sick people for twelve hours and then come home to someone in pain.

I wish you would decide to get along with Dad. You need to show him some respect and compassion. . . . He loves you. He would love to teach you to drive. We need another driver. I don't know how much longer he'll be able to drive. (Don't tell him I said that.) He's still holding on to dreams of playing soccer, but I think he'll be lucky if he walks again. . . . I'm sorry I'm grouchy and tired, but I am. Work is stressful. At least it's an escape to a different world. I'm too busy dealing with other people's problems to dwell on my own. I can imagine how Dad feels not being able to support his family. When I realized that Dad wasn't going to be able to return to work, I had an awful feeling. How can I support us? Will anyone hire me? Do I still have enough knowledge to be a nurse? I have learned and grown through all of this. Even if Dad could go back to work today, I would continue to work. I never want to feel like I can't support myself again. I have given you my love and support for years and have many beautiful memories. . . . I need your love and support now."

It's eye- and heart-opening to see how each family member is affected when one person gets sick. Each person's life becomes altered. Everyone may feel alone and misunderstood. The non-ill family members need support systems too.

Many people don't believe in back problems until they happen to them. Many people believe that they can take a medical problem to a doctor and the doctor will reach into his bag of tricks and fix it. You're sick, you go to the doctor, the doctor does something, and you get better. Right? Two surgeries fixed Mark's leg pain but didn't touch the lower back pain. Damage to his discs escalated from moderate to severe. One doctor refused to do fusion surgery, saying that the success rate was only fifty-fifty. Another doctor guaranteed Mark a 90 percent success rate from fusion surgery, claiming he never made anyone worse. Mark's plumber was lying on Mark's kitchen floor working under the sink when Mark told him that he'd finally found a doctor who could fix him. The plumber asked the doctor's name. When Mark told him, the plumber sat up so fast he nearly clunked his head.

"That's the doctor who ruined my wife's back!" the plumber said.

That's when Mark saw the light. "We think doctors are all-knowing. We think they have something special and they're going to fix us," he said in one interview. "We have to do our homework and take responsibility for our bodies and the course of our medical care. Doctors can't always tell us all our options. One doctor has a hammer, so everything looks like a nail. The next one has a screwdriver, so everything looks like a screw. If your problem is like a lock, you need a doctor with a key."

We shouldn't hand our lives over to someone else. We need to take charge and understand for ourselves. We can consult specialists, but ultimately we live with the choices we make. We deserve to be fully informed and make decisions that are right for us.

Mark walked away from the accident until he couldn't walk anymore. He walked straight into spinal hell. Nobody—not the doctors, his friends, the judge, his attorney, even his loving wife—understood. Mark was about to learn that while life isn't always fair, it has a plan. He began doing research on the Internet. On a forum he met other people living in spinal hell. They shared information—which doctors to see, whom to avoid, the latest technology, possible complications. Most important, the people in the Internet spine community understood. Mark got welcomed to the *I've Lost My Life Because My Back Doesn't Work and My Doctor Can't Fix Me* Club.

First Mark talked to the Internet gurus. Then he became one. Although he didn't know it yet, he was being groomed for his next career— walking other people through the spinal hell that he walked through alone. Mark heard about a new surgery called ADR (artificial disc replacement). Damaged discs are removed instead of fused, and artificial discs are inserted in their place. While fusion leaves people stiff, the artificial discs restore mobility. They work similar to artificial hips or knees. Although long-term findings aren't available, the probability of success with ADR is higher than with fusion. Doctors have been performing ADR in Germany since 1989. In 2002, the surgery was still under clinical study in the United States on its way to becoming FDA approved.

Mark heard about ADR surgery two years before he underwent it. Because he heard bad reports, Mark first dismissed it as an option. A woman who was supposedly an Internet guru said they were putting in the discs in Germany and taking them out in France. But when Mark pressed her for details about why the discs weren't a good choice, the woman couldn't back up her story. Mark began aggressively researching ADR, and what he discovered excited him. It didn't match what the woman said. They were putting in the discs in Germany, and many patients who had been in wheelchairs were walking from the surgery room to the recovery room—some of them walking for the first time in years. Mark learned his second lesson: distinguish rumor from fact.

The advantages of the Internet are many, but don't take everything people say as fact. Make them say who, what, where, when, how, and why, then check out their answers. Investigate. Sometimes our money is at stake. Sometimes it's our lives. Often when pushed for sources, people either say they don't know or they heard it from someone who heard it from someone else. Spreading rumors is an easy way to hurt other people and ourselves.

Mark wanted to know everything about his options, this surgery, the discs, what could go right, what could go wrong. He made e-mail contact with leading international ADR surgeons. Despite the risks, Mark decided ADR was for him. Because the FDA allowed U.S. surgeons to replace only one disc and Mark needed two, Mark and Diane flew overseas. Insurance wouldn't pay, so Mark refinanced his California home to pay for his new back. In September 2002 in Munich, a doctor put two artificial discs in Mark's lower back. But Mark wasn't one of the people who walked from surgery to the recovery room. "My recovery was hard," Mark said. "I hurt."

Two days before surgery, Mark watched what he describes as an unbelievable UEFA soccer game at Munich's Olympic Stadium. A self-proclaimed goalkeeper junkie, Mark bought the goalie's jersey and put it on. Watching the last half of the game, he wondered, *Is this a sign? Is it possible that someday I'll play soccer again?* He hadn't completely lost hope, and now hope was close to becoming real. But a week later, after the surgery and back at the hotel, Mark collapsed into Diane's arms. "Will I ever know a day without pain?" he asked. Three years later, he still chokes remembering how he felt.

But six weeks after surgery, Mark was off all pain medication for the first time in three years. Three weeks later, he took his last antidepressant. Mark didn't look back. "I could feel the life sucking back into me," Mark said. He's surprised he didn't become addicted to opiates after taking them so long. He says he undermedicated himself, and Diane vouches for that. Leading pain-management and addiction specialists insist that even when high doses of opiates are used properly to treat intractable pain, opiates aren't the enemy. "Chronic pain damages organs and the body. Pain is the enemy," says Dr. Forest Tennant. "Medication is the friend."

A few months later, Mark began doing more than playing soccer again. He got a new life. Besides becoming physically active, Mark found himself in the midst of doctors and the world of ADR. He became a cause célèbre at one spine convention. Instead of data beamed from an overhead projector, here was a walking, talking, scuba-diving, skiing, soccer-playing, pain-free human being who had successfully undergone a two-level ADR. Mark (Mr. Active) Mintzer was back untwisted. The discs worked. The physicians wanted to hear what he had to say. So did the people still trapped in spinal hell.

Mark first met Melanie from Canada on the Internet forums. After five failed spine surgeries and nineteen years of pain medication, she was diagnosed as hopeless with "failed back surgery syndrome." The doctors told her to go home, take her pain pills, and deal with it as best she could. Melanie had frequent bouts of urinary incontinence and difficulty walking. She was housebound, in unrelenting pain. The medical system said there was nothing more any doctor could do, but Mark wasn't willing to give up. He wanted to help. Mark began badgering doctors on Melanie's behalf. At first the American spine doctors wouldn't see her, but with Mark's persistence, Melanie got an appointment and a new diagnosis. It turned out she wasn't hopeless. To her and the medical community's astonishment, Melanie was treatable. Melanie became

Mark's first client. Eighteen months after meeting Mark, Melanie finally underwent ADR. Instead of getting diapers and a wheelchair, she got a new life. She's now medication-free, working, running, lifting, and stooping, even dancing the Irish jig. She says it's thanks to her surgeon and Mark's persistent, knowledgeable help.

Eventually, assisting spine patients became so time-consuming that Mark had to either find a way to make a living doing it or stop. In 2004, Mark formed Global Patient Network in Fountain Valley, California. Since then, he's helped 250 spine clients. He puts X-rays, MRIs, and medical profiles in a secure site online at www.globalpatientnetwork.com. This allows people to shop for doctors internationally and domestically, for not much money.

"Every day I'm contacted by people who are confused and frightened," Mark says. "Many of them don't understand what they're facing. They either can't work or are barely functioning. Their sex life is gone. Their friends, families, co-workers, and often their medical teams don't understand what they're going through. They get conflicting opinions from doctors they trust. Sometimes they're not told all their options or the information they receive is incorrect."

Mark helps people manage their situations and make informed decisions. He arranges spine symposiums where patients meet doctors. Mark has a direct line to top spine surgeons around the world. Sometimes he accompanies people to appointments and surgeries, especially overseas surgeries, so they don't have to go alone.

It's not uncommon for Mark to hang up the phone after talking to a spine patient, then sit and cry. Sometimes it's because he knows—often before the patient—that they have few options and little hope. Sometimes it's because he just heard, "Thank you. I can pick up my grandchild without even thinking about it." "Thank you. I just went out on my husband's boat for the first time." "I can tie my own shoelaces." Or "I'm off medication for the first time in nineteen years."

It's not the shoelaces, the activities, or the pain meds that bring tears to his eyes. The difference between having a life and not having a life is what a wounded healer understands.

It's not easy to have faith when we're burning in the fire. We're not all going to get our miracles. More times than not, the miracle we get is life as-is and no guarantees. Plain faith, the kind most of us have been schooled in, applies to tomorrow. It says, *Things are going to be okay— if and when we get our happy ending.* When we talk to someone who has been where we are, we get the courage to have radical faith—the extraordinary kind. It's powerful when somebody looks us in the eye and tells us we can do it and we are okay, because he or she has been where we're at. Our bodies respond right down to our cells. There's enough disaster and pain in our world. Make a contribution. Give people some hope.

Annually, the lives of Americans are disrupted by
40 million headaches
36 million back pains
24 million muscle pains
20 million neck pains

1,038 million workdays are lost to back pain.

638 million workdays are lost to headaches.

34 million Americans suffer annually from intractable pain.

31 million Americans have back pain at any given time.

One-half of all working Americans admit to back symptoms each year.

One-third of all Americans over 18 sought professional help for a back problem over a five-year period.

The cost of this back care is an estimated $50 billion annually.

Sources: American Medical Association, National Foundation for the Treatment of Pain, and American Chiropractic Association

ACTIVITIES

1. Are you going through a problem now and delegating the responsibility for solving that problem to someone else? Yes, we do need to trust the wisdom of physicians and other skilled personnel. But we also need to learn to gather information, sort through it, and then take responsibility for ourselves. Few problems magically become solved from outside of ourselves; life requires our cooperation and participation, even when that involves healing our bodies. Minimally, we need to participate in any decision affecting our lives. If the problem is too technical or beyond our comprehension, then we need to locate an advocate, someone to help us understand. We have a right to know, and we have the right to ask.

When I was diagnosed with degenerative disc disease, I didn't know I had any options. My doctor hadn't heard of ADR. Essentially I was told that it sucks to be me—by no means a technical prognosis, but an accurate one according to my physician. I researched and discovered the surgery that ultimately fixed the problem. Then I researched resources with the help of Mark Mintzer and Global Patient Network. Turn your problem into a research project. There are many resources. We can use the Internet—but remember to check facts. Don't forget about the library. The books are free, and most librarians are happy to help. Don't overlook all the magazines at the library too—including back issues. (Many of these magazines and newspapers are also archived online.) We can find groups for almost every problem that exists. Look in the yellow pages. Look on the bulletin board at your hospital. Pick up newsletters. Once I begin a dedicated search, I usually find that information begins coming to me. The mystery begins unraveling. Search for information, but be careful whom you trust. Ask for references, then check them. Bounce your information off people as a way of confirming that you're on track. Often by talking to other people about what we're learning, we help integrate information so that we really understand. Research until you become well informed. Participate in your life.

2. What problem is bothering or hurting you most right now? Have you found your community of peers—your club? Make it a project to find three people who have been where you are. Ask them if they'll talk to you and share their experience and hope. Or, if you're on the other side of your problem, find three people who are now where you've been and share your experience and hope with them.

A friend and colleague was at an airport waiting for a flight when she got a phone call from a woman she'd met on the Internet. My friend is a bereaved parent. Her daughter died after a brave struggle with illness. She watched her daughter get sick; she watched her daughter's death. The woman calling asked my friend to describe in detail how her daughter died and what the last few hours were like so she'd know what to expect, because her child was dying soon. "I sat down at the airport and went through the whole thing with this woman," my friend said. "I was crying the entire time. I know she had no idea how painful this was for me, but I did it," she said. "When the woman called me days later, after her child died, she thanked me and said how enormously helpful our conversation had been." My friend knows how important it is to be with people who really get us. She wants to be there for people the way people were there for her.

People who haven't been through what we're going through don't understand. They try to generalize, and it's not the same. "We can model for people that they can have this problem and still keep going," my friend said. That's what wounded healers do. It will happen naturally. We'll be going about the business of our lives and someone will pop into our path—someone who's going through a problem we had. Or we'll wake up one day and discover that we're working in a field where we're using what we've gone through to help other people; we're working to make this a better world. Don't worry about how it will happen. It will. All we need to do is be open, aware, and respond with a yes when life puts that person or opportunity in our path.

3. Are you going through a problem and not opening your eyes and heart to how the people you love are being affected? Acknowledging

what our loved ones are going through and that they are being affected—saying thanks and how much we appreciate their support—can go a long way. Sometimes family members can't be there for us. We need to figure out what we'd like from them. Then ask. It makes life easier if we don't lock in and expect specific things from certain people if they don't have it to give. Some of us have a hard time letting people take care of us. Maybe it's not an imposition; helping us might make them feel good. We won't know unless we ask.

4. Are you in unrelenting, intractable pain? You don't have to suffer. Contact the National Foundation for the Treatment of Pain at www.paincare.org or 713-862-9332.

CHAPTER 5

Breaking into Change:
Losing Someone to Suicide

It was one more day in Terri's life. Nine hours of gopher work at the television studio, stop at the dry cleaner, work out at the gym, spend forty-five minutes grinding through L.A. traffic, pick up a Chinese chicken salad, go home, gulp dinner, edit her script for the hundredth time after another round of notes, e-mail today's version to her agent, then haul her tired body into the shower. She was on a mission, a vendetta. She'd prove to herself, the world, and that ass of a boss she worked for that she could endure his abuse. He wasn't going to drive her away like he did everyone else. She'd earn his respect before she was done. She'd been climbing this ladder for years, doing everything from minimum-wage jobs so she could live in this city to stand-up for a year in the freezing Midwest—whatever it took to get a foot in the entertainment industry's door. She'd made it to the inside of a studio, but she wasn't going to be a writing assistant forever. She was going to be a real writer. Someday she'd have her own show. That break she needed was getting closer. She could feel it in her bones.

She washed off the city's dust, then let the hot water pound her. She was proud of her body. She didn't have that waiflike anorexic look so popular here; she was skinny but muscular, honed. Finally she felt herself surrender to the steamy heat. Five minutes later, she climbed into bed. The light was blinking on her answering machine. "Terri, please call me tonight." Another message from Brian. She felt a twinge of guilt. She still hadn't returned his last call. But it was already eleven o'clock. She had to get up in seven hours. Her brother was so needy now. She didn't know what to say. She didn't know how to make him feel better. *I'll call him tomorrow*, Terri promised herself. *On my lunch break.* She turned off the light and immediately fell asleep.

One hundred miles away, Brian paced his apartment floor. The gun was on the bureau—loaded, ready to go. He raged aloud while he paced. He didn't know if he was talking to God, life, some invisible person, or all the people he knew. It didn't matter. No one heard him anyway. They hadn't for a long time.

He sat down at his desk. Maybe if he wrote the things he was screaming about, someone would finally get it. They'd hear him, they'd understand. He didn't bother pouring the whiskey into a glass. He drank straight from the bottle while he wrote.

He hurt so damn bad and no one—nobody—cared.

Jason had cared. He was the only one in the world who did. Jason cared about Brian when they were lovers. Jason still cared when he got sick and their relationship changed, and they went from being lovers to friends. They never stopped loving each other. But Jason wasn't here anymore. In the month since Jason's death, Brian was utterly and absolutely alone. Brian had hurt before. He'd been in emotional pain most of his life. But until now he never understood the depth of pain that human beings could feel. He didn't know people could walk around with so little hope and so much hurt in their gut and still keep breathing. You'd think that much pain would kill you. It would make your heart stop beating or something. Brian was amazed and enraged every day when he woke up and realized he hadn't died in his sleep.

By the time he signed his name at the bottom of the letter, his scrawl was barely legible and he was making holes in the paper from pushing so hard with the pen. Brian wasn't sure if his writing was that bad because he was drunk or because he was angry.

He dialed 911. "Please send an ambulance," Brian said to the woman who answered. He told her his address. "I need you to take a dead body away."

"Who is it?" the dispatcher asked. "What happened? Are you sure the person is dead?"

"The body is mine," Brian said. "And yes, I'm sure I'll be dead. I'm killing myself when I hang up the phone."

"Oh, come on now," the woman said. "You don't want to do that to me, do you? This is the end of my shift. I've had a long day. If you kill yourself, I'll be here all night filling out forms. I'm five minutes away from going home." She had used this tactic before and it had worked. All she had to do was keep him on the line, keep him talking, until she could get someone to his door.

"Just send the ambulance," Brian said. "I don't want my body lying around stinking up the place. I don't want anyone walking in and finding that."

"You don't want to do that to me," the dispatcher pleaded. "I'm tired. It's been a long day. Let's talk about this for a while."

Brian hung up the phone. He walked to the bureau and picked up the gun. He stood in front of the mirror and positioned the barrel against his head. Then he closed his eyes.

At first Terri thought the noise was her alarm buzzer, that it was morning and it was time to wake up. Then she realized it was the phone. She looked at the clock. It was three in the morning Who'd be calling now? She fumbled for the receiver.

"Hello?"

A man who identified himself as a coroner began talking about Brian. The conversation seemed surreal to Terri. Was he really talking about her brother? She knew Brian was having a hard time. But suicide? No. This wasn't possible.

"He addressed the letter to you," the coroner said. Terri listened while Brian blamed their mother, then attacked their father. Then the coroner got to the part that Terri would never forget. The words became branded, seared into her mind with a red-hot poker iron. *And you, dear*

sister, even you weren't there for me. Mom and Dad not being there I under-
stand. I don't expect anything from them anymore. But you? I'm going
through the worst time of my life and you're too busy to call me back? I
thought you loved me and you couldn't even pick up the phone. Seeing as it's
your fault I'm killing myself, could you at least do one thing for me if it's not
too much trouble? Make sure my ashes get put with Jason's ashes. I want to
be with him. He's the only one who ever cared.

"Boy, he was one angry guy," the coroner said.

Terri went on automatic pilot. She told the coroner she'd call the rest
of the family. She wrote down addresses and phone numbers of people
to contact the next day. She said she'd be there by early afternoon to
identify the body. Then she hung up the phone, took a deep breath, and
dialed her mother's number.

Never before had Terri heard a sound like the one she heard her
mother make. It was a moaning, a deep howling wail. It sounded like a
noise an animal would make. Her mother's howl would haunt Terri for
years. It was the only emotion Terri would ever hear her mother express
about Brian's death.

The morgue was a cold, sterile place. Terri shifted from one foot to
the other while the coroner talked to her dad. "I tried to fix his head so
you can have an open casket," the coroner said. "I think I did a pretty
good . . ."

"Are those penny loafers you're wearing?" Brian's father interrupted.
He pointed at the coroner's shoes.

"Yes," the coroner said. "As I was saying, I did my best to repair his
head . . ."

"Where did you get those shoes?" Brian's dad said, still pointing at
the floor. "I've been looking for shoes like that for years."

"Nordstrom's, I think," the coroner said. He started to repeat what
he was trying to explain about the damage to the body. When Brian's
father interrupted him the third time, the coroner gave up. It was no
use. He'd seen many trauma reactions in this room when people came
to identify bodies. He'd seen people scream, faint, cry hysterically, go

numb, and beg for God's help. In all the years he'd worked at the morgue, this was the first time anyone had talked about shoes.

Did Brian kill himself because he had AIDS? Terri wondered. But the coroner's report came back. Brian wasn't sick. When Terri cleared out Brian's apartment, she found his journal. The world looked at Brian and saw a laid-back, happy-go-lucky guy. He was always clowning around, making everyone laugh. Brian was openly gay, okay with being gay. Happy to be gay. That's what he told her. Reading Brian's journal, Terri saw a side to her brother she didn't know existed. *Who's journal is this?* Terri thought. *I didn't even know this guy.*

> Just returned from a trip back East. Mom tried to fix me up with a "nice girl" again. When are they going to get it, that I'm gay? They keep waiting for me to meet a woman, get married, give them grandchildren. Mom keeps on me and on me. It makes me crazy. I didn't choose to be gay. I'd love to have children. What does being gay mean anyway? Why do I have to be anything? I love Jason. Because I love Jason that means I'm gay? Why can't I just be a human being who loves another person who happens to be a man?
>
> I keep telling Terri that she shouldn't let it bother her what Mom and Dad think. I tell her she's got a good rela-tionship, so what does it matter if she loves a woman? I feel like such a phony. It bothers me that I'm gay. I say it doesn't matter whether Mom and Dad approve but the truth is, it does. I want them to tell me they're proud of me and they love me. I want them to accept me for who I am. Do they have any idea how much I need that from them? They look at me and they don't see a son they love. They see a queer.

Brian had never let on to anyone how important their parents' acceptance was. He laughed it off. Terri thought Brian's depression started when Jason died. As she read through the pages of his journal, she saw that Brian had been depressed and unhappy most of his life. The coroner was right. Brian was one angry guy.

> There's no place for me in this world. I don't fit. I never
> have. Something is missing in me that's in other people.
> Sometimes I think about that priest. I feel sorry for the way
> they're torturing that poor guy now. In a way I liked him. He
> was the only man who ever gave me any attention when I
> was growing up—even if it was sexual. It was more than
> what I got from Mom and Dad. Then I go to church one
> Sunday and he's gone. Vanished. Like he never existed and
> nobody mentions him again. What a joke! We're in the rec-
> tory less than fifty feet away from our parents and we're hav-
> ing sex with a priest.
>
> Terri was the only one who knew. Every Sunday she'd ask
> me what was wrong. I'd tell her nothing was wrong and she
> looked at me like she knew I was lying. She always had that
> look in her eyes—like she knew the truth about everything.
> Mom and Dad are so dense. They don't have a clue now and
> they didn't back then. "You look so cute in your altar boy
> clothes," Mom would say. "I'm so proud of you." Why can't
> she be proud of me now?

It stunned Terri to read about the sexual abuse, but at the same time
it didn't surprise her. Terri had good instincts. That priest was creepy.
She could feel it when she was around him. When Terri and Brian went
to church on Sundays, something came over Brian. Reading all the dirty
details about what that priest did to her brother, Terri felt enraged. Week
after week, that little boy was all alone in the world with nobody to tell.
And he didn't even get mad at the priest! He felt sorry for the abuser and
blamed himself. Whenever Brian asked their mom if he could stay home
from church, she'd try to make him feel guilty. "Are you that selfish?"
she'd say.

The past month, ever since Jason died, Brian had been calling Terri
a lot. Between work, trying to get her career off the ground, working

out, and doing errands, it was hard to squeeze anything else into her days. A week ago, Terri and her partner had met Brian for lunch. They were sitting in an L.A. restaurant. Terri was talking about her screenplay, trying to convince Brian to move to L.A. "We could get together more often," she said. "Now that Jason is gone, why stay all alone in that apartment down there?" In the middle of the restaurant in broad daylight, Brian started sobbing. He started crying out loud, for the whole world to see! Terri's partner moved and slid in next to him. She put her arm around him, comforting him, telling him, "It'll be okay." Terri was in awe. Terri couldn't handle her own feelings. She couldn't handle anyone's feelings. Feelings made her nervous, uncomfortable. Feelings are a sign of weakness. You don't give in to them; you ignore them. *How can she just hold him and let him cry?* Terri wondered. *Why can't I do that? What's wrong with me? I don't even know how to hug my own brother.*

Brian needed so much. Terri didn't have anything to give. She didn't know how to be there for him. She didn't know how to be there for anyone, including herself. Being comforting and nurturing was as alien to her as trying to speak a foreign language. She thought about the messages on her answering machine, the ones she hadn't returned. *Terri, please call me. Terri, I need you.*

Terri flashed back to her school days. She was so scared to start middle school. Brian was in high school by then. Every day during lunch hour, he'd sneak over to the middle school just to check on Terri and make sure she was okay. Brian loved her so much. He was her big brother. He protected her. He was always there for her. Those years at home with their parents, Brian was always the one with the jokes. When Mom and Dad criticized her and made her feel like nothing, he made her smile. He told her she was beautiful, talented, smart. When she turned eighteen, Brian was living in New York. He moved her in with him without a second thought. He loved her. He helped her get her bearings, find her dreams, then get the courage to move to L.A.

Brian's right, Terri thought. *I wasn't there for him. It's my fault he's dead.* She just joined the *You Weren't Supposed to Go Away but You Did, and You Left Me Here with More Pain and Guilt Than I Know How to Handle* Club.

Terri watched as her mom wrote the obituary. The obituary didn't mention Jason, the only true love in Brian's life. She listened while her mother called other family members and friends and told them about Brian's death. "Yes, it was a terrible tragedy and surprise. He just dropped over dead at the gym from an aneurism. It happened while he was working out. Who would have suspected? He was in such good shape, so healthy, so young. Just goes to show that we never know, do we? When it's our time, we go." Without any trace of emotion, without flinching or blinking or breaking down and crying, Terri's mother told everyone—every single person—the exact same lie.

Something clicked in Terri as she watched her mother handle Brian's suicide. Her mother had the same emotional affect as if she was preparing a gathering for the women in her book club. The way she made up the story about how Brian died. The way she never, not once, mentioned the suicide to Terri or anyone else. At first Terri thought her mom was in shock, that she had gone on some kind of traumatized automatic pilot and was making things up as she went along. Then Terri realized her mom wasn't winging this. These behaviors—the complete denial of the suicide, the lies, the lack of emotion, the ease with which she was handling the death of her son—were what her mother had learned.

That's why the family refuses to talk about Grandpa's death, Terri thought. *My grandfather killed himself too. My mom watched Grandma do this. That's how she knows what to do.*

Brian was cremated. Her mom took the ashes back to the East Coast. She intended to put them in a drawer in the back room in the basement of the Catholic church. Brian had been clear about what he wanted done with his ashes, and his mom knew it. He wanted them mixed in with Jason's ashes. Jason's ashes had been in an urn in Brian's apartment; now the urn was at Terri's house. *Is the back room in the church basement where they put the ashes of people who commit suicide and are gay?* Terri wondered. Terri didn't say anything. Nobody said anything to her mother. Mother always got her way.

After her parents left town, Terri went to the park with a friend and her two children. Life had been so heavy. Terri needed to be outside and watch children play. Terri hadn't cried yet; she felt this strange numbness where her heart should have been. She watched the children play, then she decided to join them. She slid down the slide, taking turns with her friend's children. Then Terri climbed on the small merry-go-round, the one that spins around and around in a circle while you hang on to the railing. None of the children were on it. Terri made it go faster and faster, until she was dizzy and the world was spinning. Without waiting for it to stop, Terri leaped off. When she fell to the ground, she heard her leg bone snap.

Her left leg was broken. While Terri was at the hospital getting her cast, the light was blinking on her answering machine at home. Her television script had been accepted. Terri sold her first pilot.

It took her a while to understand—they were both lucky breaks.

"My family didn't do feelings. My family didn't grieve. Breaking my leg put me in bed for six weeks. I couldn't work, couldn't work out, couldn't even do errands. I couldn't keep running from my feelings. If I hadn't broken my leg, I would have carried on the family tradition. I would have pushed right past my grief."

Terri made an important decision. She would feel everything she felt about her brother's suicide for as long as it took. She didn't know how to be there for her brother. She couldn't change that. But she could start being there for herself.

Terri committed to her grief.

Most people don't like to feel; few people want to feel pain. There's a juncture we reach after a loss. We can't choose what happens to us, but we can honor how we feel about what happens to us. Committing to our grief doesn't mean we're choosing to drown in sorrow; it means we're choosing to heal our heart.

The stoic, strong woman who didn't do feelings started crying. Once she did, she couldn't stop. She lay in bed and cried for weeks. Her partner held her, comforted her, took care of her. "Would you get me a glass of water?" Terri asked about six weeks after Brian's death. Her partner gently said, "I think it's time you get up and get it for yourself."

Terri got out of bed. She stopped cocooning. She went back to work.

Every day she got up, got dressed, got in the car, and cried all the way to work. She worked all day, got in her car, then cried all the way home. Terri began to notice something she never saw before: A lot of people in L.A. were crying in their cars.

Grief is overwhelming at first. It comes in waves we can't control. None are exactly the same. We cry and sob, sob and cry, then the crying stops. It's over, we think. We barely catch our breath, then the crying starts again. Soon we begin to see that while we can't control the waves of grief, we can choose when we want to cry and when we need to stop. We can learn to give ourselves breaks. Nobody can cry all the time. We can distract ourselves, work, look the other way. We can even laugh. Don't worry. If we've committed to our feelings and our grief, the feelings will find a way and a time to come out.

Terri joined a suicide survivor's group. It helped to hear other people talk about how they felt. The thing that helped the most was being able to talk openly about the guilt. As the months passed, Terri surprised herself again. Terri—the woman who didn't do feelings—volunteered to facilitate the group. Helping other people deal with their grief helped her too.

"I was sitting on my kitchen floor one night listening to Brian's favorite CD over and over," Terri said. "I was collapsed on the floor, sobbing, when I had an awakening. My entire life I thought that ignoring my emotions made me powerful. Now sitting on the floor sobbing, I could see that by being vulnerable and surrendering to all my feelings, I was becoming stronger than I'd ever been."

A whole new Terri was being born. She says the worst part of the grief lasted five years. "I'm a different person now," Terri says. "I'm more sensitive, more intuitive, more aware. I can see and feel what people need. It's so easy in this big city to say, 'I'll call you,' or 'Let's get together,' and then not bother. That's the kind of person I used to be. Not anymore. It doesn't take that much effort and energy to be loving, to be caring, to be kind. When someone reaches out to me now, I'm there. And if they don't reach out to me and I know they're in pain, I reach out to them."

Terri likes who she's become. She's achieved a lot of success and power in the world of television and film. She doesn't take that power casually. She tackles the hard issues, subjects she would have avoided before. She writes scripts about being gay; she's written shows about abuse. She makes everything she learned the hard way count. It's one way she can honor her brother and be there for him now.

"The real irony is that because of his death, I've become the person he needed me to be back then. I'm not saying this to be narcissistic or egotistical, but if my brother were alive and hurting now and reached out to me, I could help him. I really believe I could stop him from killing himself. If I was the person then that I've become since his death, my brother would be alive. His death has taught me a lot."

Terri sat on a chair across from George Anderson, the medium who contacts the dead. Terri's a skeptical person. But like many people who have lost someone, she heard good things about George. She didn't know exactly what she believed about life after death, but she was willing to find out.

"George scribbled like he does with a pencil while he talked. He started talking in partial sentences. Then he told me my brother's name. He got it right! There's no way he could have known," Terri said. "George described—he told me—the exact details of Brian's death."

George said that Brian had some things he wanted to discuss.

"He says he's sorry about the letter," George said. "He didn't mean what he said. Your brother knows how much you love him. He says he was angry, drunk, and upset. He wants you to forgive him for the mean things he said. He says you were always a light in his life."

Forgive *him?* Brian wanted Terri to forgive him? Terri wanted *him* to forgive *her.*

"Terri, it's not your fault," Brian said through George. "I chose to end my own life."

In many instances, suicide is more like an accident than a deliberate act, George explained. Brian didn't really want to die. He wanted to stop the pain and he couldn't think of anything else to do.

Many bereaved people need to connect with a loved one who's dead. Some want to finish unfinished business. Some want to hear that the person they love is okay, alive somewhere on the other side. Some grief therapists say that when the time is right, this connection helps bereaved people heal their pain and make peace.

Terri had one more thing she needed to do. She and her partner got on a plane and headed east. Terri had a plan.

"Mom, I miss Brian so much. Won't you please let me go to the church, get a few of his ashes out, then bring them home? It would help me so much. Please?" Terri begged. Finally her mother agreed.

In the far room in the back of the church basement was a row of locked boxes on the wall. Terri searched until she found the one with Brian's name. She took a screwdriver out of her purse and popped the lock. Dang. The box broke! Terri ran out and bought a duplicate box. Terri put all the ashes from both men together and mixed them up. Then she put half of Jason and Brian's ashes in the box at the church. Then she took the other half of Brian and Jason's ashes home, where she keeps them in an urn. Now their ashes are together, even though they're split up in two locations and half of them are at church.

"What Mother doesn't know won't hurt her," Terri says. She feels good that she found a way to honor her brother's last request.

Terri forgave her brother for killing himself and for writing that horrible letter. She forgave her mother for how she handled her brother's death. "I'm beginning to see that people do the best they can do," Terri said, "even if sometimes their best isn't much." Terri says the only person she hasn't completely forgiven is herself.

"I expect I'll feel some guilt for the rest of my life," Terri says. "The guilt was so big I'm not sure it'll ever go away. I'll always love and miss Brian. Breaking my leg was the best thing that could have happened to me. It forced me to sit still and go into my grief. I could easily have handled it like the rest of my family, which means going into denial and not dealing with it at all. They still don't mention Brian—his birthday, his life, his death.

"With grief you either pay now or pay later," Terri said. "My debt to grief is paid in full."

There are 601,209 same-sex couples in the United States and Puerto Rico.

Two percent to 6 percent of the U.S. population is gay (depending on who's counting).

The average coming-out age for gays and lesbians has dropped from ages 19 to 23 to ages 14 to 16.

The official number of suicides in the United States is approximately 30,000 a year, but the actual number may be three to five times higher because many suicides go unreported.

During times of economic hardship, the suicide rate went up, but during the two world wars, the rates went down.

Most people have had casual thoughts of suicide.

People coming from a family where someone has killed himor herself are several times more likely to commit suicide.

White men age 65 and older are most likely to commit suicide.

Of the 30,000 annual reported suicides, 24,000 are men.

Sources: U.S. Census; a study by Caitlin Ryan, Director of Adolescent Health Initiatives at San Francisco State University; and *Why Suicide?* by Eric Marcus

ACTIVITIES

1. Are you willing to commit to your grief and stay with yourself and the process? Go over your Master List of Losses. Do you see any losses

where you've neglected or denied your grief? Are you willing to feel your grief now? Feelings don't disappear. Unresolved grief will come back to haunt us. We can't force ourselves to start feeling old grief, but being willing to feel what we need to feel is often all we need to do to start the healing process. Commit to your grief; it's a kind thing to do for your heart.

2. Have you learned how to distract yourself from your grief? It's an art that can be learned. We can't cry all the time when we're grieving. It's too much. Besides, we have to work, do errands, do other things. In the beginning, grief can and often is overwhelming. We sob uncontrollably much of the time. That's okay. Be gentle with yourself. You'll learn how to turn the faucet off and on. Sometimes doing something as simple as going into another room, going for a walk, watching a movie, calling someone on the phone, or even taking a shower can help us switch gears when we feel like we've been crying too much. Practice. Find out what techniques work for you. Our souls and hearts are smart, intelligent. The deep part of us that's healing knows how much we can take, what we need to do, and when.

3. Write letters of comfort to people who are grieving. It's hard to know what to say to someone who has experienced a loss. We stumble for words or we say the wrong thing. I look back at all the stupid and inappropriate things I said to people before Shane died—before I knew how it felt—and I'm embarrassed. It would have been more helpful to say nothing at all. The Jewish religion has beautiful traditions and specific rituals surrounding mourning. In his book *A Time to Mourn, a Time to Comfort*, Dr. Ron Wolfson gives a specific and helpful format for writing a comforting letter to a grieving person. He suggests acknowledging the loss and the name of the deceased; expressing genuine sympathy; listing special traits or qualities of the deceased that stand out in your mind; writing about a favorite memory of the deceased—something funny, touching, sweet, memorable, or loving; reminding the grieving person that he or she is strong and mentioning personal strengths that

will help him or her get through this; offering help by saying you'll do something specific, such as bringing a casserole next Friday evening or helping with grocery shopping; and ending the letter with warmth and love, not "yours truly." Taking the time to send a comforting letter is a kind thing to do. Most people treasure the letters they receive. Also, if you're trying to work through some old losses, why not send a letter of comfort to yourself? It might be just the trigger you need to help your heart heal from some old, frozen grief. Practice being nurturing and comforting on yourself. It'll help you feel better, and you'll learn what to do to help someone else.

4. Do you have a child or loved one who's gay or lesbian and needs your love and support? Do you need support so you can give that? Contact Parents, Families and Friends of Lesbians and Gays at www.pflag.org or 202-467-8180 for national and international chapter information.

5. Are you thinking about suicide or are you a suicide survivor? Help is available seven days a week, twenty-four hours a day. Contact the National Hopeline Network at 800-SUICIDE (800-784-2433); contact the National Suicide Prevention Lifeline at 800-273-TALK (800-273-8255) or TTY: 800-799-4TTY (800-799-4889); or visit www.suicide hotlines.com, www.suicidalteens.com, www.suicidal.com, www.survivors ofsuicide.com, or www.yellowribbon.org (303-429-3530).

CHAPTER 6

Wrestling with Change:
Losing Marriage, Career, and Home

It took only the *slightest* tug on the steering wheel.

The car behind Sarah's car slammed to a stop on the canyon road. The young couple in it watched Sarah's car crash through the barrier railing, then plunge down the side of the cliff. "Then it burst into flames halfway down," the driver said to the sheriff. "It exploded in a ball of fire."

"Did it look like she lost control of the vehicle?" the sheriff asked. "Was she swerving? Maybe driving drunk?"

"No," the couple in the car behind Sarah's agreed. "We were behind her for three or four miles. She was following the speed limit, staying in her lane. Her driving was fine. Suddenly her car just went flying off the cliff."

Sarah's car was the second car to drive off the canyon road that week and the fifth car that month. Each accident ended like Sarah's—all occupants in the cars died. One driver was a mother who left two young children behind. Suicide is suspected in all cases but can't be proven. Nobody left a note.

"I knew Sarah, but we weren't close. I don't think she was close to anyone," Maggie said. Maggie is one of the nine people who attended Sarah's memorial service and one of Sarah's only friends. "No relatives showed up at her service, just some people I rounded up. Sometimes Sarah would stop by the shop where I work and ask me to pray with her. She knew I'd been through hard times and I believed God got me through.

"I could tell she was troubled, but she didn't say what was wrong. I didn't know if I should push her to talk. Now I wish I had." Maggie said. "It's sad when someone thinks suicide is the only way out. But I understand what that's like. I spent two years driving around town looking for a building tall enough to jump from, so if I jumped, I'd die and not just be paralyzed the rest of my life."

Was Sarah's death accidental or intentional? What about the other four cars that went flying off the road that month? The canyon road leads to a beautiful California beach town that many people call Paradise. But when a person is going through loss and grief, even Paradise can feel like hell.

"You don't know how many times I'd be driving and think, *One flick of my wrists and my pain would be gone. I could drive into a brick wall and nobody would know if it was an accident or not.*" This is from a man most people think of as a good-natured guy. His losses aren't particularly tragic, but over a long-enough time, a series of disappointments has chipped away at his enthusiasm for life.

Wishing we're dead is one of the least-discussed stages of grief. When we lose someone or something important or when we lose enough smaller things, life can lose meaning. *What's the use?* we think. *It doesn't matter what I do. I can do everything right and still lose who and what I love most. I can do everything right and still not create a life I like or bring about change.* For life to lose meaning is natural after a loss, says Frank Parkinson in *Post-Trauma Stress*. On the other hand, we can endure the most devastating loss if we believe there's a purpose to what we're going through. That's the premise of Viktor Frankl's writings, *Man's Search for Meaning* and *The Will to Meaning*. Frankl survived three years at Auschwitz, Dachau, and other concentration camps during World War II. Now a professor of neurology and psychiatry at the University of Vienna Medical School, Frankl's approach to therapy is based on the belief that we need to find meaning in our lives and our losses.

The people I talk to agree. If there's no purpose to it, loss feels impossible to endure. But if we see some meaning, bring the struggle on.

I'd had many losses before my son died. I saw most as challenges to overcome, opportunities to become a stronger, wiser person. Shane's death wasn't a challenge. Some falls knock the breath out of us. This loss knocked the heart out of my chest. My desire was to be done.

While others are living life as usual, we find ourselves living in another world, one that doesn't make sense to our logical minds. Our faith is challenged. The belief that *if I do the right things, God will protect and take care of me and the people I love* doesn't fit anymore. The world becomes a confusing, dark place. We feel lost, unsure how to navigate. Our life plan collapsed. Life took us somewhere we didn't expect to go, and it's not someplace we want to be.

We're taught to trust what we know, but when we're in this dark place, the things we know don't always work. There's another way to look at it. It's something quantum physicists talk about. In *Alice in Wonderland* it's called "down the rabbit hole." Our faith is taking us to a deeper place, showing us new ideas and ideals. It might not feel like we're blessed anymore, but we are—strange blessings are underneath the grief.

Are you willing to fight your way back? Make an unconditional commitment to life? Trust what you don't know and can't see yet? Discover a deeper spirituality, one that says, *Wherever I go, God is there too, no matter how dark and mysterious that place is.* We can make the tiniest reconnection with life while floundering in the gap. When we do, our souls remember who we are and what we came here to do. We start showing up for life again. Step by step, we fight to change the status quo.

That's what this story is about. It's for the people in the *I Lost My Place in the World and Had to Fight My Way Back, but When I Did I Found My True Home* Club. It's for people who know that wrestling with angels isn't a metaphor in Genesis. Whether we're staving off the demons taunting us with *you don't deserve* or arm wrestling with God Himself, we're in the ring, it's the tenth round and, yes, it's happening to us.

Maggie spread her few remaining possessions on the tent floor: a sketchbook of drawings and poems, pencils, pens, some shells and stones she'd picked up at the beach. She had three changes of clothes piled in the corner. The last things she had been hanging on to—a brooch and earrings from her grandmother, brought all the way across the seas when her mother had come to the United States from Eastern Europe years before Maggie was born—had been washed away in last week's storm. The shells and the sketchbook were all that was left of her life. She had herself, but she wasn't certain how much of her was left. How does a career woman go from living a decent life in a nice apartment with her husband to being divorced, unemployed, and living on a stranger's field in a tent?

Thank God she wasn't living under bridges or sleeping in parks like some street people she knew. Under the bridge there was drinking, drugs, assaults. Many of the homeless people she'd met were like her—ordinary people who fell into the gap. Some were drifters or vets. Some were crazy, dangerous, and mean. The landowner had given her and Miles permission to pitch a tent here. She felt as safe as anyone could living on the streets. She had Miles to thank for that. Dear, sweet Miles. He saved her life. But even with his help, she was getting close to the edge.

Lightning crackled. The air pressed in on her. Was there a pattern to this twist her life had taken? How did she get here? The last thing she remembered, she was married, a solidly booked hair stylist in Santa Barbara. Years later, she would explain it like this: "It wasn't that I lost my center. I couldn't find it for a while. There's a connection we have to ourselves and the world." When you lose hope and your thinking gets dark, you lose your connection to life.

As a child, then as a young woman, Maggie took it for granted that she would always be blessed. She was. There's a way of being in the world where things work out for us. If we lose one job, another one appears. If a relationship ends, a better one is around the corner or we're content being alone. Many minister's children complain that their minister parent crammed faith down their throats. Maggie never felt like that. Her memories of going to church and listening to her father's sermons make her happy. Maggie would sit in the pew and listen to her dad preach to a congregation about a God who would never leave them. Her father had so much faith in God, Maggie barely needed any of her own.

"Maggie, your mom and I are getting divorced. We love you more than ever. Your mom and I still love each other. But your mom hears another call. She needs to go off on her own. The best thing is if you stay here with me. Things are changing, but we'll be fine." While many children complain about their parents' divorce, Maggie says her parents divorced with a lot of love. Maggie can't recall hearing a disagreement. She didn't even feel that uncomfortable feeling when people aren't getting along, but they're not being honest about it or talking about what's going on. All Maggie remembers feeling was safety and love in her home.

Her wedding had been an incredible celebration. Tables lined with exotic dishes from the old country. Dancing. Beautiful music. Her husband was dashing. Mother and Father were divorced, but they still believed in marriage and were happy for her. Things worked out for Maggie. She took it for granted they always would.

Maggie loved being a stylist. She thought of herself as an artist, not someone who just cuts and colors hair. Maggie enjoyed all her clients—every one. After graduation from beauty college, it was hard building a clientele. She'd stuck with it. She'd been able to make it because the salon owner had taken a percentage instead of a flat fee for rent, a standard practice when a stylist begins. After three years, she was booked solid five days a week. What had been a break for her in the beginning—paying a percentage to lease her space—was no longer a good deal. In most salons, once a stylist is established, the owner lets the stylist pay a set weekly rent. Not here. The owner collected $150 to $300 from the other stylists for rent. Maggie never gave him less than a thousand dollars a week, and most weeks it was more.

Was it money problems that started her downward spiral? Maggie wasn't that materialistic. She liked to dress with flair. She'd gotten that from her mother, a diva from Eastern Europe. No, her fall from Grace started when her husband lost his job.

"Don't worry," she told him. "You'll find something soon. I make enough to pay the bills. It's not like we're going to be out on the streets. We'll just have to watch our spending for a while." *A while* turned into a year. Slowly, her husband gave up. He stopped checking the classifieds.

The first time *it* happened, it caught her off guard. It was Saturday, payday. She stopped by the grocery store on her way home. She carried in the groceries, put them away. Then she counted out one hundred dollars for her husband and put it on the table. "Here's some pocket money for the week," she said.

He looked at the money. Then, instead of picking up the cash, he slapped Maggie across the face. "Do you know what that does to me?" he said. "Giving me an allowance like I'm a child? I'm the man. I'm supposed to support you."

She held her hand on her stinging cheek. "I didn't mean it that way," she said. She was stunned and hurt. He'd never hit her before. She walked up to him, tried to hug him. "We're a team. You're going to be back on your feet soon. I know it," she said.

He pushed her away. "Oh yeah?" he said. "When?" He stomped out and didn't come home until late that night. From then on, he slept on the couch. Their fights became more frequent. Her husband went from a man who never raised his voice to someone who regularly slapped her around. Maggie started weekly sessions with a therapist. She begged her husband to come with her. "Let's get help," she said. "I know we can make our marriage work."

Her therapist didn't tell Maggie what to do, but Maggie wasn't entirely honest about the abuse. She described it as *arguments*. She didn't mention *hitting*. She knew if she did, her therapist would tell her what her friends said: leave. Maggie took her vows seriously. She considered herself married for life.

What Maggie didn't get, didn't comprehend, and couldn't believe is how their relationship deteriorated from being a loving marriage to this. Her entire life, things had worked out. She kept believing that somehow this would too. Then she came home one Wednesday evening and found the papers waiting on the kitchen table. For a man who wasn't working, he'd somehow managed to seek a legal divorce.

"Please sign the papers," he said. "Without children, divorce is simple."

"I don't want it to be over," she said. "I married you for life."

"It's not working," he said. "I don't like who I've become. I don't like who I am with you. I don't feel like a man. I want to go somewhere else. Maybe Colorado, Montana, Wyoming. Anywhere but here."

Maggie begged him to bring her with, said she would go wherever he wanted. He wanted to go alone. She signed the papers. Then he was gone.

Lightning crackled again. The air felt so heavy. It would be a relief if it rained, even though that always made such a mess in the tent. None of her friends understood how it broke her heart to lose her marriage. Was divorce so common that it didn't faze people anymore—no bigger deal than trading in a car? Maybe divorce wasn't a big deal to anyone else, but it was big to her. She didn't plan on losing her husband. She got so low after he left; her thinking got so black. Before then, Maggie had never thought about suicide. Now she thought about it most of the time.

She drove around town scoping out buildings. *Can I get up to the roof? Is it high enough? If I jump, will I die or end up a vegetable in a nursing home?* Suicide wasn't a casual thought. She could feel herself on the edge. Earlier this week, she actually climbed up an outside stairway to the third floor of an office building. She stood looking down and thinking, then went back to her car.

"You can see me for ninety-five cents an hour," her therapist said. She was still seeing the same therapist she saw when her marriage ended. Her therapist knew she didn't have any money. She said Maggie had to pay something, otherwise she wouldn't be investing any of herself in their work. Maggie was begging money for therapy a quarter at a time. She was seeing her therapist once a month, but therapy wasn't helping. It wasn't touching this strange, odd place where Maggie lived. Life went on the same way. The only thing changing was Maggie's thinking. It got darker each day.

When Maggie heard people talk about how bad things come in threes, she used to think they were kidding. Maggie never had one bad thing happen to her before, much less three. But less than a month after her husband left, her landlord showed up at the door. "Sorry to do this, but I'm rehabbing the building. After I fix this place up, I can double the rents," he said. "You've got thirty days to get out." That pushed Maggie to ask her boss to alter their financial arrangement. She pointed out that she was paying three times as much as anyone else and that usually salon owners changed the agreement to a flat weekly fee once a stylist established a regular clientele. "It's not fair. It's not how they do it in other salons. I need that money. I've got to come up with first and last month's rent and a security deposit, and I've got to do it by myself," Maggie said. "This is California. You know I won't get any of my old deposit back. Please, will you change our agreement? I can't get another place to live if I'm giving you all my money."

"A deal is a deal," her boss said. "You agreed to pay a percentage."

"That was in the beginning," Maggie said.

"I gave you a deal then. I get the good deal now. I don't care what other people do. That's how it works with me," he said.

Maggie's boss wouldn't budge, so Maggie quit. *A dumb move*, Maggie thought, looking back. At the time it made sense, but her thinking wasn't right then. Her thinking hadn't been right since her divorce. In six weeks, she lost her husband, her home, and then her job. At first she told herself not to worry, when one door closes a better one opens. But this time things were different. Doors closed and none opened. "I lost my whole life," she said. "My world collapsed. Then I'm supposed to feel blessed when a therapist agrees to see me for ninety-five cents an hour so I can talk about how rotten I feel?

"I see what happened," Maggie said years later. "I'd been riding on the coattails of my father's faith. He loved God so much. God wanted me to find faith of my own."

Maggie counted from the time she saw the lightning until she heard the thunder. The lightning was getting closer. *Where was Miles?* She was hungry, frightened. She was trapped in a life she hated, and she didn't know how to get out. Once you lose your place in the world, it's hard to find it again. *Where did she belong? Here?* At least she still had her old van. Miles was usually home by now. One of them would come up with the food plan for the day.

It was humiliating at first. She begged for food at restaurants where she used to eat when she worked. At what used to be her favorite restaurant, the owner would let her eat pickles and sunflower seeds from the salad bar for free. Some days that was all Maggie had to eat. She felt grateful for that. Last week her father had stopped by her tent with a big tray of food. Dear, sweet Dad. *Where is God?* she kept demanding. *You said God loved me and would never leave. Where is He? Point Him out so I can see.* "God is right there with you," her dad kept saying. What did that mean?

"It's easy to take it for granted that you'll always be blessed and things will work out," Maggie said. "It's easy to judge people, to look at them and say if they just did this or did that, their lives would change and get better." After what Maggie's been through, she understands that sometimes life twists, and it doesn't matter what you do. Things don't work out the way you want, and you can't do much about it. The only way out is through.

Another lightning bolt lit the sky. Seconds later, thunder rumbled. This was the lowest she'd been since her fall from Grace. She couldn't pull her thoughts out of that dark place. She couldn't get her thinking on track. Nothing she did made a difference. She felt a numb, dull ache.

Why wasn't Miles home? Had something happened to him? She had less than a gallon of gas in her car. No money. Well, seven cents. She couldn't go driving. The last thing she needed was to run out of gas and have the police impound her van.

She couldn't believe it at first when her husband left, she got her notice to move, lost her job, and couldn't find another place to live. It was like watching a bad movie, only it was happening to her. She was riding an elevator in her life, and it went lower each day. No hope. No money. Nowhere to go. "You can come home and live with us, honey," her father said. He was remarried by then. His new wife was okay, but they lived in a tiny one-bedroom home. The last thing they needed was

Maggie sleeping on their couch. Besides, Maggie was almost thirty years old. She wasn't a little girl anymore. She was a grown woman who needed to work this out for herself.

She had couch-hopped among her friends for a while. A few nights here, a few nights there. But those welcome mats wore thin. First and last month's rent and a security deposit is a lot to come up with when you're employed. It's impossible when you're out of work. It can cost between two and four thousand dollars.

"There's this gap out there," Maggie said, "and there's a bunch of displaced people in it." Maggie didn't know about the gap until it became her new home.

A friend introduced her to Miles. She'd been at a friend's house for five nights in a row. This was the fourth time she'd stayed there, and it was time to leave. She was out of places to go. She'd cycled through her friends' homes so many times, she couldn't keep doing it. Things had to change. Then she met Miles. He was a godsend, an angel. He stopped by her friend's house one night. Maggie hadn't been in many relationships. She wasn't the kind of woman to run off into the sunset with someone she just met. But she didn't think she was the kind of woman who was a homeless street person either. You find yourself doing a lot of things you didn't think you ever would.

There was something about Miles. She looked into his blue eyes and felt safe with him from the beginning. She moved into his tent with him that night.

There's an underground culture even in wealthy beach cities. In another time, they might be called *nomads*. Now they're homeless people who live on the street. Some are ordinary people like Maggie. A series of bad breaks bumps them out of normal life and pushes them into the gap. Some of the people are dangerous, insane. Some are addicts, alcoholics. Some are veterans. It's a microcosm of society, its own little world. Most people don't see the people living in the gap. They're almost invisible. It bothers some people to see homeless people. It annoys them. Maggie barely noticed them until she became one herself.

Miles was from a well-known, upper-class family. A series of bad breaks knocked Miles out of his life. A wife who drank too much drove once too often with their child in the car. An accident happened, and the child died. His wife left, and Miles fell into the gap. He was intelligent, talented, and had a good heart, but he lost his fighting spirit. He didn't care enough to get back in the game. He came close to opportunities, but Miles would show up days late and dollars short. He was always sabotaging himself. But Miles showed up for Maggie. He taught her how to get around in this subculture. He made her feel safe. The weeks ran into months. She'd lost track of how long she'd been living in his tent. Some days they sat at the beach or walked around town. Sometimes they hung out under the bridge. That was scary.

Miles was usually back to the tent by now. Lightning crackled again.

A few months ago, Maggie ran into the owner of one of the larger beauty shops in town. They talked for a minute. Maggie was embarrassed, tried to get away. "Maggie, come work for me. I need you," the woman said. "I have to go back East and take care of my mother. She's sick, probably dying. I'll be gone for maybe six months. I know you'll take good care of my clients and give them back to me when I return."

Maggie was flattered by the offer. But when she thought about getting up every day, going into work from the tent, styling the hair of the wealthy women in this town while she was homeless—she couldn't do it. Besides, something had happened to her. She'd didn't trust herself to cut hair anymore. Maggie didn't just lose her home, she lost confidence in herself. She stood there that day wondering how to explain this to the woman. "I'm sorry," Maggie said. "I appreciate the offer, but I can't accept it." The woman didn't know Maggie was homeless. Except for the obviously homeless—the people pushing shopping carts around—most people don't know for sure who many of the street people are.

The lightning crackled again. Now it was starting to rain. Maggie put her belongings in a brown paper bag. The note she left for Miles was short and to the point. "I have to make some changes, Miles. If I don't, I'm afraid of what I might do. Thanks for everything you've done. I love you. Maggie."

Maggie had just enough gas to get to her father's house. His home was filled with the pungent aroma of his cooking. He was sitting in his recliner, watching TV.

"Dad, is that offer of the couch still open?"

"Welcome home, honey," he said. Maggie hugged him tightly. Maggie didn't just grab on to her father. That night she grabbed on to God.

"I filled my head with positive thoughts," Maggie said. "I got a meditation book from my father's library. Each morning I read a positive thought." Maggie had been going to her therapist occasionally. Now, for ninety-five cents a session, she went three times a week. "I prayed all the time," she said. "Morning, noon, and night I asked for God's help. Praying is all I did when I was awake. I'd latch onto one positive God thought, and I'd hold it in my mind all day. I'd plaster that thought on top of all the other negative thoughts running through my head." She didn't give herself a chance to think dark thoughts because she was thinking God thoughts so much.

Maggie's therapist said she didn't think Maggie needed medication. "I would have taken pills if my therapist had told me to," Maggie said. "It wasn't that I wasn't trying. I was doing everything right. Some people think every problem or situation can be fixed. Sometimes we're supposed to go through an experience because it's the only way we'll learn. It's one thing to think you believe something, to know it in your head. It's another to integrate that belief, to know something is true because you've learned and lived it for yourself. I had to see up close—by living it—what life was showing me.

"Miles found me at my father's. I told him I couldn't go back to the tent. He didn't push me to come back with him. He cared enough to let me go."

Maggie had been at her dad's house a couple of months when a friend called, someone from her old life. "I've got two tickets for a concert at the amphitheater tonight," her friend said. "Come with me. It'll do you good."

"No," Maggie said. "I can't."

There's a connection we have to life. "I lost that," Maggie explained. She didn't feel like she could socialize. She didn't feel like she fit in the world.

Maggie's friend wouldn't take no for an answer. "I'll be there in an hour."

Maggie sat in the amphitheater with hundreds of people. Stars lit the sky. Classical music filled the air. For a moment, the separation between Maggie and everyone else disappeared. "I felt that connection again," Maggie said. "I felt like part of life. I reconnected with myself." *The holidays are coming,* Maggie thought. *Stores need more salespeople this time of year. Maybe I can't cut hair yet, but I bet I could do retail sales even in the shape I'm in.*

Under the stars and listening to the music, Maggie got back a tiny bit of confidence. *Grace.* "Feeling like I could work as a sales clerk doesn't sound like a big deal to most people," Maggie said, "but believing that I could work at any job was a miracle to me."

Call it a blessing, getting healthy, or a miracle. We convince ourselves we're cut off, separate, different from everything and everyone else. Then for one second, with one fingertip, we touch the universe and we remember it's our world. Even if we don't know what it is, we remember that there's something we came here to do. There's a part of us—our spirit—that goes beyond jobs and titles and how much money we make and whether we live in a mansion or in a tent on a corner of some guy's field. That's the part of us that's real. That's what happened to Maggie that night. She remembered who she really is.

Our miracle won't happen until we get off that fence and stop driving around looking for that building big enough to jump from, or looking for that brick wall we can slam into, or quietly willing ourselves to die. No matter how much our life sucks, the ball isn't going to start rolling until we decide we're not going to kill ourselves, no matter how crappy we feel and how bad things are. We need to make an unconditional commitment to life. Then we restore our partnership with life. That's when the changes begin.

The next day Maggie went job hunting. A major department store hired her that week. She slept on her dad's couch every night, rolled her bedding up every morning, got dressed, and went to work. When the holiday season ended, her job did too. Maggie got another idea. *I bet I could do waitress work,* she thought. She still didn't believe in herself enough to cut hair. "People who haven't been through it may not understand," Maggie said. "I lost my home and myself. It took time to find *me* again."

Next, Maggie found a job working at a pizza parlor. She started taking small steps to change the status quo. Each step brought her closer to life. Her dad's house was a safe harbor, but she couldn't keep sleeping on his couch. She didn't have enough money to move into an apartment, but she could afford to rent a room at a cheap motel. Some days she made just enough to pay for the room and buy gas to get to and from work. She could eat one meal for free each day at the restaurant. She bought a cheap tent for the days when she ran out of money before she ran out of week. In the lean times, she slept in her tent at the RV park on the edge of town. The campgrounds felt safe. She had electricity, bathrooms, a shower to use. Staying there cost only twelve dollars a night.

"It was hard to stay even, much less get ahead," Maggie said. "Everything I made went to pay for the costs of that day."

Maggie kept forging ahead, seeing her therapist, and hanging on to God. She continued to read her daily meditation book. Each day she focused on one uplifting thought. Her thoughts about jumping off a building gradually disappeared. Lighter, more hopeful thinking replaced thoughts of death. "It didn't come easy," Maggie said. "It wasn't like this wonderful change just happened to me. I had to fight not to fall back into that dark hole."

One day, it was time. Maggie drove to one of the better beauty salons in the city and got out of her van. "God, my dad says you're with me wherever I am. I want to go back to work as a stylist. I'm going into this shop to ask for a job. I want my life back," Maggie said. "I'm putting you to the test now, God. You're either with me or you're not."

Maggie walked into the salon. She walked up to the owner, introduced herself, and offered her hand. "I'd love to work here," she said.

The owner clasped her hand in his. "I know you," he said. "You used to work at one of the other shops." He pointed at an empty styling chair. "There's your chair," he said. "When can you start?"

Maggie went out to her van. She opened the door and started to climb in. A man she recognized from under the bridge was hiding in her van. He grabbed her and starting choking her. Maggie screamed, fought him. She pulled loose, got away. She ran to a restaurant where she knew the police hung out. She found an officer and told him what happened. He walked back with her to her van. The man who attacked her was gone.

"It was like the last demon I had to fight. Life was throwing the final challenge at me," Maggie said. "Do you really believe you deserve to be blessed?"

It's been six years since the day Maggie put God to the test. Maggie has a cute, funky apartment in the artsy part of town. She drives a newer used car. She's in a relationship she describes as positive and light. If you ask Maggie what she learned from her years of homelessness, the first thing she'll tell you is that *every stinking dirty little thing that happens to us happens for a reason.*

She's not defined by where she works or lives or whether she's in a relationship. "My identity is that I'm a child of God. I don't worry about the future," she says. "I take each day as it comes. After what I've been through, I know I'll have enough Grace for whatever life brings. Just because God is with us doesn't mean we'll be spared from painful experiences. But the experience has something to teach us. It's our job to figure out what that lesson is."

Sometimes it's not enough to read about a subject in a book, talk about it in a group, or watch it in a movie. We need to go through the experience ourselves. That's how we learn. That's how we become who we really are.

Without any malice, Maggie explains that her ex-husband has been through dark times of his own since their divorce. "He remarried, had a little girl. One day she was playing in back of their house. She wandered into a pond and drowned. My heart breaks for the pain he and his wife are going through." She ran into Miles recently, when he was passing through town. He's still homeless, living in the gap. "I'm so grateful I had a chance to spend time with him and thank him for all he did. I'll always love him. He helped me get through the worst part of my life. I feel so badly for him. He's still homeless, wandering around without a place to live or a job. I want to do something to help him, do more for him than I know I reasonably can. I wish I could change his life for him. I know he needs help. But some of what Miles has to do, he needs to do for himself."

On rainy nights, you can see Maggie on the bridge throwing clean pairs of socks and big trash bags for raincoats to the homeless people underneath. On Thanksgiving, she's likely to show up at one of the free dinners put on by the community. She helps in any way she can, and she gives free haircuts to people who need them. Except for a few people from the old days, most people who know Maggie don't know what she went through. She's embarrassed about her past. "They don't know it, but a lot of people are a few paychecks away from being homeless. Many people are closer than they think. It doesn't matter what kind of education you have, what kind of family you come from, or what your situation is now. Being homeless can happen to anyone," Maggie said. "I know because it happened to me.

"I thought I wasn't being blessed, but when I think about all the things that could have happened and didn't, I can see that even though it was a nightmare, it could have been worse. Look in the Bible in the book of Genesis. Find the story of Jacob. He was traveling down the road trying to get back home after being gone a long time when he ran into a big man. Jacob stayed up all night wrestling with him. The man was really an angel. The angel asked Jacob to let him go. Jacob said no. When the angel asked what Jacob wanted, Jacob said he wanted to be blessed.

"Wrestle with an angel," Maggie says. "Grab hold of God. If God isn't blessing you, demand to be blessed. Hang on and don't let go until God says yes."

Of 80 communities surveyed, 80 percent prohibit sleeping or camping in public areas, but 100 percent of these communities lack enough shelter beds to meet the demands.

Fines from $50 to $2,000 are imposed on the poor because they lack housing. Because they also lack money to pay the fine, they go to jail.

As of January 2005, there were approximately 230,000 homeless war veterans in America. This number is expected to grow dramatically over the next three years.

As of December 8, 2004, Iraq veterans were already showing up at homeless shelters.

More than 3 million men, women, and children were homeless in 2005. Of these, 30 percent are homeless chronically.

Five million people in the United States spend more than half their incomes on housing, leaving them on the verge of homelessness. A missed paycheck, illness, or an unpaid bill can push them over the edge and into the gap.

The Department of Housing and Urban Development (HUD) says housing/rent costs shouldn't exceed 30 percent of income.

Sources: National Coalition for the Homeless, United Press International, and National Law Center on Homelessness and Poverty

ACTIVITIES

1. Make an unconditional commitment to life. I was talking to a friend, another bereaved mother, about finding the will to live after a big loss. "That commitment to life has to come first," I said, "before anything else can happen." She agreed. "But it's hard," she said. "How can we get that commitment to life when life has knocked out our will to live?" That's a tough question to answer. I can only say what worked for me.

It was about one year after my son's death. A friend stopped by my house. I was sitting in the kitchen doing a crossword puzzle. (That was my idea of a big day.) "I'm worried about you," my friend said. "You've lost your will to live. You're dropping out at a deep level. If you don't do something soon, it's going to be too late. Melody," he said, "you're going to die." I knew my friend was right. Every night, I was going to bed begging God to let me die in my sleep, then feeling enraged when I woke up alive. For various reasons, I didn't or wouldn't allow myself to have suicide as an option. But at a deep level, my soul quit.

When we quit, it's common for our bodies to follow. Stories of people who die shortly after someone they love dies are common. I remember attending a party at a beautiful mansion years before my son died. That was back in my poverty days, when I was lucky to bring home eight hundred dollars a month. "Wow," I said to a friend. "These people have it all."

"Not really," my friend said. "He's a successful attorney. But his ten-year-old daughter died a few years ago. Then, not long after, his wife, a young woman, died one night in her sleep."

"From what?" I asked.

"From a broken heart," my friend said. "She was a young woman, and she died of a heart attack."

We can literally will ourselves to die if our will to live is weak enough and our desire to be done is strong. When my friend told me I was on the cusp of death, it scared me. While I didn't believe in life any longer, I didn't really want to die. I loved my son, but I loved my daughter too. I was all she had. I wasn't willing to leave her alone. I knew someday I'd die, but I didn't want to leave this way—a big quitter. I asked my friend what I could do to reclaim my will to live. He didn't have any suggestions. I'm a writer, so I did the only thing I knew—I used the power of words. I wrote out an unconditional commitment to life. If you've been through a major loss, and you're on the fence about whether you want to live or die, what you need to do first, before anything else can happen—before this journey begins that will heal your heart—is make a commitment to life. There are two commitments we need to make after loss: We need to make a commitment to life and we need to make a commitment to our grief. In *Living Through Mourning*, a beautiful book about grieving, author Harriet Sarnoff Schiff writes on page 81, "In the beginning, however, there must be the commitment to life. Without that all efforts will fail." You can use the following words or write an agreement of your own. The important idea (however you do it) is that you commit.

Life Pact

I hereby commit unconditionally to life. I will live my life fully until its natural end. I claim a strong will to live. This agreement is not conditional upon me getting what I want, having any particular relationship, having any particular amount of money, getting any particular job, owning a home, or feeling a particular way. I will live my life to the best of my ability as long as I'm alive. I'll show up for whatever each day brings. I'll show up for my life. I ask God to help me find my highest good path and reveal my destiny. By signing this agreement, I realize I'm entering into partnership with life and I'm demonstrating my choice to live. If any previous negative thoughts have started deterioration in my body, I hereby command my body to stop deteriorating and order and ask it to be healthy and fit. I honor my body and my life, and I hereby turn around any damage I started and begin living life on a healthy, positive note. I forgive life for what it's done; I forgive God and other people; I forgive myself. I accept the forgiveness God gives me. I release all negative thoughts and acknowledge that I'm enough to live my life for. I promise that I won't do anything to hurt myself or knowingly or intentionally hurt anyone else. I will live my life in love and I ask for and receive all God's blessings and help.

Signed: _____

Dated: _____

After signing and dating your contract, read it aloud. Then put your contract someplace safe and sacred. Few things are more powerful than the written and spoken word.

2. Start taking steps to change the status quo. If you don't like how things have been going, take action to make changes. Sometimes we can go with the flow and change happens effortlessly. Sometimes change isn't that easy. Like Maggie, we have to wrestle with an angel to get blessed and to get life moving again. It might feel impossible to get from where we are to where we're going. The longest journey begins with one step. Sometimes that first step is the hardest. You don't have to be homeless to feel stuck, trapped, in the gap, and in need of what feels like an impossible change. Things don't have to stay the same, even if they've been the way they are for a long time. Write some goals on paper. Start with easy ones, things you believe you can accomplish. Maggie didn't believe she could go back to her old career at first. She had to start with something easy. She could only manifest what she believed she could do. Start taking steps to re-create your life. Start at your comfort level, but also be willing to feel a little uncomfortable at first.

3. For local information on housing or resources for the homeless, contact the U.S. Department of Housing and Urban Development for Local Homeless Assistance at 800-FED-INFO (800-333-4636), TDD/TTY (800-483-2209), or www.hud.gov/homeless; contact the HUDVet Resource Center at 800-998-9999; or contact the Homeless Peoples Network at the Arizona State Public Information Network at aspin.asu.edu/hpn/.

4. Make a list of your reasons to live. Suicide wasn't an option for me for several reasons. One was I didn't want to abandon my daughter, and another was I didn't want to leave a quitter. A third was that I wanted to see this painful experience through, stick around until I found some meaning in it. There was also another reason. Just in case the concept of reincarnation is true (the journalist in me doesn't know because it can't be proven) I didn't want to take the chance that I'd have to come back and face these same circumstances again until I got it right. What are some reasons you should stick around and see your life through?

5. Save. Make a commitment to put a percentage of your income away for a rainy day. Then don't touch your money until it rains. If you have to spend it, get another cushion again as soon as you can.

6. Volunteer time or money to shelters or missions in your city that care for the homeless and poor. Share some of the blessings you've been given. Bored? Wondering what to do some weekends or evenings? Feeling alone on a holiday? Look in your newspaper for local organizations that need volunteers on holidays. Also, the National Law Center on Homelessness and Poverty is looking for volunteers. Contact them at 202-638-2535 or www.nlchp.org.

7. Have you ever had an angel in your life (someone like Miles) who came for a while and helped you survive, an escort who helped you get to the next place? Have you recognized and thanked this person for the help he or she gave? Sometimes we get angry or hurt when a person doesn't stick around or the relationship doesn't last. Maybe it wasn't supposed to last; that person was sent to help us only for a while, a reason, a season. Sometimes nobody but us understands what a lifesaver this person was, but we don't need to let that stop us from being clear on what that person meant to us. It's easy to disregard these temporary relationships and not give them the honor that's due—especially if the person wasn't able to bring about change for him- or herself even though he or she helped us. Say a prayer or do something that corresponds with

your spiritual beliefs to honor, recognize, and thank the people who helped you. Then pass it on. Be there for someone else.

8. Review your Master List of Losses. Can you see how any of these (or all of them) changed you in a way that you wouldn't have been if you hadn't gone through the experience? Which losses have really made you who you are, shaped who you are (or who you're becoming)? How? Write in your journal about this. Write a story or poem about this. Or tell someone. Express the importance of the experience so its value becomes real to you.

CHAPTER 7

Destined to Change:
When Dreams Die

My friend Andy called one day. Andy was my skydiving instructor. We used to be roommates until I moved out of the Blue Sky Lodge in Lake Elsinore, California, and back to the beach. Andy still lived there with his girlfriend and some other skydivers who rented from me. I kept my room but didn't go there much anymore.

"*Airspeed* called," he said. "They want me to try out for their team." Airspeed is a national and world competition skydiving team.

"That's great," I said.

"What if I make it?" he asked. "They say I probably will. That means I lose living here and my job. I'm finally comfortable. I'm ahead on my bills. I'm even saving money. My life is stable. Team life means going back to starving and barely surviving again."

"Five years ago, you would have given anything for that phone call. Competing on a world team was your dream!" I said. "Now you don't know if you should do it? Are you crazy? That's what you've wanted to do since we met. It's what life has been getting you ready for all along."

"I'd have to move," he said. "I just bought a new car, and I'll have to sell that. I'll have to cut way back."

"You're good at cutting back," I said. "You do it well. In the end, what do you want to say you did—chose security or went for your dream?"

Andy didn't have to answer. We both knew what he'd say.

Forgetting our dreams is easy. We get a vision. We're so excited. We give it a try, but it doesn't happen right away, or it doesn't happen how and when we think it should. So we get into the grind of doing something else. *What's the use?* we think. *My dream isn't going to happen. It was just some foolish notion.* We're so enthusiastic in the beginning. We know what we want. But we're not ready for it. We don't know that, but life does. We start learning, growing, changing. We don't know that we're doing the prep work. We think life is throwing us a bone or telling us we can't have our dream. Times passes, and then one day our dreams become so distant we don't remember them anymore. We forgot what we wanted so badly and why.

Destiny is sneaky. It creeps up on us when we're not looking. Sometimes we're staring at our problems so hard we forget they're part of our destiny too. We might forget our dreams, but our dreams don't forget us. Dreams are life's way of showing us what our destiny is.

In many stories, I've changed people's names to protect their privacy. Some people said, "I want you to use my real name." Lori Yearwood is one. A seasoned newspaper reporter, Lori knows that slight changes (name, job, age, city of residence) weaken a story. What follows is Lori's story of coming to grips with her dreams and her destiny. It's for anyone in the *I Got So Caught Up in the Grind I Forgot My Dreams and I'm Not Sure I Deserve Them* Club. It's about forgetting that problems and setbacks all weave into our destiny. It's about remembering how precious dreams are.

"Horsey, Daddy! Horsey!" four-year-old Lori screams, pointing out the car window.

"Yes, honey, it's a horse," her father says.

"Please can I see the horse?" Lori begs. Most children like animals. They learn animal sounds and names—moo says the cow, oink says the pig. But from the time she could talk, Lori and horses? That's passion. It's obsession. It's a love affair. Vernon Yearwood-Drayton pulls the car to the side of the road and lets Lori pet the horse.

Lori grew up. She became a reporter, and as soon as she had enough money, she bought her first horse. Buying this horse was about more than getting something she loves. Lori shopped for her horse a few months after her father's death. Her dad had endured a long bout with brain cancer. Lori had cared for him until the end. She missed him. When her parents separated, she lived with her dad. She and her dad were close. It broke her heart when he died. Lori's gift to herself after his death was to buy a horse. She didn't have firm ideas about what she wanted other than the horse's name *had* to start with V, for Vernon— her dad's name.

Meaning is important. Certain things such as religious objects or holidays have universal meaning. En masse, we agree that something *means* a particular thing. But the meaning we attach to life events is personal. It doesn't matter if something *means* anything to anyone else. What matters is what an event or experience means to us. We can go through horrendous struggles if there's meaning to what we endure. A friend who runs an import/export business was looking for new products, and he asked my opinion about which ones I liked. I looked at the necklaces and other items in his line. "Find items with meaning attached to them," I said. "That's what people like."

Lori wanted the name of her horse to mean that the horse was connected to her dad. "Don't get your hopes up," a woman told Lori. "I've been around horses for years, and I've never met a horse yet whose name starts with V."

Lori drove to a stable with horses for sale. The woman who worked there walked Lori to the pasture. A white stallion immediately pranced over to Lori and kissed her on the nose.

"What's his or her name?" Lori asked.

"His name is Vashka," the woman said.

From the day Lori met Vashka, he became living, prancing proof of her father Vernon's undying love—a tender gesture from the other side.

"I quit!" Lori said politely but firmly, handing in her resignation. She held an enviable job as a reporter for the *Miami Herald*. She was in a good position for any writer; she was making a decent income doing something she loved. The problem was it wasn't her dream. She wanted to teach inner-city children to write. She wanted to do freelance writing from home. But she didn't want just a house; she wanted to live on a ranch with her horse. This was her dream since she was a child.

It wasn't work or duty to make the hour-and-a-half round-trip drive to the stables. It was a privilege to spend time with her horse. Lori cheerfully, gratefully, joyfully visited Vashka every day unless she was sick or out of town on business or visiting her mom. Lori was aware she was going through a time of transformation and change in her life. It wasn't only her father's death, quitting her job, and getting a horse. Her relationship with her mom was changing too. Lori was beginning to see that just as she wrote stories for a living, she told herself stories about her life, about what happened to her and why.

"I've got to get out of here or I'll go insane!" her mom screams at her dad. "I cannot stay here with you another hour."

But who's going to help me shave my legs? thirteen-year-old Lori wonders, watching her mom drive away. After a while, her mom's outbursts and disappearances don't surprise Lori anymore. But they still hurt. Why doesn't she love me? Lori wonders. What did I do wrong?

For so many years, Lori told herself the story that her mother abandoned her because she didn't love her. *It's truth, not fiction*, Lori thought. Over the years, however, with a therapist's help, Lori began to edit that story. *Mom was having a nervous breakdown. She didn't get along with my dad. It wasn't about me. My mom left because she had to, to survive. My mom loves me now and she always has.* Any good writer knows that good stories are made in the editing and rewriting—not in the first draft.

It's easy to feel like a victim. Most of us feel powerless about many things. We are. We can't stop someone from dying unless we execute a successful rescue attempt. We can't change other people. But do we have some power? Can we alter what happens to us by what we believe and the meaning we attach to events? Many people say yes, we can. Scientists and quantum physicists say that we change something (or someone) by the simple act of observing. Looking at something interacts with and changes what or who we're looking at. We can change what people see when they look at us by what we believe about ourselves.

We each have a magic wand that can change us and impact the world. It's called *our power*. People say we own our power, but power isn't something we own. It's something we step into, grow into, breathe into. Power is a force in the universe we align with. We don't pick it up like a club. We can write and rewrite stories that create self-esteem and the knowledge that we are loved. Even in worst-case scenarios where we weren't loved or we lost our self-esteem, we can write a new story or another ending.

Dear Melody: I'm working on a book about finding my power. I'd like to interview you and other women I admire to hear what you have to say about power. Thank you for considering my request. Lori Yearwood.

I get many reader requests, but this one caught my attention. Then the request to interview me for the book turned into a request from Lori to also interview me for a story for *O, The Oprah Magazine*.

"I'd like to spend a few days with you. Tag along and see how you live your life," Lori said.

We attended a seminar by the Dalai Lama in Pasadena. The next day Lori and I went to the drop zone. Lori put on a jumpsuit, and we both jumped out of the plane. Lori made her first tandem skydive.

After that, Lori and I became friends. Right before September 11, 2001, she was passing through town, and I invited her to stay with me for a few days.

We're in my living room. Lori is saying something. I'm used to this feeling by now when I'm around her. It pulls on my energy. It wants something from me, something I don't have to give. I raise my hands in exasperation. "I don't have your power Lori," I yell. "You do!"

"Oh," she says, and stops pulling.

Over the coming weeks and months, Lori began to believe in herself. I saw the change in her before she did. Her father's death was the first in a sequence of events. It had a domino effect. She found Vashka, quit her job at the newspaper, then started a nonprofit business called Storytellers Ink. She began teaching inner-city kids—the tough ones, the ones with pain in their eyes and clenched fists—how to tap into their power by writing instead of fighting. Her business generated interest. Newspapers were writing about her. Other schools across the nation inquired about her program. Children were writing stories about their experience, strength, and hope. People wanted Lori's program in their communities and schools.

Storytellers Ink was expanding, but Lori kept tripping over obstacles. Eventually, she found herself spending more time supervising employees and talking to the accountant than doing what she loved— teaching children how to write from their hearts and find their power.

The domino effect that started with Vernon's death was good, but something was missing. Lori wanted her ranch. She wanted to live there with horses. Dreams are funny living things. Do we find them or do they find us? And having our dreams come true is rarely what we expect. Dreams should come with labels: *Caution. Unexpected territory ahead.*

Lori and her friend Rachel finished loading the RV, then they herded Lori's two horses into the trailer attached to the rear. Two weeks before the move, Lori bought another horse, a miniature named Harley. Harley is slightly bigger than a dog. Again, it was love at first sight. "Horse owners know instantly when the bond is there and that horse is the right one for them," Lori explains. "I love both horses, Vashka and Harley. They love each other. They're fun horses. Harley likes to untie people's shoelaces. Vashka makes it clear that he's the boss."

Lori can live anywhere and do her business—Storytellers Ink and her writing. Her first choice for a ranch was Northern California, but that's too expensive. Across the border in a lush green valley in Oregon, Lori found a three-bedroom, three-bath house on three-and-a-half acres that she could afford. *Perfect for me and the horses*, Lori thought. *They'll eat grass while I write books.* The house was in good shape; it passed the inspection. That meant Lori could take her time building a barn and fixing the property. Rachel, a friend from Miami, wanted to get out of the city too. She loves horses. Rachel and Lori decided to move together and be roommates. Lori would buy the house; Rachel would help with chores. Together they'd make the dream work.

Lori pulled out of her driveway and took one last look at the Miami house that had been home for so long. In one week, she'd be living her dream. "I knew living with Rachel was a mistake from the beginning," Lori admitted later. "The truth is that it was such a big move I was afraid to do it alone.

"The trip was an omen, a nightmare from the day we hit the road," Lori said. She bought bad gas. The RV broke down. The horse trailer unhitched and rolled away. You can't check into a Super 8 with two horses. Most motels won't let you in with a dog. "They have horse motels around the country," Lori explains. "They're like RV parks, only you can let your horses walk around, eat, and sleep in a stall." But when the RV broke down, there wasn't a horse motel in sight.

"Rachel and I were at a restaurant wondering what we were going to do when a woman appeared out of nowhere. She overheard us. She invited us to stay at her ranch while the RV got fixed. She was like an angel," Lori said. "She fed us and gave us and the horses a safe place to stay."

After the RV was up and running, Lori and Rachel fought through storms and a tornado. By the time they reached New Mexico, Vashka's legs were swelling badly. Lori had to stop. No more traveling until Vashka healed. It was too dangerous. It was an Indiana Jones–style adventure. Every time a problem appeared, a solution did too—eventually, anyway.

Rachel had planned on buying a horse in Oregon, but when she met Sunny at a horse motel one night, Rachel knew she had to have him. Lori and Rachel squeezed, pushed, and crammed, but they couldn't fit Sunny in the trailer with Harley and Vashka. Rachel would have to send for Sunny later.

"That trip was a sign," Lori said. "A trip that should have taken a week took twenty-eight days." It was only the beginning of everything turning upside down, around, and over. From the day she left Miami, and for the next two years, everything in Lori's dream happened wrong.

"I thought moving would be like living in the city, only I'd have the same life on a ranch," Lori said. "Instead, everything about my life changed. It was nothing like what I thought it would be. Taking care of two horses was overwhelming. I had no idea what I was in for. I didn't have a clue. I knew Rachel and I living together wouldn't work. I used her for a security blanket. I had to apologize for that later. I knew my nonprofit business was having problems. But I had no idea that the rest of my life would unfold the way it did. I was shocked and surprised," she said. "I still am."

We associate grief with death, unwanted change, tragedy. But all change brings loss. We let go of the old to make space for the new. There's comfort in going to the same grocery store, coffee shop, restaurants. Each community has its own feel. It's uncomfortable and unsettling when familiar routines change. It's even upsetting when something very minor happens, like the receptionist quitting at the dentist office we've been going to for ten years. No matter what we say, we're not prepared for change.

Living our dream rarely feels the way we imagine it will. How can new parents prepare for the ways a child will change their lives? After living with a partner for years, people say marriage still unexpectedly alters the relationship. Our expectations of what it will feel like to be successful, have our own business, or get that job or promotion can be monumentally different from how these things play out.

At Lori's ranch in Oregon, before the end of the first two weeks the underground sewage backed up through the bathtubs. There were massive hidden problems with the septic system. Laws protecting home buyers ensured that Lori didn't have to pay. But it was a nightmare to live with and fix.

When Lori's furniture arrived, most of it was broken. Then the moving company immediately went out of business. Lori couldn't collect on damages even though she had bought insurance. Then Storytellers Ink collapsed. Lori had no income. She started living off her savings. She found three part-time jobs teaching writing. After a while, life with Rachel became intolerable. Rachel left, leaving Lori with Sunny (the horse Rachel bought on the trip). Now Lori had three horses—two she bonded with and loves and one that's like a foster child. Lori was on her own financially and doing all the upkeep at the ranch. She couldn't find a spare minute to write. It wasn't the sewage, cleaning horse poop, brushing the horses, cleaning the stalls, tending the land, grocery shopping, house cleaning, or worrying about the bills that finally got to her. What consumed and dominated Lori's life were the horses. All three became seriously ill.

"Some of it was diet," Lori explained. "I'd never kept horses. I thought they could live on grass and carrots. Wrong! That's a sugar-filled diet. They couldn't digest it. It made them sick. So I'm living on three-and-a-half acres of lush grass, and I've got to keep the horses away from it! Plus, the horses are emotionally stressed to the max by the move, the change in environment, and the change in the land and climate. Horses are sensitive, like people. In addition to having problems with their digestive tracts, which is serious and life-threatening, the horses began having problems with their feet. Shoeing horses is bad for them," Lori explained. "It cuts their lifespan in half. There's division about that in the horse world, but it's what I know to be true. Horses live twice as long if they're barefoot and their feet are cared for properly."

Horses that aren't shod need to be trimmed, a process that involves the cutting back, shaping, and guiding of the foot's growth. Lori had an expert trimmer in Miami. "It took me a while to catch on, but the trimmer I found in Oregon was butchering their feet," Lori said. "I took it for granted all trimmers knew what they were doing, but that's not true. There are many styles of trimming. The style this trimmer was using didn't work on my horses. It really hurt them—badly." She didn't notice the damage at first.

"Then beautiful, stately Vashka began spending most of his life lying down. That's a bad sign for a horse. I was so worried about Vashka that I didn't pay attention to Harley. By the time I noticed, Harley was so fat from living on grass and carrots he looked like a fat pumpkin with feet."

Next Sunny got sick. "One horse would start to get better, then another one would become ill. It was so bad for a while I wondered if I had Munchausen by proxy," Lori joked. (Munchausen syndrome is a disorder where a person pretends to be sick to receive medical attention. Munchausen syndrome by proxy is a disorder where a person fabricates—or even causes—disease or illness in his or her child in order to receive medical attention, procedures, and treatment for the child.) Lori had been Daddy's little girl all her life. If she needed anything, she called her father, and he instantly made it better. Now he was gone and she was living in the middle of nowhere, isolated and alone.

Lori was exhausted. It took twelve to fourteen hours each day to take care of the sick horses and the ranch. "Nobody understood what I was going through," Lori said. "Nobody got it. Even I wasn't sure what was happening. Every day I'd wake up and say, 'This isn't supposed to be happening. This is not happening the way it should. This is wrong.' I was convinced that this was all a big mistake. And the guilt! I thought I was being punished for everything I'd ever done wrong. Once I'd lied to my father," Lori confessed. "I said I needed a loan to pay off my taxes. Then I used the money for something else. I felt guilty about that. I felt guilty about everything I'd ever done wrong. I believed that my life falling apart meant I was being punished and getting exactly what I deserved. Who was I to think I had any right to live my dream?"

It's common, natural, and normal to believe we're being punished when we lose something or someone we love—or when things go wrong—even if intellectually we know different. A friend's mother was dying of cancer. She pulled her daughter aside. "The cancer is God's way of punishing me for not being a good mother," she said. Her daughter just looked at her. "What am I supposed to do with that?" she asked. "I forgave you the instant you got sick, Mom," she said. "And despite what happened when I was a child, I turned out fine. I'm happy, successful. You're not being punished. You're sick because you're sick." The guilt that comes with grief feels real, but it's not. It's a nasty, biting, stinging, and painful side effect of grief.

Lori couldn't take it anymore. She looked at her life, the ranch, the sick horses, and the bank account running dry. Something had to change. The something that changed was her. She surrendered. Instead of waking up each day saying, "This isn't supposed to be happening," Lori started saying, "Okay, God, have it Your way." She pushed away the guilt. She rolled up her sleeves. "I'm going to make this work," she said. "I deserve my dream."

When we stop resisting, we stop fighting ourselves. We become partners instead of enemies with life.

Lori changed the horses' diet. She built a barn. She fenced the yard in and kept the horses away from the grass. She connected with a group of people in the horse world in Oregon. She met people in online forums, other people struggling to learn how to care for their horses. She still hadn't found a good trimmer, so she took an intensive course and began trimming the horses herself. "It was a disaster," Lori said. "I didn't do a good job. Harley's feet were bleeding. I felt so guilty I swore I'd never trim again." So she found another trimmer.

The next trimmer did worse than Lori at trimming the horses' feet. After a few months, the new trimmer had Harley's feet so inflamed he was kneeling to eat. The online vet told Lori that all she needed to do was alter her trimming style slightly. When she saw what bad shape the horses' feet were in from the new trimmer, Lori decided to tackle trimming again with the vet's help.

"Every day I woke up and consciously surrendered," Lori said. "I'd say to God, 'Just show me what You want me to do.' I also began the practice of gratitude." Lori found five to ten things each day to be grateful for—including the things she didn't like, the things she was resisting. She willed herself into acceptance. Acceptance turned to moments of joy. Gratitude for everything as it is in our lives is the key to surrender. Surrender is the key to life.

For two years, Lori walked blindfolded through the dark. Slowly, she saw how much she'd changed. She was doing chores she never imagined she could. She was learning how to trim and how to maintain healthy horses. People began bringing their horses to her. With her online vet's help, Lori began teaching other horse owners what she'd learned. She was able to send people to reliable resources in the horse world. By surrendering, Lori aligned with her purpose. What she used to think were accidents, mistakes, and problems became an important part of her destiny. She realized there was a reason—a purpose—for everything that happened and that life was unfolding as it should.

"At first it was confusing," Lori said. "One person said do this, another said do that. One vet had me spending every waking hour taking care of the horses." Lori began to see that if she didn't adopt a moderate approach, she and her horses would starve. She had to have time to work. Lori learned the importance of balance. She's learning and relearning to trust herself and to listen to her horses about what they need.

Lori's mother bought a cottage and a plot of land next to Lori's ranch. In the beginning, Lori was chasing her losses—trying to get what she didn't get from her mom when she was a child. That didn't work. What worked was Lori forming a relationship with her mom based on who they both are now.

"You can go through anything—any amount of suffering—if you know there's a reason for it. Then even the most depleting days don't hurt. Well they do, but they don't," Lori says. "It helps when you know there's a reason for the pain."

The horses that were barely surviving are now on the road to thriving. Lori is too. She's not the same person she was. "It doesn't occur to me to think, *Oh, it's Friday night—why don't I have a date?* I'm too exhausted to go out." She's letting her dream work even though it doesn't feel the way she thought it would.

Recently she sent me this message:

> It keeps coming to me to tell you what a wonderful day I had—truly a euphoric one. This is what I did:
>
> • Picked up old hay.
> • Cleaned all the water and feed buckets with salt.
> • Talked to my Internet vet about how to trim Vashka.
> • Then had a great time with Sunny. Today is his birthday.

Since I had that heart-to-heart talk with him about being a foster child versus being chosen like Vashka or Harley, our relationship changed. He nickered for me this morning (a content sound horses make comparable to a cat purring), if you can believe it. His heart is opening to me and mine to him. I can feel it.

- Cleaned the barns, stalls, and tack room.
- Picked up old sticks in the forest, stuff from the flooding.

I'm really happy. My definition of *accomplishment* has changed. It comes from me, not from the outside world, although I'm still working to make it with my writing. Also I'm going to buy a chainsaw to finish off the tree stumps in the woods. I can do so many things I never thought I could. It's empowering.

Lori isn't a city girl anymore. She's not Daddy's little girl. She's a grown woman taking care of herself, a ranch, and three horses. Her body is fit, lean, and strong. Even if the horses aren't perfectly healthy, she can accept where they are in this moment. She knows they're healing. "I have to let go a little and realize they're horses; they're not people," she says. Whether she's lying in the field breathing in sync with Vashka or smiling because Harley untied her shoes, Lori knows that everything she's been through is worthwhile.

A year ago she would have told you she was going through life alone and unguided. Now she knows she's being led. It was her destiny to be transformed. It was what life had in mind all along. "Caring for these beautiful creatures is an honor and a gift," she says. It hurts to risk having dreams. What if they don't work? The death of dreams is as painful as the death of someone we love. But living without dreams is a living death.

Lori didn't find her power. It found her.

This is a story about Lori and horses, but it's a story about more than that. This can be a cruel world. Lori took care of her dad until he died.

My skydiver friend Andy was the one who walked in and found his brother's dead body when they were teenagers, and his older brother had killed himself by shooting himself in the head. It can be really ugly here. I don't know why it's that way. Maybe someday when we're face-to-face with God, He'll tell us. Until then it's a mystery.

We have dreams. We dream about keeping our parents around for a long time. We dream about watching our child grow up, get married, see what he does for a living. I know Shane would have been a great dad. We have dreams when we commit to a partner or get married of our marriage lasting happily forever—and maybe having a houseful of children.

Sometimes our dreams are simpler. We dream—plan on—being healthy, being able to walk without crutches or a wheelchair. And those basic dreams about life get shattered, ripped apart. Or we dream of having a mom and dad who love us for who we are, and they don't. For whatever reason, destiny sees fit to rip our dreams away and we don't get a say. No matter how much power people tell us we have, we can't do a thing about it.

But there's one thing we can do. It doesn't make the ugliness disappear, but it helps. We can bury the old dreams and have the courage to find new ones, whether it's to live with our horses or open our heart and love again or care enough to write a book that helps people heal instead of pounding out empty words. If and when those dreams die, we can let them slip away and have the courage to find new ones again. It's not being loyal to the person we love and buried or to that family we wanted when we keep ourselves miserable, unhappy, and living in pain. We might think it keeps us connected to them if we walk around hurting, but that's not so. As much as we'd sometimes like to not be here, we might end up living for a long time. It won't make our loved ones happy to see us walking around hurting and living without dreams. If it were the other way around, we'd want the people we love to be happy. We'd want them to go on with their lives and make the best lives that they can.

There's something we can do to make our world a more beautiful place. Go for the gold. Let God plant the seeds of dreams in our hearts and see what destiny grows.

There are 9.2 million horses in the United States. Two million people own horses.

The horse industry has a direct U.S. economic effect of $39 billion annually.

Of all horse owners in the United States, 34 percent have annual household incomes of less than $50,000, 28 percent have incomes over $100,000, and 46 percent have incomes between $25,000 and $75,000.

More than 70 percent of horse owners live in communities of 50,000 or fewer.

There are horses in every state, and 45 states have at least 20,000 horses each.

There were 31,276 members of the United States Parachute Association in 2005.

In 2005, 2,177,007 skydives were made. In those skydives, 922 people were injured and 27 people died.

Eight million people suffer through the death of someone in their immediate family in one year, including 800,000 widows and widowers. Of people under 25, 400,000 suffer from the death of a loved one.

Sources: The American Horse Council, the United States Parachute Association, and the National Mental Health Association

ACTIVITIES

1. Find meaning in your life and value the meaning you find. Review your Master List of Losses. What did you learn from each one? What did each mean to you? Do you believe there's purpose and value in what you're going through right now? Can you at least be open to seeing what that purpose is? Are you resisting the daily experiences in your life, telling yourself that what's happening is a mistake, that it's wrong? In Victor Frankl's books and the therapy he invented—logotherapy—he talks about the absolute importance of finding meaning in our losses, our suffering, and in our lives. We can endure tremendous pain and suffering if we believe there is meaning to what we're going through. On the other hand, if we think we're suffering for no reason or good purpose, even small losses can become unbearable.

Ask God (or the Higher Power of your understanding) to show you the meaning in your losses. Ask your losses to show you the meaning. Grapple with this part of your healing until you find meaning in your pain. It doesn't matter what it means to someone else—it's the meaning you derive that matters.

One woman was in a bicycling accident. It shredded her lips and parts of her face and sent her into a severe depression. She was a beautiful woman; she still is. Several reconstructive surgeries have repaired the damage, but for the longest time, it bothered her because when she tries to use her mouth to smile, her lips don't form a smile. Instead, her mouth oddly quivers. The damage to the nerves was severe. "This was the worst loss I'd been through in my life," she said. "I felt like God was picking on me, punishing me. I felt like God had pulled the rug out from under me. Slowly I began to understand. We don't smile with our mouths. We smile from deep inside of ourselves; a smile is the feeling we have in our hearts toward the person we're greeting. A smile comes from our eyes, from our hearts, from our soul. I began to practice expressing a smile using all of me—not just my lips. When I began to learn that, I slowly came through my depression. I found meaning in my loss." Now when you greet this woman, you wouldn't guess that her lips don't actually form a smile. You'd swear she was smiling using her mouth, but her smile is actually coming from her heart. Allow your losses to mean something to you.

2. Practice gratitude daily. Make it part of your regular routine. If possible, find a gratitude partner. Otherwise do it by yourself. Each day, make a list of at least five things that you're grateful for. It doesn't have to be—and shouldn't be—only the things you think are good or blessings. Start looking at everything—every single thing that happens in your day—as something to be grateful for even if you don't feel that way. Be grateful for the problems, the things you think are mistakes, the things you don't like. I call it *nonresistance gratitude*. Be thankful for that unpleasant way you feel. Be thankful for the depression, the confusion, the anger. You don't have to feel grateful. You can will gratitude. The gratitude will eventually become real. Make a commitment to do this for forty days. After forty days, you might not want to stop. Let life and destiny transform you.

3. Are you telling yourself a story about something that happened in your life, and the way you're telling the story hurts? Does the end of your story leave you feeling victimized, with low self-worth, and feeling unloved? Go through your Master List of Losses. Become aware of the story you're telling yourself about what you've lost. Is it possible that you could change your story and have a happier ending—an ending that leaves you aligning with your power and purpose instead of being a victim?

4. Be a helper (when giving feels right to you). I'm not suggesting we rescue the world or put ourselves in dangerous situations. That's being codependent. Be smart. Be safe. But God needs us to help people. In your prayer and meditation time, ask God to use you as an instrument of love.

5. Do you have a dream? Did you have a dream that you forgot? Ask

God to help you remember your dream. Ask for the courage to dream and to help make your dreams come true.

6. Bury dead dreams. Remember to include dreams that died on your Master List of Losses. Grieving the loss of old dreams is a good way to make space for the new.

7. Get rid of grief guilt. Go over your Master List of Losses. Which losses make you feel guilty—like you deserved them, caused them, or did something wrong? Do you feel like any of those losses are punishment? Be honest. Are you ready to let go of your guilt? Ask God to forgive you and help you forgive yourself. Every day for one month, each time you look in the mirror, look directly into your eyes and say, "I forgive you." If you're still feeling guilty at the end of the first month, repeat this exercise until you're guilt free. You deserve to be at peace.

CHAPTER 8

Betting on Change:
When Childhood Grief Makes an Encore

This chapter began as a story about aging. Barbara Suzanne was stunningly beautiful when she was young. She's still beautiful, but she's getting old. I wanted to talk to her about how she felt about that. She agreed. But when we sat down over dinner, she had something else on her mind.

"How do you feel about getting old?" I asked.

"So you think I'm old?" Barbara said. "How old do you think I am?"

I couldn't tell if she was being defensive or coy. The question put me in a bind. If I answered the wrong way, the interview might end. "We're both getting old," I said. "I know I despise parts of aging, but that's me. I want to hear what you have to say."

"The secret to aging is taking care of ourselves," Barbara said. "Eat right and exercise every day."

I didn't ask for her secret. I don't think she has one; I don't think anyone does. Yes, she looks younger than she is. But the "secret to aging" is a billion-dollar marketing technique. "This isn't a story about how to look young when we're not," I said. "We're all getting older every day. What bothers you most about aging? How do you feel about it? What's the hardest thing?"

"I've been sober for a long time," Barbara said. "A few weeks ago, I came closer than I ever have to getting drunk. I really got into trouble."

She shook her head in disbelief. "I still can't believe this happened to me."

"What happened?" I said. "What did you do?"

This is the story Barbara Suzanne told me. It started at the hospital the night before her father died.

Barbara's dad had been sick with cancer for years. When he went into the hospital this time, he knew he wasn't going to walk out. He was dying. He knew it, and so did everyone else. Barbara had some business she wanted to finish with her dad; he'd never once told her he loved her. When she was young, he'd call her "daddy's little girl," then he'd stick some money in her hand. She wanted him to say the words, tell her he loved her. They were running out of time. If he was going to say it, it had to happen now.

She moved her chair closer to his bed and looked into his eyes. "Do you love me, Dad?" she asked.

He didn't respond.

"Do you love me?" Barbara asked again. She wasn't letting him off the hook.

Her father turned away, deliberately averting his eyes. "I don't know," he said after a long silence.

Barbara felt like he'd stuck a knife in her heart, but she didn't cry. She didn't cry when he said that. She didn't cry when he died the next day. She didn't cry at the wake, the funeral, at his grave. Not one tear came out. "I don't know how to grieve," Barbara said. She had been through hard times in her life. She had ended relationships. She had difficulties in her relationship with her son. She wasn't a stranger to pain or loss, but when it came to grief, she felt like she was walking on foreign ground. This was the first person she loved deeply who had died.

Not long after the funeral, Barbara stumbled into something while she was on the computer, surfing the Internet. Barbara doesn't consider herself highly computer literate, but she can get around. She can send and receive e-mails, look things up, shop. She signed up with several online dating services. She enjoys playing computer games like solitaire.

Now she discovered something better than that. On her computer, she could log in to a virtual casino, sit down at a table, and play cards with other people. She could gamble online, just like at a casino. An animated character represented her. Other animated characters represented the other people who sat at the table and played cards with her. By moving the mouse, she could operate her online character, tell it how much to bet, when to hold. It was like gambling in Vegas while wearing her pajamas in the privacy of her home. She could choose whether she wanted to play for money or not. She chose to play for fun.

Her dad had been a gambler. When she was young, he taught her to play poker. Texas hold 'em was their game. Now Barbara could play Texas hold 'em online. She won and won and won, but because she was playing for free, she won pretend money. After a couple of weeks, she'd won thousands of dollars. *If I'd been playing for real money*, Barbara thought, *I'd be rich by now*.

One night, Barbara Suzanne got out her credit card and put two thousand real dollars in her casino online account and switched to the "play for money" game. It was stupid to play for free. She was obviously good at the game. Look at how much pretend money she won.

Barbara was excited. This was fun. Except when Barbara started playing for real money, something changed. She didn't win as often as she did when she was playing for free. No matter how good Barbara's cards were, somebody at the virtual card table got dealt a better hand. Did her luck change when she gave the casino her credit card number? Was this coincidence? Was it paranoid to think the casino was cheating her? Someone was walking away from the virtual card table with the winnings. Each animated character represented a real human being— didn't it? Somebody else sitting at home in front of his or her computer was winning—even if it wasn't her. She probably hit a losing streak. No matter how good someone is at gambling, nobody wins all the time. Luck comes and goes. That's why they call it *a winning streak*. If she stayed with it, Lady Luck would eventually come around again.

By the time Barbara went to bed the first night she started playing for money, she'd lost a thousand dollars. She wanted to keep playing until she broke even, but she needed some sleep. Tomorrow she would double up her bets until she won back what she lost. She'd gotten some money when her dad died, but she wasn't going to get the bulk of her inheritance until after her stepmother's death. She couldn't afford to lose the money she lost. She couldn't stop gambling until she won it back.

First thing next morning, Barbara was back at the computer playing poker again. From then on, online gambling became the center of her life. No matter where Barbara went, she couldn't wait to get home and play cards. She stayed up past her usual bedtime playing cards every night. She couldn't wait to wake up and get back on the computer in the morning. Barbara had a reason to get out of bed and a reason to come home. For the first time in a long time, she felt alive.

One afternoon when Barbara returned home from the grocery store, she found a dead pigeon on her porch. It was lying in front of her door. Something about it bothered her. It made her feel uneasy, but she didn't make the connection. Later she remembered something her dad taught her. *At every card table there's a pigeon—a sucker, a mark. If you look around and can't see who the pigeon is, then it's probably you.*

Barbara maxed out one credit card, then she started using another. No matter how long she played, how well she played, or which table she sat at, she couldn't win. She couldn't get ahead. She also couldn't stop. She had to win back the money she lost. Any minute her luck would change, she thought. It would be like it was in the beginning, when she had such good luck playing for free. But by the time the bank called Barbara two weeks later, she'd lost twelve thousand dollars at the online casino, and her checking account was four thousand dollars overdrawn.

"A month or so before my dad's death, a woman said she lost one hundred and fifty thousand dollars gambling online," Barbara said. "When she told me that I thought, *How could anyone be that dumb?*" Now she understood.

"I thought the animated characters sitting at the table represented real people—like me. I thought I was playing cards with real people. Even though the game was computerized, I thought the game was legitimate and I had a chance. Those weren't people I was playing against!"

Barbara said. "It was all rigged! Nobody was winning except the online casino site. It wasn't like Vegas, where a dealer has to deal you the cards that come up and play by the rules. It was a computer game that was rigged—programmed—so I'd lose. At least in Vegas, I would have had a chance. I know better than to gamble anyway—online or not," Barbara said. "I grew up around gambling. I know you only gamble what you're willing to lose. I've got enough money to pay my bills each month, but I'm not rich. I ended up losing all the money my dad left me plus some of my own."

Chasing our losses isn't a good idea in any area of our lives. It's normal to react to a loss by thinking, *I can't afford to lose that. I have to stay and make it work*, whether we're talking about a love relationship that's gone bad, an investment, a move to the wrong city, or gambling. But chasing our losses doesn't usually recoup what we lost. We end up losing more.

Barbara still couldn't believe this happened to her. Gambling in casinos can be seductive and troublesome for someone with a gambling problem. Barbara Suzanne found online gambling even more insidious and seductive. "It didn't feel real," Barbara said. "It felt like I was playing a video game, until it was time to pay my credit card bills."

When Barbara went to the bank, she learned that not only had the odds of the game changed when Barbara switched from playing for fun to playing for money, the online casino had also attempted to fraudulently run the same check through her account and collect on it more than once. She had written an online check for two thousand dollars. After that check cleared her account, the casino ran the same check through her account again and collected another two thousand. When the casino ran the check through a third time to collect another two thousand, Barbara's banker called to alert her. Barbara had banked there for years. The bank employee knew something was wrong.

Gambling switched from being something that made Barbara feel alive to a living hell. She was filled with remorse. "I couldn't believe what I'd done," she said. "Sure the casino was trying to defraud me by running the check through more than once. But I'd gambled away a lot of money—money I couldn't afford to lose. I was gambling when I didn't have a chance to win because the computer was programmed for me to lose. How could I be so stupid? I was furious with myself. When you're gambling, you'd give anything to feel that winning streak again. You think it's right around the corner. Then when it does come, you play through it until you start to lose again. It's hard to stop and take your losses. You think any minute your luck will change and you'll win, but then all you do is lose more. Twelve thousand dollars and I had nothing to show for it! This wasn't fun. I'd been sober and in recovery for a long time, but now for the first time in years, I wanted to get drunk."

Barbara didn't drink. She called her Alcoholics Anonymous sponsor instead. After talking about what happened, Barbara realized that what she stumbled into was more powerful than her. It was time to take her losses. The situation was out of control.

Some losses happen to us; others we create. It's hard to lose something when we've done it to ourselves. We gain control when we admit that whatever we're trying to control is controlling us. As bad as it feels to admit defeat, when we surrender to the loss, we start winning.

Barbara's bank reversed four thousand dollars of fraudulent charges—the funds the online casino had illegally withdrawn—so her account was no longer overdrawn. Then Barbara had a friend take the gambling software off Barbara's computer. She stopped gambling, a day at a time. She consulted an attorney and learned she wasn't alone. A lot of people are in the *I Stumbled into an Online Casino and Was Dumb Enough to Lose Thousands of Dollars* Club. Teenagers are using their parents' credit cards and creating monumental debt. Online gambling is a billion-dollar industry, and the casinos are the ones winning. The attorney told Barbara that even though the computerized gambling was rigged so she'd lose, there wasn't anything he or she could do about it. Barbara was out all the money she lost. She was distraught, but at least her life was back on track.

A few weeks later, Barbara began to see the incident in a different light. In her family, money equals love. "I didn't know how to cry about my dad's death. I didn't know how to mourn. I think I set up this gambling situation so I'd have a reason to feel bad," Barbara said. "I didn't cry when my dad said he didn't know if he loved me, and that really hurt. I didn't cry when my dad died. But I sure knew how to grieve about losing that money. I cried about that. I think losing the money symbolizes losing my father and his love.

"You asked what I dislike most about aging. I'm not sure what I dislike the most, but I know what I miss: it's the feeling of being in love. I miss it a lot. It hurts. I can't remember the last time I felt that way, it's been so many years. I watch television and see people falling in love. I see people in real life walking around holding hands. On the computer dating services, I list my age as fifty-one," she said, winking. "But we both know I'm older than that. I don't know if I'll ever be in love again. Who knows? Maybe I've had my last kiss. This gambling filled up a big empty space in my life. That's a part of aging that hurts."

No matter how bad gambling losses are today, those losses can and will get worse tomorrow if we don't stop now. Barbara didn't get her father's love, and that hurt. He died, and she's grieving that too. When her stepmother dies, she'll get a substantial sum of money from her father's will. In the meantime, she can work on learning the difference between money and love. She can believe she deserves both. She won't have to lose again.

When Barbara Suzanne stopped gambling and got help, she started her own lucky streak.

Online gambling grew from 30 sites and bets of $17 million in 1996 to approximately $3 billion in wagers in 2000.

In 2003 U.S. gamblers bet an estimated $6 billion.

Gross gaming revenues for online betting will reach $48 billion by 2010.

Online gambling revenues will reach $125 billion by 2015.

"There are approximately 10 million problem gamblers in the United States today—10 million people who are jeopardizing their lives, their families, and their futures for gambling."

Sources: AngelCiti Entertainment, Merrill Lynch, Online Gambling Research and Markets Group, and www.problemgamblingstudy.org

ACTIVITIES

1. If you have a gambling problem, call 213-386-8789 (International Service Office for Gamblers Anonymous) for a meeting near you. If you love someone who has a gambling problem, call 718-352-1671 (Gam-Anon International Service Office). Get help stopping gambling; turn your luck around.

2. Go back over your Master List of Losses, the one you did for the first activity in chapter 1. Do you see any significant losses that you experienced but haven't yet grieved? You don't have to do anything about this, just be aware. Remember, ignoring grief doesn't make it disappear. Sooner or later the feelings will emerge. Maybe they'll show up in a similar loss situation we create. Maybe the feelings will turn into an illness. Many professionals suggest that emotional pain can become physical pain. As much as it hurts to feel emotional pain, it's better to take our losses as soon as we can.

3. Write about your thoughts and feelings on the subject of getting older. Buy a journal and devote it to that subject. Write about how you feel about being your current age. What do you dislike the most about aging? Then make another list. What are your favorite things about being your current age? Many people, places, and things become more valuable *and* valued with time.

4. Is there a loss in your life that you're chasing right now? Is there

something that's not working out, but you're telling yourself you can't afford to lose it so you've got to make it work—all the while losing more? Sometimes situations do turn around. But most of the time, losing situations only get worse, and the longer we stay in them, the more we lose. When we surrender to our losses is when we start to win.

CHAPTER 9

Spare Change:
Making the Most of What We Have

While sitting on a bench in front of the flower shop, I noticed a beggar sitting on the sidewalk out front. He didn't know I was behind him, watching. I could see what the people walking by him couldn't. He had used both sides of white poster sheets to make a hinged book of signs covering various sympathetic situations. "HAVE CANCER, HUNGRY" read the sign facing passersby. "DISABLED VET NEEDS MONEY AND RIDE" read the sign facing me. I couldn't see the other eight signs. *That's really funny*, I thought. *He turned begging into a business. He could get a job with those skills!*

How would you like to make a million dollars? That's not an invitation to an Amway meeting. How would you like to make a million dollars doing something you love? You might think it's odd to include finances in a book about change and grief. But how much pain and stress stem from money problems? "I'm a broken man," one bankrupt man said after years of living on credit cards while watching his business fail. One man committed suicide after losing his home. He had refinanced it to the hilt. Credit card interest rates soar to usury rates after we default on payments; it's in the fine print. Some folks who went through the Depression are still afraid to throw anything away—from bread bags to rotten food—whether it has value or not. Counselors daily see the bruises when people let money stress bring them to blows. Most

SOS calls I receive are frantic pleas for *money please*. People betray, kill, and risk prison for money. They identify happiness with cash so much that they allow the lack of it to ruin their lives.

The only time money isn't a problem is when we have enough. Even then it can be a worrisome thing. Many books claim to teach *anyone* how to create abundance. But an eleven-year-old working in an Egyptian sweatshop probably won't be able to create wealth. Or could she? What about elderly people who don't have enough money to eat and pay bills? Can they manifest anything they want? Soon the elderly will outnumber the young. By age eighty-five, one in three will have Alzheimer's. The Social Security pot may be dry. What will our elderly do? They're not taken care of that well now.

"My mom has Alzheimer's. I hired a caretaker to stay with her during the week," one woman said. "I walked in unannounced one afternoon. The caretaker was sitting on Mom's bed, staring at the TV. She had put Mom in the shower; Mom had had an accident in her Depends. Mom was huddled in the corner of the shower. She was scared, touching the water, saying, "Es ist heiss, es ist heiss." (It's hot, it's hot.) It broke my heart. I fired the caretaker on the spot. The family does the best we can, but we have financial limitations. We have to work. We can't be there all the time."

Abundance—including investments and financial management after money is earned—is something we create, but it's also part of being blessed. The Bible says the poor will always be with us. Not everyone can create wealth, but many people can. With the way real estate has gone up, if we own a home and have retirement funds, our net worth is probably already close to a million dollars. Unless something drastically changes in the current economy, a million dollars isn't that much anymore. With all that said, this is a story about what I've learned about money, abundance, and wealth.

Secret number one: Be grateful for what we have, no matter how much or little that is. We don't have to feel grateful; we can will or force gratitude until *acting as if* makes it real. To those who have, more will be given, but if we believe we have nothing, that's what we'll get. Treating what we have with gratitude is like giving a seed soil, water, and sun. It can grow us a money tree.

I followed my husband up four flights of steps. I didn't want to take the elevator and risk running into someone we knew at the welfare office. I was so ashamed. This wasn't supposed to be happening. My husband was a chemical dependency counselor when we met. I'd been clean and sober for years and wanted to be a counselor too. I had this dream that someday we'd work together helping other addicts get sober. Our marriage wouldn't be just for us. It would benefit others. We'd be a recovery team, and we'd be of service to the world.

There were two things he didn't tell me until it was too late. He wanted out of the chemical dependency field because counseling didn't pay enough. He wanted to be rich without working for it. "I'm an idea man," he said. The other thing he didn't mention was that he wasn't really sober. He'd been drinking and lying about it for years. At home he spent most of his time in bed. He always complained about insomnia and feeling tired. He was always trying to catch up on lost sleep. Years later he admitted that he hid liquor bottles all over the house. He stayed in bed because he was drunk and needed to hide that from me. I felt disappointed that he didn't want to help people and my dream of us working together to help others wouldn't come true. But lying about drinking? That betrayal hurt. I knew ultimately it would cost us our marriage if he didn't get sober for real.

I looked around the welfare office waiting room at the others waiting for handouts. All my husband's schemes, from selling necklaces made out of Mount St. Helen's volcanic ash to hustling krugerrands (South African gold coins), had landed us here at the welfare office. We had two children, no money, no food. My mom had loaned us the down payment on a shack of a house, but we couldn't make the payments on that, and they were only $350 a month. Spare change scrounged from under the couch cushions and turning in bottles was all we had, and we barely had any of that. I wasn't lazy, but he didn't care if he wrote bad checks. He didn't care if bills went into collection. There'd probably be a parking ticket on the car when we went outside because he didn't care about things like that. We had so many judgments against us that when I worked, my paychecks were instantly garnisheed. The battle was lost before it began. I had good credit when I met him. I paid my bills on time. Financial responsibility was important to me, but I couldn't put a leash on this man, and God knows I tried.

Early in life, my mom had shown me that a woman could work, run a business, make good money. She could invest in real estate and make money work for her after she earned it. She could buy herself what she wanted. She didn't have to wait for a man. She could and should save for old age. The only thing Mom, who grew up in the Depression, didn't show me was how to spend money. I learned that for myself. I didn't doubt my earning ability. The problem was, I didn't understand the concept of being unequally yoked. Marriage is a legally binding contract. If we link with someone who writes bad checks, doesn't pay bills, overlooks taxes, doesn't treat possessions with respect, and squanders what he has, those behaviors affect us. If he believes he doesn't deserve abundance, his beliefs contaminate us. I was trapped in money hell. The only way out was divorce.

I wasn't ready for that yet. I loved my husband. My marital commitment was important to me. I had been divorced once and still felt guilty about that. Our children, Nichole and Shane, loved their dad. I finally saw that his drinking episodes weren't slips. A slip was when he stayed sober more than a month. I believe in recovery, but it doesn't happen for everyone. "There but for the grace of God go I" is more than a cliché. I kept hoping that someday David would get sober. The thought of breaking up our family made me ache.

David was a kind, funny man. "He made me laugh," my sister-in-law said at his funeral. "I'd see him at the grocery store. I'd be cringing and hiding and he'd yell across the aisles and ask, 'What are you buying with your food stamps?'" After David died, my daughter discovered in his paperwork that he'd been sponsoring a child in a third world country. Even though he was drinking and broke, he sent his thirty-five dollars faithfully each month.

David did the best he could. Some people have the alcoholism disease so badly they cannot stop drinking no matter how much you want them to and how hard they try. For some reason they don't get the Grace. In the movie *Bruce Almighty*, Bruce whined when he didn't get the promotion he wanted. "Stop acting like a victim," his girlfriend said. "I'm not a victim, I'm a martyr," he said. That's how I felt. I couldn't see what I was learning. All I knew was that we were broke and it was because of him. I didn't know I was in a real-life financial school. By the time I graduated, I'd have a Ph.D.

Secret number two: Don't starve from pride. Ask if you need help, then humbly accept it when it comes. Don't take more than you need. Pay it back as soon as you can.

I tried to believe that things would work out, but that Christmas keeping the faith was difficult. It was Christmas Eve day. We still didn't have a tree or presents for the children. Late that afternoon, a friend knocked on the door. She gave me a stack of wrapped toys. "Santa sent them," she said. That night we found a discounted tree we could afford. I found lights and decorations from last year. I wound popcorn and cranberry strings around the tree. I found an angel and put her on top. It was a scraggly tree, but it looked pretty when it was lit. We didn't have money. My husband's drinking was destroying our marriage. But my children were with me. Shane was still alive.

"Remember when you made that skating rink for us in your backyard?" a neighborhood child said thirty-two years later, when she had a child of her own. "You'd take us to the drive-in movies and let us sit on top of the car. I'll never forget some of the great times we had." Often we don't realize until we look back how happy we really were.

Why wait to be happy? We waste so many moments thinking happiness is a step away. We're like a donkey with a carrot on a stick attached to its head, always chasing the carrot but never reaching it because it's permanently one step away. We tell ourselves any number of things constitute the missing piece that'll make us happy: a relationship, a change in the relationship we're in now, money, improved health, losing weight, a bigger house, a more expensive car, or living in another state. Meanwhile, living like this donkey becomes a way of life. We think we'll be happy when we get the next thing, but we're still miserable when we get it because our ideas about what will make us happy aren't true. Sometimes we become more miserable after we get what we want. If getting what we want doesn't make us happy, what will? Getting something else? While acquiring something may be a timely decision, no *thing* is the key to being complete. The missing piece is spelled p-e-a-c-e. There's another way to be happy. Realize we're happy now instead of looking back and seeing it later, after the moment is gone.

Another Christmas, the children and I were in the kitchen when we heard a knock on the door. In came a group from church. It was a Sunday school teacher and all the children in her class with a box of food and gifts. They watched as we opened our gifts: a sweater that didn't fit, a toy that needed batteries (without the batteries), a doll for a girl years younger than my daughter. Then they sang Christmas carols and looked around our home. "It's the thought that counts," I told the children. But we were embarrassed by everyone looking at us and looking around our home. My children and I made a decision: If and when we had money, we'd help anonymously and try to give people what they want. And if we gave a toy that needed batteries, we'd include the batteries too.

Secret number three: Everything we need is provided—*everything.* I didn't get exactly what I wanted the way I wanted it, but we didn't go naked or die from starvation. We had clothes to wear even if they were secondhand or didn't have designer labels. I learned a verse from the Bible. I said it then, and I repeat it like a mantra whenever I'm money-scared now: "My God shall supply all my need according to His riches in glory." I say it until peace comes. We don't need look to any agency, person, or employer to meet our needs. Our Higher Power is our Source, and God's resources surpass what we can see.

Secret number four: We should be careful who we marry or choose for a partner. Their money beliefs and behaviors affect us. The person with the most dysfunction wins.

For a long time after I got sober, I felt guilty about being an alcoholic and addict. For years, I didn't believe I deserved to even own and drive a car. Finally, one day, I couldn't endure taking the bus any longer. I looked up at the heavens and said, "I want a car! Please?" Within a month, I was driving a car that belonged to me. God didn't care if I had a car or not. Life was waiting until it mattered to me.

Secret number five: We don't get what we deserve; we get what we believe we deserve. Ask God for help releasing beliefs blocking financial stability and abundance. There aren't limited funds so some people get a little and others a lot. There's more than spare change for us even if other people are rich. We live in an abundant world. Ask and you shall receive. Don't envy. We get what we wish for other people and nobody has what's ours. Be happy for other people's success. If they can be successful, so can we.

My husband had been dragging me to Amway meetings for months. I was trying to pay attention to the speaker, but I drifted. He was talking about the millions he made selling soap, then he hollered, *he didn't sell soap, he sold hope and so could we!* "Multilevel corporations are a way to make money and help people," he said. "We're being of service by teaching people how to become rich." He told us how to get people to come to the meetings so we could sponsor them, and they could sponsor people, and the people on top could profit from all the soap sold by the people underneath. He knew people wouldn't come if they knew it was an Amway meeting. (So did we.) "Ask if they want to become wealthy working three nights a week," he said. "Don't say *Amway* until they're trapped in the room, then they'll have to hear the pitch." I didn't want to ask one more person if they wanted to make a million dollars and hear, "I know what you're talking about. It's Amway. I tried it and it didn't work."

Then the speaker began talking about *Think and Grow Rich,* a classic book on wealth. Suddenly what he said made sense: set goals, let your subconscious guide you into achieving them, envision already having what you want because believing you have it makes it real. What didn't make sense to me was using these principles to sell soap. I had to do something I felt passionate about, something that intuitively felt right, like it was God's will for me. Then these principles might work.

David and I drove home. I headed out in the ten-degree weather and knocked on a neighbor's door. "What is it, Melody?" he asked.

I held out my white crate filled with cleaning products. "Want to buy some soap?"

Secret number six: While patiently waiting for destiny to reveal itself, do the best we can.

I felt sad a few years later when I heard that the main speaker at that meeting died. He really had been successful selling soap and hope. He died a wealthy man.

I want to be a writer. I was painting a wall in my house when I remembered that dream. Since I was a child I wanted to write, but I had forgotten that. I looked at the ceiling. "God, if You want me to write, You're going to have to show me how to go about it because I don't have a clue." Within twenty-four hours, I had my first job writing for a community newspaper. It paid five dollars a story. Two years later, my first book was published. I made nine hundred dollars for two years of work. I had doubts about whether I should pursue writing, but then the book won a small award. The validation was exactly what I needed, and I learned how to write a book.

Because I'd been sickly so much of my childhood and had missed so much school, I learned to teach myself whatever I wanted to learn—there's an upside to most experiences. I spent the next seven years learning to write by self-study, attending workshops, and writing. I continued writing, and I worked any job where my wages wouldn't be garnisheed: babysitting, handing out food samples at the grocery store, running family groups at chemical dependency treatment centers, whatever came my way and offered money I could bring home.

Secret number seven: Know what we're passionate about. Hang on. Don't let go of the dream, but let go of the need to control how it comes true. Be willing to pay our dues. Then do whatever it takes (legally) to support ourselves until our dreams come true.

When I wrote my second book five years later, I made a decision. If

I ever wrote a book again, I'd write it because I was passionate about what I had to say and not for the money. I was still married then. I'd moved up the ladder from working for a community paper to a daily. We're taught to write what we know, which is only partially true because sometimes we write what we're learning. What I knew was that it hurt to be married to an alcoholic who wouldn't stop drinking. The only thing that helped me was to detach in love and take care of myself. I decided to write a book about that. I was apprehensive about saying what I thought, but I decided to speak my truth. I figured nobody would read the book anyway. We're free when we have nothing to lose.

Secret number eight: Do the work for the sake of the work. Don't attach outcomes. Work with the enthusiasm of beginner's mind—the fresh outlook we have in the beginning when we're so excited that we'd work for free or almost nothing because we're not cynical or disillusioned yet. If we can't do the task with love, either change our hearts or our jobs. Working for fame and fortune doesn't work. Purpose isn't a burden; it's a privilege. Find joy in what we do.

I was in my basement office writing the manuscript that was to become known as *Codependent No More* when I typed, "You don't have to stay in relationships that make you miserable." I stopped typing and stared at what I'd written, my eyes riveted to the computer screen. My husband and I were approaching our tenth anniversary. Did I want to go for year eleven? I went upstairs. "Our marriage has been dead for years," I told David. "It's time to get divorced."

He kept reading the newspaper. "Sure thing, dear," he said. He didn't hear a word I'd said. I rented an apartment and loaded a U-Haul with furniture, a television, a stereo, his clothes. I drove him to the apartment. "Don't come to the other house at night," I said. "This is where you live now." Then I went home and finished writing the book. I kept the children, the house—and the bills. It's kinder to get divorced than count the years until someone dies and we're free.

Women often do their grieving while they're still in the marriage. They repeatedly tell the husband, "What you're doing hurts. If you don't stop it, I'm gone." If the husband doesn't stop, the woman feels angry, hurt, confused, and depressed. For a long time, it looks like she's sticking her head in the sand. One day the confusion lifts. What was inconceivable and unacceptable feels clear. She did her mourning while she was married. She didn't plan it that way, but that's how it worked. She went through the stages of grief: denial, anger, bargaining, sadness. Now she's accepted divorce. The man is devastated. How can she just walk away like that—without looking back? He didn't hear her begging him to change. He called it *nagging*. He didn't hear her crying herself to sleep at night. He was snoring. When she leaves, her grief is almost over. His has just begun.

It should have been a quick divorce, but the judge looked at the paperwork and scowled, "I don't see anything here about child support." I surprised myself and my attorney when I flew to my feet. "With all due respect, Your Honor, in the years we were married, this man hasn't paid the bills. Why would he start now? Whether you tell him to pay me twenty dollars or two thousand dollars a month, he can't give me money he doesn't have."

"Case continued until adequate child support is written into the order." The judge banged the gavel. Four months later he granted the divorce, giving me four hundred dollars of child support a month. Ha! Once when the children were hungry, I tracked down my ex and begged him for three hundred dollars. Four months later, he manipulated me into giving it back by whining about how he didn't have money to pay his rent and how could I let the father of my children sleep on the streets? I could have made a fuss about child support, but he didn't have the money to pay me; it wasn't like he was withholding it. It was easier to rely on God and myself. At least I knew what to expect.

It was a quiet night. The children were sleeping. I'd finished writing *Codependent No More* and was back working for the daily newspaper. Lying in bed, I asked myself a question. Maybe my guardian angels asked me. *If I could have anything in the world and it wouldn't be wrong, what would that be?* I wrote a list. New clothes for the children. Pay the bills from the divorce. Make thirteen hundred dollars a month by writing, with a little extra for emergencies, Christmas, and birthdays. *Is that*

all? What I'd really like is to have one million dollars after taxes in the bank.
I wrote that, put the list in the Bible, and went to sleep. I didn't think
about the list for years. I didn't understand the significance of that event.
It was a turning point—the beginning of letting go of believing that I
deserved to be punished by not having enough money, life had to be a
struggle, and I'd never have enough. I stumbled into a nearly perfect
attitude for success. I didn't attach extreme importance to having money
by feeling like I couldn't be complete without it, and I wasn't blocking
myself with limiting beliefs.

Secret number nine: Write our goals. Be certain they're what we desire
and believe we deserve. They have to feel solid—like they're something
we can really have and what we want (not a foolish whim). There's a certain feeling we get when our goals are right. Put life in our goals by
including what we want to do, not just what we want to get. Then let
go and be content with what we have. Take guided actions. Live a surrendered life.

I didn't know I had to write *keep my children alive and healthy* on the
list. I thought that went without saying. Maybe we don't get everything
we want. Sometimes we get what we get.

I was furious about the bills from the marriage. I owed fifty thousand
dollars for David's irresponsibility. He had incurred many of the bills in
his business schemes, but if I wanted good credit, I had to pay them. I
earned one thousand a month. It was all I could do to pay necessary
expenses. Paying these old bills would be a stretch. Thinking about the
bills gave me anxiety. Once I had a panic attack, hyperventilated, and
called 911.

One day it was time. I was sick of creditors hounding me, tired from
living with all the anxiety that having unpaid bills creates. What if I took
all the principles I'd learned about sobriety and applied them to money:
admitted I was powerless and my financial life was unmanageable,
turned my financial life and will over to God, did my part, then asked
for God's help? That's the day I stopped feeling like a victim and took
responsibility for myself. I made a list of creditors. I contacted every

creditor and said I would send something each month until the bill was paid in full. Then I did what I said. Miracles happened. I got a letter from a hospital where I owed five thousand dollars and was paying off ten dollars a month; they wrote, "We're happy to inform you that you qualify for an assistance program. Your balance has been reduced to zero." Some creditors reduced the amount I owed by 50 percent. All the forces in the universe conspired to help when I surrendered and took responsibility for myself. Paying my bills turned into a snowball rolling downhill. It went faster and faster. One day I would even pay the welfare department back.

Secret number ten: No matter how unfair or overwhelming our situation feels, take responsibility for ourselves and our bills. Bills aren't an all-or-nothing situation. Don't wait until we can pay the entire amount. Stop hiding. Pay something every month.

I learned more about money. Spend less than we earn; live under our means. Don't spend money we don't have; *never* write a check until the money is *already* in the bank. Don't use credit cards for credit; use credit cards like checks, then pay the entire balance each month. Give when we have a little, when we have enough, and when we have lots. Don't give away our rent money. It's like using oxygen masks on planes; pay our necessary bills first, then help others, otherwise someone will have to help us. Sometimes give money, but also give of ourselves. Our hearts will tell us when to give, how much, and to whom.

Remember, not all charities can be trusted. Ask how much money actually gets to the people we want to help. Charity can be a lucrative business for the people at the top. "What percentage goes to administration?" I often ask.

"I don't know. Call the main office and ask," says the solicitor.

"That's not my job. You're asking for something from me," I say. Then I hang up the phone. Once I reported an organization that was pestering me for thousands of dollars. The state discovered it was a scam! Some days, everywhere we turn there's a hand reaching out or a charity calling for a donation. It's too much! I know one man who *never* answers his phone because he knows it's an unsolicited business trying to sell him something or a charity after his money. Having so many people after our money makes us want to not give at all. Other days we can't give away money fast enough.

"After the Christmas 2004 tsunami, I ran to my computer to find legitimate charities," one man said. "My heart was so burdened, I had to help." Worldwide, millions of people felt the same. We opened our hearts and checkbooks instantly. Nobody had to ask. Money and good wishes poured out as we grieved together, whether we personally know anyone injured or not. Many wanted to give more than money but weren't sure how. "I want to help," a friend said, "not just give a few pennies. I want to volunteer my life to be of service to people around the world. But how do I do that? Where do I go with this urge?"

She was sincere—not codependent. She genuinely wanted to be used as a force for good to help people suffering from disasters: earthquakes, floods, wars, tsunamis, hurricanes, and diseases. According to the World Health Organization and the *New York Times*, millions of women—girls—in Africa's sub-Sahara are plagued by fistulas. They live as outcasts after unsuccessful childbirths tear up their insides, leaving them incontinent, dripping feces and urine. Suffering is rampant. So is communication so we know about the suffering that's going on—sometimes know more than we want. "Ask how you can help and be of service," I said. "You'll be shown." So will we. Opportunities to give will appear in our path. We decide when to say yes.

Giving is crucial for living. The key is understanding we're not obliged to say yes, but we can. It's as codependent to feel that we have to say no as it is to feel that we have to say yes. Bypass, go above, under, around, in front of, or behind guilt, fear, and ego. Let life help the people it wants to through us. Being of service is a good way to live. Sometimes the best thing we can do—for someone else and ourselves— is help someone by giving or loaning money. Sometimes giving money isn't helpful. It annoys us and it prolongs a problem the person is eventually going to have to solve. Boomers are accused of being the "me generation." I disagree. We followed the people who lived through the Depression. Many of us inherited a legacy of feeling undeserving. We weren't sure we were entitled to anything. The me generation? Getting to *me too* took many of us a third of a lifetime or more.

Pay taxes diligently. Give Caesar his due or he'll become a relentless burden. As soon as we can, save for emergencies and old age. If an emergency arises—the furnace breaks or the car won't start—pray like the dickens. Stop everything and beg God for help. Money can't buy happiness but poverty is a lot of work. No matter what happens, don't forfeit responsibility or ethics. We'll be guided about what to do.

Years ago, I drove to the food shelves one night. Food shelves are community programs—small, free grocery stores. People donate nonperishable goods like peanut butter and macaroni and cheese. If we're broke, we take what we need. When I pulled into the parking lot, the building was dark. The sign in the door said, "Closed until Wednesday." It was Monday. I was tired. Tired from the years of struggling and praying and begging. Tired from the years of being afraid about having the lights or the gas shut off. Tired of not being able to take my children out to eat or buy them new clothes. The years of struggle caught up with me that night. I laid my head on the steering wheel and cried.

Soon you'll never have to worry about money again—unless you want to. I heard that as clearly as if someone said it in my ear. Simultaneously a peace filled the car, a peace so big that my exhaustion disappeared. It wasn't a feeling that sometime in the future things would be okay. Everything was okay now.

I drove home. I didn't win the lottery. Something better happened. My self-worth disconnected from my net worth. I stopped struggling and stepped into peace.

I don't know how much time passed. It might have been eight months, a year, or three. Shane came home from school, kissed me on the cheek, then headed for the fridge. "High five," I said, holding up my hand.

He slapped my hand. "What for?" he asked.

"We've got a million dollars in the bank," I said.

Secret number eleven: Be so peaceful with what we have that we barely notice when our income changes. Some things don't change when money increases. We still have to pay bills and file taxes. Our happiness and peace won't change by getting money either. Rarely do we get what we want until we know that getting what we want doesn't matter.

There were more lessons. I learned when to buy real estate, when to sell. I gained a basic understanding of mutual funds and investments. More than that I learned (the hard way) how to discern whom to trust and how to not trust too much. I learned to continually trust myself although I could let some people help. I learned money is like candy. Don't leave it unguarded with hungry people. They'll help themselves. One of my first investments was annuity life insurance policies on my children's lives. But I found the idea of life insurance on my children so repugnant that I canceled the policies. I'm glad I did before my son died. Many people deserve to be compensated for their loss. No amount of money could compensate for losing Shane. How money comes to us matters. Oh, and as long as I was paying my credit cards in full each month, why not use a credit card with a good rewards program? Then I can use the rewards to get things from appliances to airline tickets for free. Make pennies count.

In many cultures, begging is an honored tradition. Beggars position themselves by tourist sites, holy spots, or merchants—places people with spare change might be and preferably places that invoke guilt. On the steps to temples in China, women and men sit hunched over deliberately displaying their missing or wounded limbs to prove they're not kidding; they can't get a job. Hard to look at? Much harder to live with, I bet. Some parents send the children to beg. It's a family vocation. It's hard to refuse a scraggly girl when her stomach is bulging from malnutrition and you're on vacation. "They keep showing the pictures of big-eyed, starving children hour after hour on television," a friend said. "I've got to change the channel. I can't lie in my big soft bed eating a sandwich and look at that!" Even if we don't have much money it makes us feel guilty, incompetent, and sad when we see all the poverty and disaster in the world.

She was standing by the freeway entrance. A big bandana covered her head. "Homeless and have cancer. Please help!" her sign read. True? Who knows? I keep spare change in the car for situations like this. I grabbed some money and put it in her hand. "God bless you," I said and meant it. "God bless you too," she said.

Spare change is important. I used to live on it too.

Remember the dream I had for my marriage? I wanted my husband and myself to be a recovery team, then I discovered he didn't want to be a counselor. He didn't want to work at all or be sober. As it turned out, my marriage was the classroom where I learned the ideas I wrote about in *Codependent No More*, a book now published in fifteen countries. Our relationship did help the world. My husband was also a catalyst for me learning about abundance and wealth.

Secret number twelve: Keep an open mind and don't become bitter, so you can see when your dreams come true. Likely it won't happen the way you expect. How would you feel if you had a million dollars? Can you feel that way now, just as you are? I don't mean write checks and buy on credit. I'm talking about how we feel inside. Don't you know the whole world already belongs to us?

The average hourly earnings of nonsupervisory workers was $15.54 in 2004. The average wage for workers in the private sector was about $520 a week.

The number of people declaring bankruptcy has steadily increased over the past 30 years and shows no sign of slowing down. Last year 1.5 million Americans filed for bankruptcy.

Nearly 95 percent of those who declared bankruptcy did so due to a job loss, family breakup, or medical crisis, as opposed to financial irresponsibility or living beyond their means.

Public response to the hurricane devastation on the Gulf Coast in 2005 is about to become the biggest charitable outpouring in U.S. history, surpassing the relief effort that followed the September 11, 2001, attacks. Private donations totaled nearly $2.7 billion just 11 weeks after Hurricane Katrina struck. The total amount given to September 11 charities was $2.8 billion.

Funds received by the American Red Cross for relief and recovery efforts for the tsunami that hit Asia in December 2004 totaled approximately $567.3 million as of September 30, 2005.

On January 5, 1914, Henry Ford, head of the Ford Motor Company, introduced a minimum wage scale of $5 per day.

Worldwide, 1.3 billion people live on less than $1 a day; 3 billion live on under $2 a day.

2005 U.S. Poverty Guidelines
  $9,570 for one person, $11,950 in Alaska, $11,010 in Hawaii
  $12,830 for a family of two, $16,030 in Alaska, $14,760 in Hawaii
  $16,090 for a family of three, $20,110 in Alaska, $18,510 in Hawaii

The number of millionaires in the United States was up 10 percent in 2004.

The number of high-net-worth individuals (HNWI—those with at least $1 million, not including home equity) jumped from 2.27 million in 2003 to 2.7 million in 2004, surpassing the European HNWI population of 2.6 million for the first time since 2001.

Sources: White House Bureau of Labor Statistics, U.S. Courts, a Harvard study, American Red Cross, Indiana University's Center on Philanthropy, *New York Times*, "The Other Crisis" address by James Wolfensohn, Federal Register, and Capgemini 2005 World Wealth Report by Merrill Lynch

---

ACTIVITIES

1. Let go of money fear. Do you have money fear? Some people have it more than others; usually people who have been through long stretches of poverty (or whose parents have been poor) suffer from it. The fear may be realistic, but many of us have money fear even when we have enough. If you have money fear, acknowledge it for what it is. Then use the affirmation "My God shall provide all my need according to His riches in glory." Say it out loud. Or create and use another comforting affirmation—one that helps you find peace and corresponds to your spiritual beliefs. On bill day, people with money fear can take as much time having anxiety about paying bills as they take to write checks. If that's the case, try playing soothing music in the background while you're paying bills. Thank God you have the money to pay your bills instead of being upset about writing checks.

2. Get your financial situation under control. If your financial life is out of control, try working the principles of the Twelve Steps on money: admit powerlessness, believe God will help, surrender our life and will to the care of God. Take a fearless inventory of what we have and who and what we owe, then be honest with ourselves, people, and God about where we're at. Take an inventory of our financial beliefs and behaviors. Become entirely ready to live a new way. Humbly ask God to take whatever character defects, sabotaging behaviors, and beliefs have been getting in our way. Contact creditors. Make a reasonable plan for paying what we owe. Then stick to it. If the plan changes, don't hide. Let the creditors know. Continue to take inventory on a regular basis—are we spending too much or too little, living under or above our means? Are

we comfortable with whom we're giving to and how much we're giving? Are we being good to ourselves and saving for our future and emergencies? If we get off track, get back on as fast as we can. If we need to, go back to Step One. Daily and as needed, ask for guidance about what to do—to earn money, to spend, to save, and to invest after money is earned. One day we'll have an awakening: We'll be happy and know we're complete, and it won't be attached to how much money we have—although by then we might be a millionaire. There are agencies (legitimate ones that have our best interests at heart) that can help us create budgets, consolidate and prioritize debts, and contact creditors so we don't feel so overwhelmed. There are also agencies that won't be as helpful, and will charge high fees and high interest rates to help. Be careful. If it sounds too good to be true, it probably is. Debtors Anonymous (DA) is a free, nonprofit Twelve Step group for people who compulsively go into debt. Contact Debtors Anonymous General Service Office at 781-453-2743 or www.debtorsanonymous.org for help. Credit Guard of America is an independent, nonprofit credit counseling agency that provides debt counseling and financial education. Contact Credit Guard at 800-500-6489 or www.creditguard.org.

3. Is someone else's financial instability and irresponsibility affecting you? Consider getting help for yourself. Contact Co-Dependents Anonymous at www.codependents.org or Al-Anon (if drinking is involved with that person's financial instability) at 888-4AL-ANON (888-425-2666) or www.al-anon.alateen.org.

4. Write your money goals. Do a new goal sheet once a year or as needed. Put life in your goals by writing what you want to do and create, not just what you want to have.

5. Do an inventory of your beliefs about money. What do you believe you deserve to earn monthly? Annually? Do you have a ceiling on what you believe you deserve to have saved? Do you believe you can only have money if someone gives it to you (such as your husband) or if you win

the lottery? Do you believe you can't earn more than your parents earned? Do you believe you have to struggle and fight for every penny you earn? Do you believe you should be punished for something in your past by not making much money? Do you believe it's wrong to have money, or that there's a limited amount of money in the world and someone else has yours? Do you feel guilty because you have more money than friends or family? Be aware of the power of our beliefs. When we change what we believe, our world changes too. Success is an inside job.

CHAPTER 10

Dying to Change:
Facing Death

"Are you only going to include stories in the book where people do the right thing, stories with happy endings?" a friend asked.

This is a self-help book. It should have stories with positive outcomes. But we're only human. How many times have we heard that? It's an idea we know intellectually. It's an important idea to integrate because when we know it that deeply, it affects what we do. Accepting our humanity makes a difference. It's a prerequisite to forgiving others and ourselves. It helps us surrender and ask for help. Sometimes it's only after we do something wrong that we're able to do it right.

While there are behaviors that are right and wrong—behaviors that lead to desirable results and behaviors that lead to negative unwanted consequences, behaviors that are legal and behaviors that are illegal, behaviors that are morally sound and behaviors that are immoral, behaviors that are in harmony with life and behaviors that break natural law, behaviors that are sane and behaviors that are crazy—right and wrong are often judgments we make when we're trying to cram life into a tidy box.

Soon after my friend asked if it was only going to write stories with happy endings, I heard about Andrea and Jeff. In a society with labels for so many disorders—manic-depressive, chronic-depressive, ADD, ADHD, obsessive-compulsive, alcoholic, drug-dependent, codependent, borderline, and bereaved—it's important to remember that people are human and sometimes life is more than a label.

There are all kinds of losses in life. Some losses happen to us. We're walking through life, and *bam*, we get hit by a car or with an illness or with someone's death. Other losses we participate in creating. An example of that might be the disease of alcoholism. The alcohol won't jump into our mouths and force its way into our stomachs; we have to pour it in and swallow. There are other losses we participate in creating. Maybe we made a bad choice about whom to marry. Maybe we weren't paying attention and the accident was our fault. Sometimes we create losses by breaking the law.

Some stories don't have happy endings. People don't always do the right thing. This is a story about people in the *I Didn't Get It Until It Was Too Late and I Was Facing My Own Death* Club. It's about remarkable courage in the face of miserable odds.

When four-year-old Brian spiked a fever and started coughing one October night, his mother, Andrea, was concerned. She had a bowling tournament scheduled that evening. Her husband, Jeff, urged her to go. He said he'd take care of Brian. Jeff called the pediatrician. The doctor told Jeff to give Brian cough syrup and baby aspirin. Jeff did what the doctor said, but by morning, Brian was worse. The three of them had been up most of the night. Brian's cough sounded horrible, that hacking croupy sound. A neighbor volunteered to take their six-year-old daughter, Michelle, to school so Andrea and Jeff could take Brian to the emergency room. The doctors immediately admitted Brian. He had the croup, but the doctors said it wasn't that serious, and soon they'd have Brian's illness under control.

The doctors told Andrea and Jeff there was nothing for them to do there. Brian needed to be in a steam tent. He needed medication and rest. Andrea wanted to stay, but she decided the doctors were probably right. When she was there, Brian didn't want to lie in the steam tent. He wanted to cuddle in his mother's lap. Reluctantly, Andrea agreed to go home. She'd drop Jeff off at work on the way.

Walking out of the room, Andrea turned and looked at Brian. Her little boy looked scared.

Two hours later, the pediatrician called. Could Andrea and Jeff please come to the hospital immediately? Andrea asked what was wrong, but the doctor wouldn't say. Andrea raced to the hospital; Jeff took a taxi from work and met her there. When they walked into Brian's room, his crib was empty. His throat had swollen shut from the croup, the doctor explained. Then Brian had aspirated—vomited. Because his throat was closed, the fluid backed up into his tiny lungs. This caused a form of fatal pneumonia. Brian was dead.

"When Andrea was at her bowling tournament the night before, I watched a show on TV about the Great American Funeral," Jeff said. "I had no idea that within twenty-four hours I'd be planning a funeral for my son."

It was like walking through a nightmare: buying a miniature casket and a cemetery plot, writing the obituary, choosing what Brian would wear. Andrea and Jeff made decisions that no parents should have to make. Before Brian's death, Andrea had drunk alcohol occasionally, but her drinking wasn't a problem. She'd have one drink and stop. Jeff still isn't sure when Andrea crossed the line from social drinker to alcoholic. It could have been hours, months, or years after Brian's death.

"My wife got so good at being drunk that you couldn't tell when she was drunk and when she was sober," Jeff said. Alcoholics get good at hiding what they don't want you to know.

Jeff didn't yell or attempt to control Andrea's drinking. He worked, took care of their daughter, and held the family together. He didn't have his head in the sand; he wasn't in denial. He knew Andrea was drinking too much. Jeff had an instinctive knack for practicing loving detachment; he's a sane, caring, stable guy. But the day came when something had to be done. Jeff called a local treatment center, and they helped him plan an intervention. With professional help, Jeff and Michelle (by now fourteen) told Andrea how her drinking affected them. They told her how much it hurt. Andrea agreed to attend outpatient treatment, but in less than two weeks, she started drinking again.

Andrea knew other people lost children. She knew she had a daughter who needed her, and she loved her daughter. She loved her husband.

But she wanted to stay drunk. She wanted to numb the pain. She didn't have anything to give.

Many grieving people go through a cycle when they have nothing—no energy, attention, or love—to give anyone in their lives. That doesn't mean they don't love those people. It means they're depleted. There's nothing left to give. Intellectually, they know they should do different and better. But they're only human, and their humanity shows. Sometimes we need to accept and forgive others and ourselves because our best wasn't very good. Sometimes we go crazy—insane—with grief.

It was that look in Brian's eyes that haunted Andrea the most. Did Brian know he was dying? Maybe if she had stayed with him at the hospital there was something she could have done. For God's sake, a mother is supposed to protect her child. What was that crap Andrea heard about how the angels came when you died? That wasn't what she'd seen in her baby's eyes. He looked helpless, frightened, and alone.

Sometimes parents can't protect their children. After all, parents are human too.

Andrea knew life wasn't fair, but nobody told her life was going to kill her son. Where was that written—in the fine print? There weren't words to convey her rage. The only thing she could do was drink at it—drink at life. One day Andrea woke up and started drinking the same way she had each day for the past ten years. The difference was that after she drank her first drink this day, she immediately got sick and threw up. Andrea wasn't done with alcohol, but her body was. Her liver was done.

Wasn't that just like life? Now it wouldn't let her drink herself to death. Her body forced her into sobriety. She checked into inpatient treatment because she didn't have any other choice, but by the time Andrea completed treatment this time, she truly wanted to be sober. She wanted to start showing up for life instead of running away. If we wait for life to entice us into living, coax us into believing in it again, we may wait a long time. Making a commitment to life starts the ball rolling. We'll still have more grief to go through, more emotions to feel. But when we commit to life, we stop the downward spiral. Pieces start falling into place.

We've all heard stories about wives who die shortly after their husband's death, or husbands who follow their wives in death. Well, it's not uncommon for parents to die after losing a child either. When we lose someone we love, it's like we're standing in the middle of a river. On one side of the river is life. On the other side is death. We may have loved ones on each shore. Which way are we going to swim? We've got to pick, and not choosing *is* making a choice.

Andrea probably should have paid more attention to the bulge in her stomach and the yellow tinge in her eyes. By the time she went to treatment, her distended stomach signaled the beginning of liver cancer and cirrhosis. Her bones were fragile and brittle from advanced osteoporosis. She had diabetes. Her body was a mess. Andrea changed her life and got sober, but it was too late. Her death sentence was firmly in place. As sick as she was, after committing to life, Andrea lived for what Jeff describes as another ten wonderful years.

"Andrea and I traveled all over. We took cruises to Alaska, Antarctica, the Caribbean," Jeff said. "Michelle forgave her mother for not being there for her. We were a family again. Andrea was sick, but let me tell you—that woman was full of life."

We'd prefer to be in perfect health. Sometimes alternative healing brings miracles—no matter what the doctors tell us, our bodies reverse the illness. But sometimes we pass the point of no return. The illness cannot or won't reverse. It's normal when we're diagnosed with any disease to feel incomplete until we've healed, until the illness is completely gone and we're in perfect health. But some of us might find ourselves waiting the rest of our lives if we're not going to be at peace or live until our illness is gone.

Once, on a skydive, I couldn't get my body in the correct position during freefall. I kept trying to stop spinning. The harder I tried, the more I spun. My body was out of control. Finally, my instructor Andy flew over to me. He tapped my pull cord. Oh, I forgot. It was way past time to pull. If I didn't get my parachute open soon, it was going to be too late. After Andy and I got down on the ground, he walked over to me. "So what are you going to do?" he asked. "Spend the rest of your life trying to gain control?"

For some of us, if we spend all our time trying to make the illness go away, we'll waste all the moments we have left. We can find healing in the moment exactly as we are. We might not be in perfect health, but we can still be whole and complete. We can make the best of what we've got. Surrendering gets us some Grace.

When Andrea was diagnosed with liver cancer and cirrhosis, her doctors put her on the transplant list. She was sober, so she qualified. For a time, she and Jeff were hopeful. Then the doctors discovered the cancer had spread to her bones, so they took her off the list. The doctors told her to get her affairs in order.

Andrea lived life as long as she was alive. She sponsored other alcoholics. She and Jeff traveled. She lived each moment fully. Some people think making the most of every moment means spending our time smelling the roses. I think it means letting each moment be what it is.

As Andrea deteriorated, she and Jeff learned about hospice care, help that makes it possible for us to die as we want. The hospice workers asked Andrea how she wanted to die. "Pain free and at home," Andrea said.

"Thank God for hospice," Jeff said. "They did for my wife what I couldn't do."

Andrea learned to use a wheelchair, but the last few months, she spent most of her time in bed. *I should be peaceful. I should be okay with this*, Andrea thought. That's not how she felt. Tracey, one of the women Andrea sponsored in Alcoholics Anonymous, was a young woman who worked at a center for people with Huntington's disease, a terminal neurological disorder. From their conversations, Andrea knew that Tracey helped people die regularly. It was part of Tracey's job. She also knew that Tracey's daughter and father had died. Tracey wasn't afraid of death. She talked about it with ease.

"I need your help," Andrea said. "People talk about what a wonderful experience death is—angels, a tunnel with light, seeing people you love who have crossed to the other side. But I saw my son right before he died. It didn't look like anyone was waiting for him. He looked scared and alone. Tracey, I'm afraid to die."

"I can't tell you what it's like to die because I'm not dead," Tracey said. "But I've been with a lot of people when they died. From everything I've heard, dying isn't that bad. I'll be with you," Tracey promised. "Jeff and Michelle will be here too. Whatever happens, you're not going to go through this alone. There will be people—guardian angels or people you know who have died—waiting for you on the other side. Brian will be there too. They'll take you to the light."

"I didn't see any angels in Brian's room," Andrea said. "My son died alone." Even saying those words filled Andrea with guilt.

"Let's take each moment as it comes," Tracey said. "Then while it's happening, you tell me what dying is like."

"What about my cats?" Andrea said. "Who'll take care of them when I'm gone?"

Tracey and Andrea laughed. Jeff brought Andrea's two cats into the room. Andrea nuzzled her face into their warm fur. "I promise you," Jeff said. "The cats will be fine."

Tracey sat next to Andrea. "You've had quite a life. A lot of it hasn't been the life you wanted. Some of it has. But your body is worn out now. It's tired. It's okay if you go."

Andrea relaxed. Her breathing became shallower. Jeff, Tracey, and Michelle took turns sitting with Andrea. Then Tracey went home. Late that evening, Andrea pointed to the corner.

"They're here," she said.

"Who?" Jeff asked.

"The angels," Andrea said. "They want me to go with them."

The fear that had been in Andrea's eyes was gone. There was a glow on her face.

"Then go." Jeff kissed Andrea good-bye. "I love you, and I'll see you," he said.

Jeff says he's a lucky guy. "My daughter is alive. I had Brian for four years. And those last ten years with Andrea, those were the best. Maybe it's good we can't see ahead and don't know everything that's coming. We'd spend all our time being afraid. Sometimes it's easy to judge people, say they should have done different. But who's to say that any of it is a mistake?"

All we can do is make the best of what we've got. Sometimes living in the mystery and loving it means learning to say, "Who knows?"

Until 1936, pneumonia was the number-one cause of death in the United States. Because of the use of antibiotics, it and influenza are now number six or number seven.

Two million people worldwide consider themselves members of Alcoholics Anonymous.

Heavy drinking for as little as a few days can lead to fatty liver or steatosis—the earliest stage of alcoholic liver disease.

Up to two drinks per day for men and one drink per day for women and older people causes few if any problems.

One drink equals one 12-ounce bottle of beer or wine cooler, one 5-ounce glass of wine, or 1.5 ounces of 80-proof distilled spirits.

People who should not drink at all include
- women who are pregnant or trying to become pregnant
- people planning to drive or operate high-speed machinery or engage in any activity requiring alertness
- people taking certain prescribed or over-the-counter medications
- people with certain illnesses (including hepatitis)
- recovering alcoholics
- people under age 21

Sources: American Lung Association, Alcoholics Anonymous, and National Institute on Alcohol Abuse and Alcoholism

ACTIVITIES

1. Are you a bereaved parent, grandparent, or sibling? The Compassionate Friends is a worldwide nonprofit organization dedicated to supporting people who have lost a child. They also offer support for other relatives— like siblings and grandparents. You don't have to go through your grief alone. Check out their Web site at www.compassionatefriends.org or call toll-free at 877-969-0010.

2. Make peace with the imperfections of your life. We'd all like our lives to be perfect. Who wouldn't rather live without an illness or any of the limitations many of us face? While some people have fairy-tale lives, most of us don't. In any situation, at each step of our lives, we'll have limitations and strengths, things we can do and things we can't. What are the limitations or imperfections you're challenged to accept? Do you have a physical problem that's making your life less than perfect? Maybe a loved one has a problem that's creating an imperfect world. If we wait for our lives to be perfect before we decide to live them and be happy, we might spend (like my friend Andy says) the rest of our lives waiting to gain control.

The actor Christopher Reeve did more with his life in the years following the equestrian accident that left him paralyzed than most people do who are healthy. He started a foundation that helped other paralyzed people; he acted in and directed movies, including scenes teaching people about the latest technology for spinal cord injuries. He wrote books. He made the best of his family life. He didn't love his life. In his book *Still Me*, Christopher Reeve talked openly about how he hated his life, hated his limitations, and had to work daily to maintain a good attitude. We don't have to be Pollyannaish. We can accept how we feel about our limitations and our imperfections. We can hate our situation. We can get angry. Then we can make the most of what we have left. Christopher Reeve said the secret to getting through his ordeal was surrendering to each moment and thinking of other people instead of himself. What can you do with what you've got left—the time, the resources? When we stop waiting for life to be perfect, we get a life that's excellent instead. Challenge yourself to make the most of what you have. To motivate yourself, you might want to read *Still Me* by Christopher Reeve. It's hard to read that book and not feel blessed. All clubs have business to tend to; I hereby nominate Christopher Reeve as unofficial president of the Grief Club. His life shows us all how to live with whatever hand we've been dealt.

3. Are you or is someone you love facing death? Have you decided how you want to handle your death? It's helpful to put instructions in writing (a living will) so people will know exactly what we want. Make your last wishes known. Also, we should consider writing some letters, making a scrapbook, or making a videotape if we know death is near. That will give our loved ones something to cherish after we're gone.

4. If you or someone you love is dying, you don't have to go through the experience alone. Hospice care is available. You can die where and how you want and get sufficient medication for the pain. Contact the National Foundation for the Treatment of Pain at www.paincare.org or 713-862-9332; the International Association for Hospice and Palliative Care at www.hospicecare.com or 713-880-2940; or the National Hospice and Palliative Care Organization at www.nhpco.org or 703-837-1500.

5. Deal with alcoholism or drug addiction as soon as possible. Many people begin drinking to self-medicate pain, but then the "cure" becomes a disease of its own. Get help for yourself, whether you're the person who's drinking or whether you love someone who's drinking. Contact numbers and Web addresses include the following: Al-Anon

Family Group Headquarters at 888-4AL-ANON (888-425-2666) or www.al-anon.alateen.org; Alcoholics Anonymous World Services at 212-870-3400 or www.aa.org; National Council on Alcoholism and Drug Dependence, Inc., at 212-269-7797 or www.ncadd.org; National Institute on Alcohol Abuse and Alcoholism at 301-443-3860 or www.niaaa.nih.gov; Co-Dependents Anonymous at 602-277-7991 or www.coda.org; Adult Children of Alcoholics at 310-534-1815 (leave message only) or www.adultchildren.org.

CHAPTER 11

Cool Change:
When Doctors Aren't Enough

I met Bradley when I was a guest on his radio show. Understanding I was probably crossing lines, I later sent the e-mail anyway. "Have you been tested for hepatitis C?" I asked.

"No," he replied. I'm familiar with his objections: no insurance, not enough time, and I don't feel sick. Who wants to know we have a potentially fatal and incurable disease?

Most of us are sick to death of scare tactics about diseases—everything we should and shouldn't do, drink, and eat. "Everyone's so worried about Big Brother," a member of Generation Y says. (He calls it Generation Why?) "Who'd want to watch us anyway? All they'll see is people worrying about carbohydrates, cholesterol, and this month's fatal disease. Besides, we're all so busy working to raise money for $300,000 starter homes—what's to see?"

Despite his resistance, I continued sending Bradley e-mails telling him where to get tested. He continued to ignore me. Finally I broke. "Okay, you get tested and I'll pay," I said. "Then let me use the results in my writing."

Bradley agreed. He went to a doctor. In a few days we'd know.

This story is for anyone who wonders if it's okay to question the doctor. It's for people who didn't question the doctor and wish they had. It's for people in the *I've Got Hepatitis C and I Just Want It Out of Me* Club. This story is about overcoming the barriers to healing, no matter what disease we have. It began on Talk Radio KRLA 870 AM—the show that's right here, right now to help you help yourself.

I sat in the studio waiting for my cue. *By the time he's eight, he lost five siblings. At nine he's left for dead only to awaken from a coma paralyzed. Now he's here to share his path from skid-row junkie to successful talk show host.*

"This is the Bradley Quick Experience brought to you by the Cool Change Foundation and Hepatitis C Free. Joining us to kick off the Hepatitis C Awareness Campaign are HCV survivors Lloyd Wright and Melody Beattie." Then Bradley asks his trademark question. "Lloyd and Melody, do you have opinions on recovering from a hopeless state of body and mind?"

"Yes, Bradley, we do," we chime like well-behaved kids.

"Why the campaign?" Bradley asks.

I describe a conversation I had with a woman at the local chapter of the American Liver Foundation. "The people at our hepatitis C support groups complain of discrimination," she said. "People are afraid to touch them, hire them." Lloyd and Bradley recalled attending a dinner event for writers. A woman sat next to Lloyd, saw his book about hepatitis C, then quickly moved to another table.

"She thought I had hepatitis and was afraid of catching it," Lloyd said. "There's a tremendous lack of information. People need to know the truth."

"When did you decide to start the campaign?" Bradley asks.

"Ten years ago," Lloyd says and begins to tell his story.

Lloyd drives his shiny yellow tractor around a remote site in the Santa Monica Mountains. A home builder, on this September day in 1979, twenty-nine-year-old Lloyd is building an avocado farm. Suddenly the tractor's hydraulic reverser fails. In one-sixteenth of a second, the tractor lunges into reverse, tossing Lloyd onto the ground. Then the 16,000-pound machine runs over him on its way to rolling off the cliff.

Lloyd relaxes into a warm pool of his blood. While he waits for death he sees a vision—angels whispering to people telling them what to do. Meanwhile, a lone guy on horseback sees Lloyd's tractor fall off the cliff. The rider calls for help on his CB radio. A medical helicopter is dispatched. It transports Lloyd to Los Robles Hospital—the only hospital then with hyperbolic chambers, a new technology that saves crushed tissue.

"Your right leg is broken in six places," a doctor says. "You've undergone massive crush injuries. We don't know if we can save your leg. Even if we can, you'll probably die from kidney failure. Do you understand what I'm saying?"

Over the next month Lloyd undergoes nine surgeries and four blood transfusions. When Lloyd's insurance runs out, the doctors give him a choice: raise some cash and stay at Los Robles or go to the county hospital, where they'll amputate his leg. Lloyd begins selling property, gold—whatever he can for whatever he can get. He wants his leg.

To the doctors' surprise, Lloyd lives. His leg re-attaches. Also to their surprise, the blood they gave Lloyd contains a potentially lethal virus. The virus doesn't have a name yet. When it's identified years later, it won't have a cure. It is pandemic. What will become known as HCV is inflaming the livers of 170 million people around the world.

Bradley repeats his question. "So, Lloyd, when did you come up with the idea to take information to the streets and the media about HCV?"

After he gets out of the hospital, Lloyd gets a job pumping gas for five dollars an hour. By 1983, Lloyd's liver is so inflamed that doctors accuse him of being an alcoholic. Lloyd says he's not. Eventually Lloyd returns to building homes, but his energy flags. In 1991, Lloyd has surgery for malignant testicular cancer. During radiation therapy, Lloyd's liver is so inflamed that doctors again insist he's an alcoholic. Meanwhile, a virus called non-A and non-B hepatitis becomes known as hepatitis C, something junkies get from sharing needles. A test for it is developed. Lloyd tests negative. What doctors don't know is that this first test is unreliable. When the test is perfected, nobody thinks to tell Lloyd.

By then it's 1993 and Lloyd is building a home for himself, a project he normally enjoys, but he can't summon the energy to saw wood or pound a nail. Lloyd sees a gastroenterologist after a dentist gives Lloyd antibiotics that cause bleeding lesions in his colon. This doctor decides that Lloyd's liver is inflamed because he has too much iron in his blood. He prescribes phlebotomies—bloodletting to reduce iron content. The phlebotomies are performed at a local blood bank. Lloyd's blood accidentally ends up in the donated blood pile, a lucky mistake for Lloyd. By now the world knows that people don't get HCV only from infected needles and shooting drugs. They get it from doctors, dentists, hospitals, tattoos, snorting coke, and blood transfusions. Blood banks have begun screening blood for HCV. Lloyd's blood finally gets tested using a reliable test.

When Lloyd gets a letter telling him he can't donate blood because he has hepatitis C, he calls the blood bank to find out what it means. A technician says it means he'll either die from HCV or liver cancer, a complication of HCV, but no matter what course the disease takes, it'll be a slow, painful death. Lloyd see two doctors and asks what to do. One doesn't know; the other tells Lloyd to use interferon, the only treatment approved by the FDA at that time. The doctor mentions that interferon has side effects—Lloyd might feel like he has the flu—but it's worth it because it offers an 80 percent chance of a cure. Before Lloyd can start treatment, he has to get a liver biopsy, a procedure where a needle is inserted through the stomach and liver tissue is removed for examination. The biopsy hurts; sometimes the needle perforates a lung. Anesthetic and pain meds are recommended. Because Lloyd is a cash patient, he receives neither. When Lloyd screams in pain, the doctor relents and gives him one pain pill. Afterward, Lloyd drives to the pharmacy and picks up his first batch of interferon, a two-week supply for $692.

Within one week Lloyd is changed "into a monster," he says. At first I think he's exaggerating. Product information lists interferon's side effects as flulike symptoms, fatigue, digestive discomforts, mood disturbances, hair thinning, injection-site discomfort, and blood disorders. Not bad in exchange for a cure. But years later, information will reveal that all patients receiving interferon will have mild to moderate side effects including neutropenia, fatigue, myalgia, headache, fever, chills, and increased SGOT. Other frequently occurring side effects are nausea, vomiting, depression, diarrhea, alopecia, and thrombocytopenia. Interferon also causes depression, suicidal behavior, suicidal ideation, suicide attempts, and completed suicides.

When I read that, I think it means: I'll feel tired, nauseated, and may wish I was dead—not much different than I've felt other times in my life. SGOT, neutropenia, alopecia, and thrombocytopenia don't register. My mind skips the words. I don't know what they mean.

When I research the words, I learn increased SGOT means increased liver inflammation—the opposite of an HCV patient's goal. Neutropenia is a blood disease that causes painful ulcers in the mouth and persistent lung, sinus, ear, and gum infections. Alopecia is an autoimmune disorder that makes body hair fall out. Thrombocytopenia means the body is low in platelets. The body needs platelets to make blood clot. Without enough platelets, people bleed to death—usually from the stomach or brain. Suddenly interferon doesn't look so harmless.

Researching further, I learn interferon's cure rate isn't 80 percent; it's between 12 to 56 percent, depending on who's talking. Some people will have more debilitating side effects than flulike symptoms. They'll have heart attacks or heart failure, strokes, renal failure, or blindness. Other side effects are pulmonary fibrosis, serious thyroid disorder, pneumonia, respiratory failure, hypotension, fatal and nonfatal colitis, fatal and non-fatal pancreatitis, autoimmune disorders, rheumatoid arthritis, and lupus. Sometimes the HCV gets worse instead of better. Some people undergo personality changes—they get aggressive, homicidal, psychotic, or bipolar, whether they have a history of psychiatric problems or not. Recovering addicts and alcoholics may start using again during treatment. "Life-threatening" is how interferon is described. It can cause other problems, but I don't have to keep reading. I get it. Interferon is a dangerous drug.

But now they've come out with pegylated interferon, the doctor says. It's safer. Pegylated interferon is the same drug in time-released form.

There are four (going on five) FDA-approved treatments for HCV; all involve using some form of interferon. Interferon can be used by itself (Schering-Plough's brand is Intron A). Interferon can be used in combination with ribavirin (Schering-Plough calls it Rebetol). The FDA has approved pegylated interferon (Peg-Intron) used by itself or in combination with ribavirin. Ribavirin can cause hemolytic anemia, birth defects, and the death of an unborn child.

"But all drugs have side effects," the doctors say.

Pegylated or not, interferon is black-boxed by the FDA. That means it can kill or harm you. It can cause you to kill yourself or someone else.

Lloyd's doctor suggests cutting his dose in half. Lloyd does so but continues to suffer. He loses his career and his girlfriend. He destroys every relationship, including his relationship with his dog, and he still has hepatitis C. "I felt like I was dying," he says. "I was so miserable I wished I would."

Between January and August 1995, Lloyd takes two weeks of whole doses of interferon and eight weeks of half doses, but by the end of treatment, he's sicker than when he began. The doctors begin saying he'll die in three to five years. When Lloyd was crushed by the tractor, he was willing to die. Now he wants to fight for his life.

The maharaja's photographer lives in a house Lloyd built. "I know a natural doctor—John Finnegan," says the photographer. "I think he can help." Finnegan gives Lloyd a list of supplements to take. As the people in Lloyd's life leave because he's so insane, the empty space is filled with finding and taking supplements and brewing teas. Lloyd recalls something he heard or read somewhere—maybe in the Bible: No matter what disease we have, God puts something natural on the planet to cure it. Lloyd is on a mission. He wants to find those things. In 1997, after eighteen months of supplements and teas, Lloyd has another HCV test. The HCV is gone. His liver scores are normal. When Lloyd tells the doctor what cured him, the doctor says, "Yeah, and Elvis is alive with two heads."

That's when Lloyd started his HCV campaign.

Lloyd writes *Triumph Over Hepatitis C*, a book that talks about his experience with HCV and interferon. He shares the recipe of supplements he took that got him well. He puts up a Web site for advertising, makes twenty copies of the book, sells those in two days, then makes twenty copies more. When the book sells faster than he can make copies, Lloyd begins self-publishing. People beg Lloyd to sell them the same things he took, so Lloyd offers supplements for sale at www.hepatitiscfree.com. By 2006, his book sells more than 200,000 copies, and Lloyd has either talked to or exchanged e-mails with 70,000 people.

"It takes a long time to get anywhere," Bradley comments. Lloyd agrees.

"How did you get HCV?" Bradley asks me.

In the late sixties and early seventies, I'm running around Minnesota shooting cocaine, morphine—anything I can get into a needle and into my veins. In 1976 (I'm clean and sober by then) I get a blood transfusion after giving birth to my daughter. Both behaviors—shooting drugs and getting a transfusion before 1992—are high risks.

"Most likely from shooting drugs," I say.

"How did you find out you have it?" Bradley asks.

In 2002, I write two books and I've got plans. I'm going to get cosmetic surgery—hold back the effects of gravity and time. Then I'm going to travel, have fun. I go in for a pre-op physical. Five days later, I get the call. A doctor furtively asks if I'm alone, can we talk, have I ever shot drugs? Then he tells me he's got bad news. I have hepatitis C. I go through the stages—denial, rage, bargaining. I'm scared. All I can see when I read about HCV is that some people who get it die. I have visions of lying in a hospital bed half conscious, with my stomach swelled up like I'm pregnant. I decide not to use interferon. The cure looks as bad as or worse than the disease. Interferon doesn't feel right for me. I'm attracted to Lloyd's Web site. I begin to understand what some of the HCV jargon means. I learn I have a low viral load. My liver scores are in the normal range. I'm fatigued, but it could be from working so hard. Maybe from getting old? I'm feeling a pain under my right ribs where my liver is. I'm angry I have the disease. Couldn't God have spared me this one thing? I'm infuriated that I know I have it. Now no cosmetic surgery. My vacation turns into two years of talking to Lloyd, begging for reassurance that my liver won't explode and taking up to 150 supplements a day.

A doctor pushes me to use interferon even though I have a low viral load and a normal liver—conditions which should preclude him from giving me the drug. I've read about it. I know. I tell him no. Thinking I'm worried about the side effect of depression, the doctor says he'll prescribe antidepressants. I tell him I don't want to take interferon or antidepressants. Then the doctor looks closely at my history. "Why do you care if you have HCV?" he asks. "You're a skydiver." If my odds of being injured or killed from skydiving were as great as they are from interferon, I wouldn't jump out of a plane.

I refuse to have a liver biopsy after studying that procedure. I have an ultrasound instead (a noninvasive test). My liver looks normal. But I've been taking supplements since 1990. Coincidentally, many supplements I've been taking are what Lloyd took to get well. There's been some kind of cosmic guidance going on even if I didn't understand it.

When I first learn I have HCV, I feel contaminated, untouchable. I want it out of me. It takes two years before the fear goes away. I realize that having HCV—like anything that happens to me—isn't a mistake. My liver isn't going to explode. HCV becomes part of my destiny, and learning I have it isn't a bad thing. It gives me an opportunity to take care of my liver. I realize I'm not dying from HCV—I'm living with it. If I live with HCV the rest of my life, so what? I'm still me.

Bradley plays the commercial I recorded for Lloyd for the *Howard Stern Show*. "Four times more people have HCV than AIDS. Your doctor will tell you there aren't any options besides interferon. Not true." I think about people I've met. One woman is cured after three years of using interferon. She's glad she did it even though she looks like the walking dead. A man takes one shot of interferon and dies from respiratory failure, a documented side effect. His prescribing doctor still hasn't called him back after the man called to say he felt sick. His mom shows me a note he wrote before he died. "You were right, Mom. I shouldn't have used interferon." Another man does two interferon treatment courses with few side effects and is cured. One usually gentle man tries to kill his wife and children during interferon treatment. His HCV isn't cured. Even though he has been sober for years, he begins drinking again. I meet a man who used interferon, wasn't cured, and is hospitalized every six weeks to stop internal bleeding—another interferon side effect. Side effects can continue years after interferon treatment ends. Another woman uses interferon, isn't helped, and like Lloyd, looks for a natural remedy. She says she's cured and now sells the herbs she took at www.godsremedy.com. I meet some people who had HCV and recovered spontaneously when they stopped drinking and started leading healthy lives.

Lloyd says taking interferon is like playing Russian roulette.

"Are you hepatitis C free too?" Bradley asks me.

"I'm not," I say. "But I'm healthy. I have the liver of a two-year-old. Most likely, I'll live long enough to die from something else." Lloyd is in his fifties and still tests negative for the virus. "HCV isn't a death sentence," he says. Sometimes it can be reversed. Or people can live comfortably with it by good nutrition and taking the right supplements—if they catch it in time."

"Stay tuned," Bradley says. "We'll be right back with the symptoms."

Some people get the classic yellow eyes and orangey skin from hepatitis. They turn jaundice and feel nauseated right away. Sometimes it sneaks up on them. Thirty years after getting HCV, people feel fatigued. "They get out of bed long enough to walk to the couch," Lloyd says. "They think it's from getting old." Some have brain fog. Others itch, feel pain under their right rib cage, or their ankles swell. Dark urine, loss of appetite, and abdominal pain are other symptoms, says the Centers for Disease Control (CDC).

The most common symptom of HCV is no symptom at all. Three percent of the world's population has HCV. Most people who have it don't know it. That's why it's called the Silent Killer. It's silent because everyone is ignoring it, Lloyd says. It's silent because people are ashamed of having it and don't want to talk about it, I say. It's silent because you can have it for twenty or thirty years and not know you have it.

Bradley takes a call from a listener. "Can HCV be transmitted by body fluids, saliva, or sweat?" a woman timidly asks. "Can I get it from having sex?"

"After dealing with 70,000 clients and not having one of them say they gave or got it by sexual transmission, I can say no, it's not a sexually transmitted disease," Lloyd says. "I also have a study in front of me done in Italy about the risk of sexual transmission among monogamous heterosexual partners. After ten years there wasn't one occurrence of hepatitis C." Lloyd quotes another study of gay men done in San Francisco that says sexual transmission there was nil too.

The CDC doesn't rate monogamous sex with someone with HCV as a high or even intermediate risk and doesn't recommend that those people get tested. HCV isn't spread by hugging, kissing, exposure to body fluids, coughing, sneezing, or sharing drinking glasses or eating utensils. It's blood-to-blood transmitted. Blood from an infected person has to get in another person's bloodstream. If they're monogamous, people with HCV don't need to use condoms, but they need to bandage bleeding cuts. It's the responsible thing to do. People with HCV shouldn't share toothbrushes, razors, tweezers, or fingernail clippers—anything that might have dried blood on it. People shooting drugs shouldn't share needles. You can get HCV again after the virus is cured. Some people—up to 30 percent—don't know how they got the virus.

In the studio, I look across the desk at Bradley. *Has he been tested?* I wonder.

"What's up with interferon?" Bradley asks. "Is it a scam or the best they can do?"

If there's a potentially fatal disease with no cure, and a drug company develops something even partially effective—it doesn't have to be safe—the FDA approves it. That's how the system works. "Some people are frightened by their doctors into using interferon," Lloyd says. "They think they'll die if they don't. Some of it's about money. Interferon was first used on throat cancer. It didn't work, so they started using it on HCV." Interferon is a drug looking for a disease to cure, and HCV isn't it, one doctor told Lloyd.

On June 27, 2004, the *New York Times* published an article, "As Doctor Writes Prescription, Drug Company Writes a Check," by Gardiner Harris. The drug company writing the checks was Schering-Plough; the main medication it was paying doctors to prescribe was medicine for HCV. Schering-Plough claims such practices have stopped. The article called the clinical studies done on drugs—the ones people rely on for data about safety, efficacy, and side effects—thinly disguised marketing efforts.

Lloyd says he runs into three basic responses to HCV: interested, disinterested, and people who won't do anything unless their doctors tell them to. If he was in the latter group, Lloyd says he'd be dead. Many people think doctors are God.

I receive an urgent e-mail from my sister Jeanne. "You know how I've been going to the doctor for months and he thought it was sinus then he thought it was asthma? Well now he found nodules on my thyroid and wants to do a biopsy," she says. I'm still not sure where she's going. "What I'm wondering is this," she finally asks, "do you think doctors can be wrong?" My sister is thirteen years older than me. She's a licensed practical nurse. Sometimes we talk about acupuncture and supplements, but she's Western-medicine oriented. She knows doctors make mistakes; they've made them on her. One doctor wouldn't listen to her after surgery when she said she had an infection in her body at the surgical site. By the time he listened, she was so sick she had to be hospitalized for months and given IV antibiotics. Part of her still thinks doctors are God.

She watched what I went through the past years. Four days after I surrendered to having hepatitis C, I began having symptoms of a urinary tract infection. I took many courses of antibiotics. Didn't help. I still had to pee every two to five minutes. It was driving me insane. My lower back hurt, but it had for most of my life. My doctor sent me to a urologist. My daughter, Nichole, went with me. We were in the waiting room looking at brochures. "Is Nature's Call Overwhelming You?" We were giggling, but it wasn't funny. The doctors suspected interstitial cystitis, an incurable disease that destroys quality of life. I didn't feel like I had that. I know my body by now. I have researched everything that might occur at the doctor's office today. The test I'm dreading and am certain the doctor will suggest is a cystoscopy: a camera is inserted through the urethra (a slim canal) into the bladder so the doctor can look around. I don't like painful, invasive tests. Everything I've read about this test says it hurts and shouldn't be done without anesthetic. The doctor tells me to put on a gown and go into an exam room. "I'm going to do a cystoscopy," he says.

"Will you hurt me?" I ask, already knowing the answer.

"Not any more than I have to," he says.

I ask him if he'll use anesthetic. He says no.

The incident with the urologist coincidentally happened during a time when I'm working on healing old trauma. One similar trauma happened when I was sixteen. "You're pregnant," Mom said to me one day. It was 1964 and abortions were illegal. Two weeks later, she takes me to a doctor in Mexico. His fingernails are grimy. I look at her, begging her with my eyes not to do this. "Never mind," Mom told him. Days later I'm lying on a table in a doctor's office in Beverly Hills. The doctor gives me a shot. It relaxes me, but I'm still tense. He says he's going to put a needle through my stomach into my uterus. He tells my mom I'll start bleeding soon. When I do, she should take me to a hospital and say that I'm miscarrying. They'll call him; he'll do a procedure and the pregnancy will be done. I watch the needle pierce my stomach. My mother doesn't look at me. Nobody holds my hand, says it's okay. Nobody has ever said it will be okay or asked if I was scared. Trauma is the flight-or-freeze response. When I get traumatized, I freeze—I don't speak up for myself.

Now at the urologist's office, I start shaking. The doctor leaves. A nurse enters. My daughter thinks I should do whatever the doctor says. "You don't have to consent to a test you don't want," the nurse says.

I'm crying. "I don't want the test," I say.

My daughter is angry at me. The nurse pats my hand. "I'll tell him you said no," she says.

The doctor returns. "I'd really like to do the procedure," he says.

"I bet you would," I say. Then I stop the sarcasm. He doesn't mean to hurt me. He's just doing what he does. It's my responsibility to make decisions about my health.

As it turns out, my problems aren't even connected to my urinary tract. Two discs in my back have been degenerating for years. Now they're bone on bone, pinching the nerves to the bladder. The bladder is fine. This after sixteen wrong prescriptions, visits to five doctors, and thousands of dollars in tests. The doctors didn't discover it! One morning I remember what a doctor said years ago about the discs in my lower back degenerating, and I'd be in pain or on pain medication for the rest of my life. I had said neither option was acceptable. That's when I found alternative medicine. I'd held the problem at bay so long I'd forgotten about it. Now I research degenerating discs. They can cause the symptoms I'm having—what the doctors think is interstitial cystitis. I go to another doctor—not the urologist—and ask for X-rays of my back. "I think that's what's causing the problem," I said. He shows me the X-rays. Yes, that's it! But it was my intuition that took us to my spine. I'm not sure if or when the doctors would have gotten us there. Do doctors make mistakes?

"Jeanne," I said. "You just watched me go through a horrible course of misdiagnosis, so sick from the wrong medications I was stopping the car by the side of the road and puking. I read in the New York Times this morning that doctors seriously misdiagnose fatal illnesses 20 percent of the time. It said millions of people are treated for the wrong disease, and doctors' rate of accuracy hasn't changed since 1930."

"I guess I needed to hear you say it," she said.

Doctors. God bless them. They can save our lives. But yes, sometimes they can be wrong.

"So what can people with HCV do besides use interferon?" Bradley asks.

Four or five quality products usually do the trick, Lloyd says. Milk thistle, dandelion root, lipoic acid, selenium, and live-cell thymus helped him. Other products are available for energy. People can spend one hundred a month or ten times that much. They can buy from a health food store, but quality is essential. If people do the basics, they can get off the couch, get off disability insurance, and go back to work. "Don't forget the teas," I say. The body absorbs milk thistle and dandelion root teas more readily than pills. The people who drink the teas are the ones Lloyd sees get better.

Some people who use interferon use alternative medicine too. Even conventional doctors agree that milk thistle helps. A report by the Mayo Clinic states that while most studies are small and poorly designed, there is still good scientific evidence that milk thistle causes improvements in liver tests of people with HCV, and increased liver function and decreased number of deaths in people with cirrhosis (scarring of the liver associated with liver disease). There's no magic bullet in conventional or complementary medicine for HCV. It's a combination of things that work. Some people diagnosed with HCV think, *No big deal, I'll just get a liver transplant.* Liver transplants aren't fun, Lloyd says. The virus immediately attacks the transplanted liver. It's better to keep your own liver—if you can.

Seventy percent of the people with HCV are going to die of old age or something else, Lloyd says. "People don't have to use interferon or die. They have choices. They need to know what those choices are. Most people accept what doctors say as truth. Or they stop reading the medication inserts because the print is so small." Lloyd doesn't just sell supplements; he gives hope. He listens to people, calms them. What he says isn't always good news. Some people are almost dead by the time they find him. He doesn't say there's no hope, but he discourages buying if he thinks the products won't help.

"I can't begin to tell you how much your kindness and compassion mean," Debra C., one of Lloyd's first clients wrote. Debra's frantic search for help for her husband led her to Lloyd the last week of her husband's life. This was a case of too little too late. She slept on a cot by her husband's side at the hospital the last month of his life. He went into his first coma on Good Friday. When he regained consciousness Easter Sunday, Jamie, their twenty-one-year-old daughter, asked her dad what he saw when he was gone.

"Jamie, I know this might sound crazy, but it's true what they say," her dad said. "In a flash, I found myself in the most beautiful world you could ever imagine. I was dancing and playing and singing. I have never felt so free and happy in all my life. The white light was there, but it was unlike any white light you could ever imagine in this physical world."

"This was the gift he gave us," Debra said. "He let us know that his passing didn't mean he was fading off into oblivion or some deep, dark hole. It was the absolute knowing that he has passed on to some wonderful, magical world that comforts us during our terrible times of missing him. No amount of money could put a price on this gift."

We're heading into the final segment of the Cool Change show. "Tell us," Bradley says to Lloyd. "How did you get the spiritual insight to develop this program?"

Lloyd tells the story of being out of hope after Western medicine failed and how the maharaja's photographer kept pushing him to see Dr. Finnegan. "I kept resisting. He kept insisting. Finally I gave in," Lloyd said. The spiritual insight Lloyd talks about is the guidance many of us get. We don't know what to do, then someone makes a suggestion. At first we say no thanks. But that person pesters until we give in. Spiritual guidance is often ordinary, not at all like we associate with getting a message from God. Guidance can come from someone we know or somebody we just met. Frequently we resist. Or we may get a gut feeling to do something. We can't explain it logically, but taking a certain action feels right. Other times, we find ourselves naturally doing the next thing. Guidance often happens when we surrender to this desperate place of no hope.

Lloyd doesn't talk about miracles with white light, but he saw a vision when he was lying in that remote field of the Santa Monica Mountains bleeding to death. It looked like angels whispering in people's ears. Who knows? Maybe what we call intuition and guidance is when the angels whisper to us. Lloyd doesn't wear his spiritual beliefs on his sleeve, but I know he believes in God and the power of prayer. I do too.

I'm eight years old. My glasses are thick and getting thicker. I hate them. The doctor says my eyesight is worsening and I'll likely go blind. One day I watch a church show on TV. A minister says, "If you need healing, join me now in prayer." I ask God to please heal my eyes. Soon my vision tests almost twenty-twenty. I don't wear glasses again until I'm in my forties and need them for reading the way many people that age do.

Now in my fifties, I spend two years staring at my liver results, frantic about HCV. Then overnight I go from making peace with HCV to discovering I need surgery on my back unless I want to be in a wheelchair. I make plans to go to Germany for surgery. My friend Heather wants me to see a healer she met—a man named Howard Wills. He lives on the East Coast but sometimes passes through town. I resist. It's not that I don't believe in healing and prayer. But sometimes I get tired of the latest hot healer or new alternative medicine craze. Or I become closed. Before I go to Germany, Heather gives me a gift certificate to see Howard. I go. He prays and talks about forgiveness. He doesn't say, "Your liver needs healing." He asks, "Are you ready to forgive everyone who has ever hurt you? Are you ready to be forgiven by everyone you've hurt? Are you ready to be forgiven by God? Are you ready to forgive yourself?"

What does forgiveness have to do with getting well? Howard says we get so much negativity piled up around us that we start getting sick and can't get well. "We need to humbly go to God and ask for help," Howard says. Even recovery programs say cleaning our slate is crucial to getting well. I answer yes to Howard's questions about forgiveness. Howard prays. It's a pleasant healing session, but I still have hepatitis C, and I still need to go to Germany for surgery. The surgery is traumatic, invasive, painful, but successful.

Then I return to the United States, spike a fever, come down with double pneumonia. Heavy doses of antibiotics don't help. It's two months after surgery, and I'm getting sicker every day. I see fear in my doctors' eyes. My friends and family are frightened. I'm too sick to be scared. Then Howard's assistant calls. Howard is passing through town and his assistant has a feeling I need a healing. "I can't," I say. "I'm too sick to get up and answer the door."

"That's why we need to see you," she says.

Soon Howard and his assistant are sitting in my bedroom. We talk about forgiveness again. Then Howard asks if I'm ready to be healthy. Yes!

We pray together. That's the moment I start to get well. Prayer works.

On the radio show, I interrupt Lloyd. "I want to say something to anyone who's sick, but especially to people who got HCV from using drugs. It's easy to think we deserve to be sick because we did it to ourselves. That's how I felt. It's easy to believe any illness or loss is punishment, but that's not true. We deserve to be as healthy as we can be."

Complementary medicine? Conventional medicine? A combination? We can choose what's right for us. It's tempting to sit back and wait for a cure to come from a doctor, a pill, a healer—something outside of ourselves. We may need what a doctor or healer offers, but healing begins within us. Are we ready to get well? Prayer can be the best medicine there is—the magic bullet that makes any therapy work. No matter what we're going through, ask for God's help. That's when the really cool changes occur.

It's been a year since Howard stopped by the house. The back surgery is a success. I've still got HCV. I'm not happy I have it, but I'm not sick. I drink my teas and take some supplements. I listen to my intuition about what to do. "Stop staring at your liver," the lab tech reminds me when I go in for blood work. "Go live your life."

There's a promising new treatment on the horizon for HCV. Protease inhibitors are being fast-tracked by the FDA. If approved, they'll be ready for marketing in 2007. (Fast-tracking means the testing period is shortened.) Schering-Plough is talking about using the new treatment with interferon and by itself. When I first heard about protease inhibitors, I wanted to fly to Europe, where the drugs are being used, and immediately take the cure. Then I took a deep breath. Maybe I should wait. Dr. Tennant agreed. "Wait and see how it works and what side effects people get," he said.

Don't forget to read the fine print, no matter how small, because the words that are the hardest to read might contain the information that saves your life.

Lloyd hopes they find a cure for HCV even if it means he'll be out of work. He knows God will show him what to do next. Until then, he'll keep telling people what they can do to love their livers and love themselves.

Bradley? He tested positive for HCV. "How you knew I had hepatitis C I'll never know, but I'm sure glad you suggested I get tested," he said. "I was clean and sober eighteen years at the time. I hadn't used drugs, alcohol, or needles since 1987. As far as I was concerned, I wasn't even a candidate for HCV. Getting tested changed my life."

Like Bradley says on his radio show, "The life you save may be your own."

Hepatitis C is one of five identified hepatitis viruses—A, B, C, D, and E.

Hepatitis A, B, D, and E are different from C.

Hepatitis A and B are highly contagious. A is spread primarily from fecal matter. It's usually contracted from contaminated drinking water, food, or direct contact with an infected person. Most people recover in about a month. Hepatitis B is highly contagious and is spread by contact with body fluids. B can become chronic. Most people who get B will recover within six months and can never get it again. Once they recover, people with B aren't contagious, although their blood will always show they had it. They cannot donate blood. Other people with B become silent carriers. They don't get sick, don't know they have the virus, and unknowingly transmit it to others.

Hepatitis D usually occurs with B.

There are blood tests to diagnose all hepatitis viruses and vaccines for A, B, and D.

Hepatitis E rarely occurs in the United States and is spread by contaminated water and food.

In one survey reported by the National Institutes of Health, 39 percent of the people surveyed with HCV said they're turning to alternative medicine for treatment by itself or in combination with conventional medicine.

According to a Vancouver survey of people attending an outpatient clinic, 60 percent of HCV clients said they use complementary medicine for HCV.

The majority of people with HCV will not die from the virus, but with the virus.

Chronic HCV can cause liver disease, cirrhosis (scarring of the liver), liver cancer, and liver failure. Serious illness or death from HCV is not inevitable, especially if people take care of themselves and get the health care they need.

Drinking alcohol is the worst thing to do for the liver or HCV, according to all private, public, governmental, conventional, and complementary sources for liver health and HCV.

HCV is the most common reason for liver transplants in the United States.

There are now more than 20,000 people waiting for a liver in the United States. Only 4,900 livers become available each year.

The HCV virus can live at room temperature (in dried blood) on environmental surfaces at least 16 hours, but no longer than 4 days. Blood spills can be cleaned with household bleach diluted with water at a 1:10 bleach-to-water ratio. Wear gloves.

One in fifty Americans test positive for HCV.

Eighty-seven percent of Americans believe in heaven and 84 percent say they believe in miracles.

Sources: National Institutes of Health, Hepatitis C Caring Ambassadors Program, American Liver Foundation, and Fox News Poll

———

ACTIVITIES

1. Are you at risk for HCV? Did you have a blood transfusion before 1992, shoot drugs (even once), or share a cocaine-snorting device (even once)? Did you have an organ transplant prior to 1992 or receive hemodialysis? Did you ever use the razor, toothbrush, or nail clipper of someone who has HCV (or might have HCV but doesn't know it)? Are you a health care worker exposed to needle sticks? Did you have an invasive procedure or one involving blood products done in a hospital prior to 1992? Did your mother have HCV when you were born? Was your mother at risk for HCV when you were born but hasn't been tested? Remember, most people with HCV don't know they have it. If you might be at risk, get tested. The sooner you know, the sooner you can take care of your liver so you can die from old age instead of HCV. The only way to determine the presence of HCV is a blood test done by a doctor's prescription. Contact the American Liver Foundation at 800-465-4837 or www.liverfoundation.org for information about where to get tested (if you don't have a doctor) or for information about local HCV support groups.

2. Take the next steps if you're HCV positive. Get a liver panel (AST and ALT) done to determine how well your liver is functioning, and get tested for amount of viral load. These blood tests are different than the blood test that determines if we have HCV. Many doctors recommend liver biopsies. A liver biopsy is an invasive procedure with possible side effects. The federal government is currently funding research to develop cost-effective, noninvasive alternatives to liver biopsies. Do your homework. Research the treatments. Read the fine print. Talk to people. HCV progresses slowly. If you have HCV, the sooner you discover it, the

more time is on your side. Unless you've waited until you're very sick, you can take the time you need to find the treatment that's right for you. Remember, our doctor doesn't have to live with the medicines we take and the procedures we undergo; we do.

3. What's your opinion about medicine, treatment, and healing? Allopathic or conventional medicine sees the body as a machine. It's either sick or well. If it's sick, you give it pills, give it treatments, or operate on it. Or you take pills so the symptoms don't bother you as much. Alternative medicine wears a different pair of glasses. It sees the body as a somewhat mystical apparatus that's connected to thought, emotions, and beliefs and sees it as either in balance (well) or out of balance (sick). Complementary medicine seeks to assist the body in regaining balance. Are there emotions that need to be released? Is the body deficient in a particular substance? Does it have too much of something or is it being exposed to a toxicity it doesn't like, such as aluminum, smoke, or emotions?

My opinion is that the best approach to health is a sane combination of conventional and complementary medicine. Complementary medicine includes chiropractic care, acupuncture, herbs, nutritional supplements, Chinese and Eastern medicine, hands-on healing, Reiki, homeopathic remedies, ozone therapy, massage, prayer, and more. Even conventional medical institutions like the National Institutes of Health recognize complementary medicine as valid and important forms of health care. We each have our own take on the body, illness, what constitutes health, and how to maintain it. What's right for another person may not be right for us.

4. Learn to speak up to your doctor. Ask questions. Do your homework. Get a second or third opinion, especially when you're dealing with invasive procedures, powerful medications, and serious or life-threatening illnesses. If you have a difficult time talking to your doctor, write your questions on a piece of paper, then bring your list with you. Don't leave until the questions are answered to your satisfaction. Or bring a friend or

relative to your appointment who will help you talk and give you the support you need. Make sure you understand what your doctor is telling you. Take notes on what the doctor says. If your doctor can't explain to your satisfaction, find someone who will help you understand—an advocate. Research any procedures, surgeries, or medications before you submit to the procedure or take the medicine. Find out if the procedure will hurt. If it will, you have a right to pain medication or anesthetic if you want it. Many doctors prefer not to give anesthetics or pain medications because of the time and liability involved, even though the procedure hurts. Remember, it's your body, and you have a right to refuse medications, refuse treatment, and get the care and pain meds you legitimately need. Report any side effects from medications—alternative or conventional—immediately. Remember that there are side effects from complementary (holistic) medicines and procedures too. Complementary medication can interact with conventional medicines. Check out what you're putting into your body. Watch for interactions between drugs. Take an active and informed role in your health care.

5. Add the power of humble, sincere prayer to whatever medical treatments you use. It's easy to forget to pray. Many people make sure to bless food before eating. People are beginning to recognize the importance of blessing any medications or treatments they use too. One alternative medicine professional told me she worked with people using interferon. She prayed and asked God to bless them and protect them from any side effects of the interferon, and it appeared to help. We don't need to save prayer for medical problems. Ask God or the Higher Power of our understanding to help with any problem. Write a letter to God. Specifically ask for the help we need. Then put the letter someplace private. Prayer is one of the most effective medicines we can use.

6. Wait for guidance. Learn to trust your intuition about what's right for you. When we get a problem, our first response is often to tell ourselves it's a mistake and frantically try to make it disappear. The worse the problem, the harder we try to make it go away. Before we know

what's happened, the problem has sucked us in and we're obsessively trying to control it, fixated on it instead of fixing it. It's like the Chinese finger cuff thing—the harder we try, the more entangled we become. One of the hardest things to do is step back and wait for guidance. It's hard not to know what to do next. It's hard to have an illness and no cure. It's hard to trust what we don't know yet. Sometimes immediate action is called for, but other times backing off and waiting are the most powerful actions we can take. Living in the mystery and trusting it means being comfortable saying, "I don't know what to do next." The more relaxed we are, the easier it will be to hear the answer when it comes. Trusting ourselves means we trust our sense of what feels right for us instead of obsessively trying to do anything and everything— sometimes all at once. Some people live only by intellect—by rational decisions. Some live by intuition. The best response is a balanced combination of both. If we're not sure what our body needs, ask it. Then listen for the answer. Watch for the guidance that comes.

7. Do you believe you deserve to have an illness or the loss or problem you're going through? Go over your Master List of Losses. Are there any losses on that list you believe you deserve or that you believe are punishment for something you've done wrong? If we're in prison, our loss of freedom is a consequence or punishment (unless we're truly innocent). Sometimes loss is a consequence of something we've done. Are you willing to forgive yourself? If you're sick, are you ready to get well? Sometimes when we've been sick for a long time, we begin to identify with our illness, calling it "my HCV" or "my cancer." Some alternative health care professionals say it's very important to stop claiming the illness as ours and begin to claim our health. In the book *The Worst Is Over* by Judith Acosta and Judith Simon Prager, the authors talk about the power of words and how our bodies respond instantly to them. Tell your body that it's healing, that it's okay to heal. My acupuncturist, Hank Golden, recommends talking to our bodies, telling our bodies that it's okay to stop hurting and time to get well.

8. What do you believe about life after death, or life after life? Someday we will all die. Many people feel that knowing what they believe about life after death helps them to deal with the loss of loved ones and face their own death. If you're unsure what you believe, begin a search for Truth.

CHAPTER 12

Facing Change:
Losing a Parent to Alcoholism

A friend and I were talking about why so many powerful, beautiful, talented, successful women are in relationships with guys who don't bring much (at least that we can see) to the table.

"What's that about?" my friend asked. She wasn't looking for an answer. We weren't being judgmental, gossipy, or mean. The women we were talking about aren't complaining or being victims about their relationships. They aren't behaving in codependent ways. But it looked like many of our friends are going through a phase of being with men who aren't their equals. Some are hanging on for dear life. It's confusing. We genuinely didn't understand, but then it's so easy to see the imperfections in someone else.

A lot of people throw around the phrase *everything happens for a reason.* They say it when they can't think of anything better to say and they want to help a person in pain. But often it's not a comforting thing; it has the opposite effect. We infer that God has this plan for us, and this unpleasant thing that happened is an integral part of that plan, so we should buck up and like this thing that happened. That may be true. But it's still not comforting. It's only a comforting concept when we discover it for ourselves, when after months or years of frustration we see we've been learning something important and valuable, that these painful events have been preparing us for something grand. We've been in specialized training, but we didn't understand until now. Then the *every-thing happens for a reason* concept uplifts us. We're able to connect the dots and draw a picture. It makes us feel good inside. We trust life again.

There are other ways to interpret *everything happens for a reason*. There is a natural cause and effect, a reason for everything that happens, including the decisions we make. If we saw or understood the motivating force, then the confusing thing we're looking at would make sense. We'd understand why beautiful, successful, talented women link themselves to men who aren't their equals or the other way around.

There is a valid reason women do that. In her book, *Trauma and Recovery: The Aftermath of Violence—from Domestic Abuse to Political Terror*, Judith Herman spells out that reason. "The pathological environment of childhood abuse forces the development of extraordinary capacities, both creative and destructive," she writes. The abuse suffered doesn't have to be extreme—such as being forced to eat dog food or being beaten. Trauma does strange things to people, and many life events are traumatic—divorce, death, neglect, having alcoholic parents, accidents, killing people when we're soldiers at war. Trauma may be involved with any sudden disruption of life as we know it. The woman or man who is abused and traumatized may be forced to trust, love, and live with people who have sick behaviors, forced to do things that go against the grain. A soldier is trained to kill enemies whom, in a moment of insight, he sees not as enemies but as brothers—his fellow men. People who live with craziness or abuse learn to normalize abnormalities for survival's sake. We have an incredible talent for making horrible things okay. We often become highly skilled at psychically tuning into the needs and moods of the people around us. To stay safe, we become mind readers, and we do it well. To stay alive, we become experts at managing and caring for other people, but this training doesn't include how to take care of ourselves.

If we do see what we need, we don't bring it up. "I'd rather die, take pills—do anything—than say what I need and want," one talented, successful woman says. When we should have been playing with dolls or trains, we were running households, fending off blows, parenting Mom or Dad, going to school, and often earning money too. Meanwhile, we hid our feelings, needs, and reality from ourselves and the world.

A bitter, unhappy childhood is one effect of trauma and abuse. But another probable effect of a stressful childhood, reports Anahad O'Connor in a *New York Times* article entitled "Sick of Work," is the ability not only to endure but to thrive in stressful work environments as adults. We're able to function in situations where others, such as people who had protected and happy childhoods, can't. Trauma and traumatic childhoods can be training—boot camp—for entrepreneurs. There's an upside to the pain we endure. Becoming highly successful is a positive side effect for many people abused as children, including children of alcoholics. Many abused or traumatized people become superachievers as adults. Some people call them overachievers, but that's demeaning. Many abused children and children of alcoholics have created superb careers that have contributed much to the world. So if these recovering codependent women (or men) trudging the road of *progress not perfection* have a difficult time sorting out whom to trust as adults because they had to trust untrustworthy people when they were children, if they're so used to wearing blinders that they have a hard time taking them off now, if they're torn between pushing people away because intimacy is threatening and keeping jerks close to them because they're terrified of abandonment and being alone, maybe it's wise and compassionate to allow them these imperfections while they're out there superachieving and truly making a difference in our world.

Giving people slack is a kind thing to do for them and ourselves.

In the 1980s, we saw an uprising of abuse victims who were willing to name their pain and do the work to move on. These people included adult children of alcoholics and those who suffered from emotional abuse, neglect, and sexual abuse. We identified abuse in all its forms. Abuse has been going on for God knows how long, but we started pointing at it and figuring out ways to heal from the ways the abuse affects and impacts our lives now. We saw the birth of Co-Dependents Anonymous groups. People were ripe to deal with codependent behaviors. We identified survival behaviors such as caretaking, controlling, manipulation, excessive neediness, difficulty setting boundaries, inability to identify our needs, and low self-esteem—the behaviors people formed in response to childhood or adult dysfunction. Although some people went to extremes and some went on witch hunts in the beginning, this was and still is a positive movement overall. But a shortcoming is the tendency of traumatized people to hang on to their victimization long after the abuse stops.

Even if they don't use the words *I'm a victim*, their personas reek of victimhood from the tone of their voices to their frequent sighs. This is some of what's diminished the movement's reputation. It is understandably difficult to surpass the belief that we're victims. Many of us were legitimate victims, sometimes for years. We were children, and we couldn't defend ourselves. But long after the abuse or trauma stops, many of us are still pointing at the parents or perpetrators, itemizing the injustices, pains, and wrongdoings we endured. Not only are we still whining about it, it's our excuse for not being happy and living a fulfilling life now. We miss the slight adjustment of focus that allows us to see and appreciate what we did get, the perfection of the universe to supply the missing pieces, and in many circumstances see the perfection of each incident, including the painful events. It's as harmful to deny the good things and the ways we were taken care of as it is to deny the trauma and the feelings generated by abuse.

It's a sign of healing when we admit that even though our loss is severe, we're protected and guided now. We didn't get what we wanted, but somehow we got what we needed—eventually. Even when we're so furious with God we can't pray, God is still on speaking terms with us and leading the way.

I had a sponsor in Al-Anon who began lecturing me about making sure I felt bad enough about all the wrongdoings I'd endured from others. She insisted I place more focus on the injustices I'd encountered since birth (and maybe conception). She firmly stated that I needed to feel outrage and indignation about these traumatic events. I said I'd try to feel as bad as I could. I sat down to meditate on my life, my childhood, and the painful things that happened. I sat cross-legged, eyes closed, with a CD of Tibetan monks chanting in the background. It was a rare and delightful meditation when my body was still and my mind stopped chattering. It was my intention to focus on these injustices and my outrage as my sponsor urged.

Instead a light filled me, then surrounded the area where I sat. I became flooded with a feeling that started as peace, then turned to gratitude, then blossomed into joy. I saw the absolute perfection of even the most insignificant incident. All the events in my life had chiseled and shaped me with the artful precision of a master sculptor working on a chunk of clay—even the events that hurt. The times when I hadn't had my needs met by someone or in a way I expected, my needs were met by someone else. Throughout my entire journey, God nurtured and sustained me and held my hand. I'd been guided the entire way even when I felt alone. I intended to feel angry, but I didn't. I felt a joyous bond with all the people I encountered and the Sculptor who so brilliantly shaped me. I felt awe instead. *Wow,* I thought. *Everything really is perfect, even the imperfections. Every single thing does happen for a reason. We can trust the slightest blowing of the winds. It is all part of a plan.*

Later I called my sponsor and told her what happened. She said obviously I hadn't done my meditation correctly or I'd be outraged at all the monsters I'd met. I said she was probably right, but since then, I haven't asked for her advice.

I've met many people who belong to the *I'm an Adult Child of an Alcoholic and I've Been Abused* Club. I've met many who belong to the *I'm a Codependent (No More)* Club. Of all the abuse stories I've heard, of all the stories of successful women (and yes, we still may have imperfections) who have not just made lemonade from lemons, but made lemon bars and lemon meringue pie too, this is my all-time favorite one.

Kate Somerville is an inspiration, a shining example of what it means to recover. She's another person who asked me to *please* use her real name, even though she's visible. "I really am proud of what I've walked through and my success," she said. "I hope my story helps someone who has it hard to not give up and to believe that happiness and success is as possible for them as it is for me."

The phone rings. Kate's receptionist covers the receiver. "It's *People*," she says. "They want to know what time we'll be ready for the photographers tomorrow. Kate checks her calendar. Her facial products and anti-aging techniques have been written up in *Us*, *Spa*, *Allure*, *In Touch*, *InStyle*, and *WOW* and featured on *E!*, *Extra*, *Access*, and *Fox News*.

She walks over and introduces herself to me. She's medium height and thin with a long mane of curly dark locks. She's pretty and naturally sweet. There's something about her—such innocence and light—I immediately feel it. It pulls me in. Kate agreed to tell me her story. We decided she'd talk while she gives me one of her famous facials. Her business, Kate Somerville Skin Health Experts, is based in a bungalow on Melrose Place in Los Angeles. I'm going to have her noninvasive procedure Titan, a dream come true. Titan is a nonsurgical way to shrink-wrap the skin on knees, the stomach, the face (which is what I've been saying I needed for years). From Titan to Quench to eyelash extensions, Kate's products have been flooded with publicity. She's been called the secret weapon behind some of Hollywood's most gorgeous complexions: Paris Hilton, Sharon Stone, Annette Bening. She barely has time for herself.

Good problem for a businesswoman to have.

"It's my angels," Kate says. "They bring me luck. They take care of me, guide each step I take. They bring the things and people I need. They've been protecting me all my life."

We start walking to one of the private skin-care rooms when the phone rings again. I already know enough of Kate's story to know that each time the phone rings, Kate prays it's not another call about her mom. While Kate is enjoying her success, her mother is wandering around Hollywood, a homeless, hopeless drunk. That's the story I'm here to listen to today—Kate's story of living with the ongoing loss of being first the child and now the adult child of an alcoholic, especially when there's been abuse.

I change clothes and lie down. Kate enters and begins working on my face. Her humility and modesty is admirable. She's married, has a little boy she loves and adores. "My success just happened," she explains. "People really like my techniques and products. They wanted to finance me and my business, so a partner and I opened this store. Business boomed from the start. Now this," she says referring to the Melrose place.

"At least for today my mom isn't homeless," Kate says. "She's in a motel. Her leg is broken. The doctors put on a cast. She's drunk. I got a call earlier about her hacking off the cast, the bone sticking out or something. I can only do so much. She won't let anyone help. I can't commit her to an institution," Kate says. "They declared her competent. She's not violating any laws. It's hard watching my life go so well while she's on the phone drunk, crying, and sick. I don't know what to do. I never have." Ever since Kate was a child, this has been her routine: Kate wakes up in the morning, cries about her mom, then gets on with her day.

Some losses have a beginning and an end. The loss occurs; it's done. We grieve, then move on. Other losses don't have an end in sight. We need to figure out how to move on with our lives while living with an ongoing and sometimes worsening loss. The way we deal with that is called *letting go* or *detachment*. Letting go doesn't mean we don't have feelings about the loss. It means we surrender to the situation and accept the feelings we have. We do what we can, what's in our power to do, what's our responsibility to do for the other person, but we also take care of ourselves. We get on with our lives even though the loss is currently taking place. Some losses are unsolvable problems that cause sadness for years. If we wait for the problem to be solved before we go on with our lives, our entire life might slip away.

Kate's mom and dad met in college. Her mom, Sigrid, was a cheerleader, her dad a football hero. "They were absolutely gorgeous, beautiful people who loved to party," Kate says. "They became teachers. They still loved to party, but the partying turned on them. They became addicts, alcoholics." Then they had Kate—their only child together. Kate said her mom hoped that by having a child, she would finally get the love she'd never had. Sigrid's mom was found outside naked, wrapped in a blanket, and frozen to death, when Sigrid was twenty years old. Sigrid never got the love she needed until Kate came along. Then Kate was the one who gave love to her mother instead of being loved the way a child should be.

"Mom let me do anything I wanted," Kate said. "I could drink or use drugs at home. There was always a party and I was invited. The thing is, it wasn't fun. The only thing I had going for me was my guardian angels. They took care of me, and I took care of Mom."

Kate was eight when her mom and dad divorced. Kate lived with her dad. He immediately remarried a woman with two children. The stepmother had no time for Kate—only her children and Kate's dad. Kate got lost, and not just a little. Kate was invisible from then on. The parents of Kate's friends began asking her to live with them. Her dad's friends began asking him, "Why don't you let Kate live with us?" Everyone could see Kate wasn't getting what she needed, except the people who should have been protecting and caring for her—her dad and mom.

"I was on the edge of a nervous breakdown my entire childhood," Kate said. "After the divorce, I spent every other weekend with Mom. When it was time for me to visit her, I'd break out in hives. I'd go to her house, and she'd go out and get drunk. So many times she left me sleeping all night on a park bench or at a bus stop. It's a miracle I never got kidnapped, killed, or really hurt. Once my mom came back after leaving me alone and being gone all night. She lifted up her skirt. She wasn't wearing any underpants. She told me she'd been raped by a gang of Hispanic men. She showed me the cigarette burns all over her private parts and upper legs."

It's hard for a child to see that, to know that about her mom. One day Kate's mom decided it was time for Kate to learn about sex. Kate's mom was drunk. So was her mom's boyfriend. Sigrid brought Kate in the bedroom and made Kate take off her clothes and get in bed. Then her mom brought her boyfriend into the bedroom and told him to get naked and have sex with Kate. Her mom wanted Kate to "learn to have sex the right way," she said. She thought the way to do that was by having her boyfriend do it to her. Kate laid there terrified. Her mom's boyfriend undressed, then got on top of her. "He was so drunk he couldn't do it—couldn't—well, you know what I mean. It didn't work." Kate's angels protected her again.

Kate and her dad went through three counselors while Kate was in high school. When each counselor got to the part where they told her father he should let Kate go live with someone else, someone who would love and care for her—which each counselor inevitably did—Kate's dad fired the counselor.

"In all my years of counseling, I've never told a teenager this before," Kate's third counselor said to her. "Even though you're a teenager, I feel that you should leave home. See if you can live with a friend or something. It would be so much better for you than where you are now."

That's what Kate did. At age sixteen, she left home and moved in with her boyfriend and his mom. Later, he became Kate's first husband. "His mom was a real-life angel," Kate said. "She had cancer. She was sick, but she helped me change my life. I was beginning to go down the same path as my parents—the whole negative lifestyle thing. I thought because my life had been miserable that's how it would always be. I started going in the wrong direction—drinking, experimenting with drugs, running with the wrong crowd. All this miserable stuff had happened to me my whole life. I didn't know it was my mother and father's problem and not mine. I thought there was something wrong with me. I thought I had to be a failure as an adult. When your life has been headed in a bad direction, you keep mindlessly going that way whether you like it or not. I didn't know I had a choice."

Her boyfriend's mother helped Kate learn she didn't have to accept the legacy of suffering, pain, and unhappiness. Life didn't have to be hard and a struggle. Kate could be what she wanted. She could set her own course. "I read some books on codependency, about adult children of alcoholics and personal growth. I read your books too," Kate said to me. "I realized that no matter what happened in the past, I didn't have to be a victim anymore. I could do or be what I wanted. Now the choice was mine."

There's a difference between knowing that in your head and knowing it in your heart. When Kate Somerville got it, she integrated it in a way that changed her life. This awareness was a turning point. "It was my first awakening," Kate said.

This woman gets and lives what recovery is about.

That's when Kate became involved in the skin-care business. It's something she has a gift for. It's what she always wanted to do. Kate says once she made the decision, her angels did the rest.

I'm not touchy-feely. Normally I don't give people hugs unless I'm close to them and the hug comes from my heart. But I wanted to hug her. I wanted to get up off the table and hold her and tell her how wonderful she is—the way her mom should have done, should be doing right now.

"Lie still," Kate says, rubbing something delicious on my face. "Relax. Let me take care of you."

That's how we are, us codependents—even the recovering ones (unless we get militant like the ones who claim to have their black belts in Al-Anon). We like to give to people, nurture them. Some people misinterpret recovery from codependency. They think recovery means we shouldn't give to people or be nurturing, but that's not it at all.

One day, a woman told me this story. She was finishing her day's work at a social services agency when a woman walked in who had just been released from chemical dependency treatment. The woman had nowhere to live and no money. She needed help. But the social services agency was closed for the day. There was nothing this woman (the one telling me the story) could do. She told me how badly she wanted to give the woman twenty dollars out of her own pocket, but she didn't. She stopped herself from giving money to the woman because she thought it would be codependent. Then she said how proud of herself she was for not helping the woman even though she wanted to, and how watching the woman walk out knowing she had no place to go broke her heart.

What she does and who she gives to is entirely her business. But I said it sounded like she really wanted to give, and if she wants to and it feels right, that's what she should do. That's what healthy giving is: knowing when giving feels right to us, whom to give to, and how much. Healthy giving is conscious giving. Codependent giving is mindless, obsessive caretaking because we feel guilty if we don't. Nurturing, loving, and giving are important parts of mental, emotional, and spiritual health.

There's giving that sustains us and giving that drains us. We don't have to get something back from the person we give to. Sometimes we get good feelings from doing the act. It's better, though, if the giving in ongoing relationships is balanced—but each person doesn't have to give the same thing at the same time. It's not about keeping score. It's about balanced, mutual, reciprocal love (in ongoing relationships). If I give from my heart, life balances the giving and receiving in the end. We can give when we're guided, and our needs will be met. We don't look to a person; God is our Source.

Giving that drains us is when we feel manipulated or coerced, or when the person we're giving to is using us, or when we're giving to manipulate the person into doing something for us. We give secretly hoping that the person will see how wonderful we are and how much he or she needs us, then the person will come into our lives and make us feel good. That type of giving doesn't work—it's giving to control. It's also unhealthy giving when our giving prevents the people we're giving to from being appropriately responsible for themselves. That diminishes them and sends the message that we think they can't take care of themselves. It puts us one up and them one down. It can make them dependent on us. People eventually resent whomever they're dependent on. Giving puts us in control. We feel safe when giving and vulnerable when we receive.

Kate insisted that the facial was complimentary. I thanked her. I could tell that Kate genuinely wanted to give to me. I felt comfortable accepting although sometimes it's still difficult for me to receive. Giving is good. The thing we want to avoid is that compulsive, obsessive giving and giving motivated by fear and guilt. Our ability to nurture and give isn't sickness; it's a beautiful part of who we are as long as we're giving in love.

Not long ago, Kate had a second awakening, one of those Buddhist things. "I feel so bad about my mom," Kate says. "I vacillate between being angry at her for being a drunk and feeling sad because she's in so much pain. I know I'm supposed to detach, but it's not easy seeing your mom living on the streets. It's been hard not to take all this personally.

One day when I was praying and meditating, I realized that even though she's my mom, she's just another human being. She's the woman I came through in order to be here and have my life."

This was a true letting go of ego. The lack of love from her mom isn't personal; her mom likely would have treated any child she had that way. It wasn't directed at Kate. Kate just happened to be in the way. When Kate stopped taking her mom's alcoholism personally, it still hurt, but not as much. Yes, it's about Kate, but it's really about her mom and the illness her mom has. Kate didn't detach in that unhealthy way where we freeze our feelings and go numb. It's the awareness Kahlil Gibran wrote about in *The Prophet*. Our children don't belong to us. Our parents aren't *ours*. We're all people walking down the street, human beings struggling through lessons, doing the best we can, and sometimes we fall short of the mark.

Whether we believe it or not, life hasn't singled us out for tragedy. Depersonalizing a loss helps us detach and lessens the pain.

After the facial, Kate and I went out to lunch. I told her what an incredible woman she is. I'm not sure she believed me. That's the thing about us codependents. We see the beauty in other people, but it's hard to see in ourselves. While it might be hard for some people to understand, there's a good reason for that too. Side effects of loss—and having an alcoholic or crazy parent is a loss—are low self-esteem and guilt. If the people we're involved with aren't feeling guilty for their behaviors, we pick up their guilt. Even though we know intellectually we aren't the person drinking and causing problems, we feel bad about ourselves. This is the story we tell ourselves: We must have done something wrong, or else this bad thing wouldn't have happened to us. There must have been something we could have done to prevent it, to make the story turn out another way. Thinking that way is a survival device. Feeling responsible and guilty gives us a sense of control. If we feel like random tragedy has rained down on us, we feel too vulnerable and unsafe in the world.

There's a natural order to life, we think. If we do good things, then good things will happen to us. Carrying this thinking forward, if something bad happens to us, then that means we did something wrong. At least that's what we erroneously believe. We did something to bring tragedy on ourselves. It's difficult to accept that painful, horrible things happen to children and adults, and there's no good reason these things happen, none at all. They happen because they happen, and life doesn't always make sense. That's a tough concept to grab for a child or an adult.

It's normal to go through loss and let it create low self-esteem, to tell ourselves we don't deserve whatever it was we lost, and that's *why* we experienced that loss. It's easy to follow that by thinking that what we do doesn't matter because bad things can happen to anyone—even us— no matter what we do. Then we give up on ourselves. This doesn't happen only to children of alcoholics. This syndrome can happen with any loss. One woman I know was a health fanatic. She exercised, ate right, didn't smoke or do anything "wrong." When she was diagnosed with cancer, she thought, *What good does it do to take care of myself? I can take great care of myself and still have bad things happen to my health.* For a while, she stopped taking good care of herself and said that what she did didn't matter. But we know—and now she does too—that's not true.

Are we willing to surrender to how vulnerable we are and still take care of ourselves? Are we willing to live by our code and create the best life we can—knowing in one moment for no good reason it can all be taken away? Something mysterious and wonderful happens when we take the high road knowing how vulnerable we really are. We connect with a deeper spirituality. We connect with our destiny when we choose to show up for life fully aware of how unfair life is and can be, knowing life has disappointed us before and that it may do that again. We'll know a new freedom and power.

The *whys* can be endless. Why does Kate's mom have this illness? Why doesn't her mother get well? Why was this Kate's destiny? People turn themselves inside out coming up with explanations trying to make sense of loss—everything from karma, to past lives where we did the same thing to someone else, to being tested or punished by God. Most loss experts agree that asking *Why?* isn't a question; asking *Why?* is similar to saying *Ouch!* It's also a stage we may need to go through until we're ready to take responsibility for ourselves and our lives and get back in the game.

Sometimes the reason for our loss isn't one we'll ever see—at least not while we're here. In *Ambiguous Loss*, author Pauline Boss says the people who live with ongoing loss most successfully are people who find a spiritual way of life and let go of their need to control. That's why groups like Al-Anon, Adult Children of Alcoholics, and Co-Dependents Anonymous work. The Twelve Steps help us find a spiritual way of living. Working the Steps helps us detach. Healthy detachment means we care, we feel our feelings, we do what we reasonably can, and we let go of what we can't.

There's an unhealthy form of detachment—when we freeze, coldly deny having any emotions, and say "I don't care" when we really do care. (And we may need to do that for a while.) We can be more than survivors of abuse and alcoholism. Surviving means we're waking up alive. We deserve more than that. We can thrive, but to do that, most of us need some help. Being around other people who have similar problems and goals gives us that magic mirror. We see ourselves in others. They see themselves in us. Together, we trudge the road of happy destiny—well, it's happy *some* of the time.

I've heard people talk about guardian angels and about angelic interventions in their lives. Kate doesn't talk about an incident where her guardian angels helped her. "They raised me," she said. "I know they'll be there every day guiding, protecting, and helping me."

We talked about "mom love," what it would feel like to have it, how it's so hard to imagine. "It would be nice to be loved like that, to be taken care of and feel safe," Kate said. "For once I'd like to have someone say, 'It's going to be all right. I'll take care of you,' but I doubt that will ever happen. I've always had to fend for myself. My strength can be tiring sometimes."

Kate knows God and her angels will take care of her, but she doesn't have that one person she can count on no matter what. "I wish I did," Kate says. "I try to be that for my son. We always want to make it better for our kids. The older I get, the more I realize parents are just people too, trying to make it the best they can. I have survived and I love my life."

Kate knows happiness is her choice.

I ask her one more question before saying good-bye. "Do you think your karma with you mom is done?"

"I don't know what's going to happen," Kate said, "but I know my future is good."

After the facial, I write some notes on the interview, then set the story aside. I kept waiting for it to be time to write Kate's story, but that time doesn't arrive. Then one day I wake up, start thinking about Kate, and can't stop. *I should call and have another facial, get in touch with her,* I think. I'm due for another Titan treatment; I love the way it shrink-wraps me. But I'm busy writing the book and don't have time to pamper myself now. Just then the phone rings. It's Kate. "I've been thinking about you," I said.

"I'm thinking about you too," Kate said. "I'm on my way to hospice. My mom is there. I expect she'll die soon, probably tonight." We talk a while, then she says to make an appointment for next week.

A week later, I'm back at Kate's place. Kate pops into the room. She looks lighter. I can tell she's not carrying a burden anymore. She leads me to a treatment room. Soon she's working her magic on my face.

"The last time we talked, you asked if my karma with my mom was done," Kate said. "I realized I am her karma. I'm the legacy she left. I've had a lot of pain from my mom, but I got good stuff too. I got so much from her—her free spirit, her creativity, her sense of humor. It's a dark sense of humor, but one that can find something funny in any situation. My mom was such a beautiful soul. I want you to see a picture of her someday," Kate said. "I want you to see her smiling eyes before all her pain.

"It feels strange," Kate said. "It's so final, so sad now that Mom's gone." Kate said she asked her dad to help with the cremation and other final details. He refused. "He said my stepmother was mad at me for even asking him to help. I started to get angry, then I picked up a book. It talked about taking the high road. I was able to call my dad and step-mother and speak my piece. I could say what I felt, but not say it with anger or resentment. Somehow what I need always comes to me—in business, in spiritual growth. I'm so blessed," Kate said.

"I got the phone call that my mom was in hospice in Santa Barbara. They told me she didn't have long. Five minutes later, a friend called—sometimes angels come in human form. When I told my friend what was happening, she said she'd be right over. She stayed by my side through it all." Kate said she and her friend drove to Santa Barbara. Her mom was dying—and dying now. Everything was going wrong with her body. It was worn out, broken, done. But at least Kate's mom wasn't underneath a bridge somewhere. She was clean, safe in a bed.

"I'm scared," Sigrid, Kate's mother, said to Kate.

"Just relax and let go," Kate said. "Go be with your mom. Go be with your friends. You've had such a hard life, Mom. It hasn't been a party for a long time. Go be free. You won't have to struggle anymore or try to survive. Go be happy for the first time."

Sigrid held her daughter's hand.

"Mom, after you die, will you please help me with a few things? This is what I want," Kate said. "I need more time with my son. I need some guidance about my marriage. I need to get back to the beach, the water. I need more time for myself. Please keep an eye on me."

"I'll be your guardian angel," Sigrid promised. Then she died.

Every day for as long as Kate can remember, she'd wake up and won-der how her mom was, where she was, which institution was going to call. The police? The hospital? Was her mom homeless? Sick? In jail? This was all happening while Kate had this wonderful success going on.

"You know those moments—for me, minutes—when you snuggle up to your mom in bed and feel safe and know you're loved? That's how it feels all the time for me now," Kate said.

For the first time in her life, Kate finally has the love and the mom she wants.

About 43 percent of the U.S. adult population—76 million Americans—has been exposed to alcoholism in the family.

Almost 1 in 5 adult Americans (18 percent) lived with an alcoholic while growing up.

About 1 in 8 American adult drinkers is alcoholic or experiences problems due to the use of alcohol. The cost to society is estimated at in excess of $166 billion each year.

There are an estimated 26.8 million children of alcoholics in the United States. Preliminary research suggests that more than 11 million are under the age of 18.

About 2 out of 1,000 children in the United States were confirmed by child protective service agencies as having experienced sexual assault in 2003.

Among high school students nationwide, 9 percent reported they were forced to have sexual intercourse.

Near-fatal abuse and neglect each year leave 18,000 permanently disabled children, tens of thousands of victims overwhelmed by lifelong psychological trauma, thousands of traumatized siblings and family members, and thousands of near-death survivors who, as adults, continue to bear the physical and psychological scars. Some may turn to crime or domestic violence or become abusers themselves.

Fifty percent of adult children of alcoholics marry alcoholics. Seventy percent develop patterns of compulsive behavior as adults, including abusive patterns with alcohol, drugs, food, sex, work, gambling, or spending.

Adult children of alcoholics are 3 to 4 times more likely to become alcoholics than the general population.

Fifty-five percent of all family violence occurs in alcoholic homes.

Incest is twice as likely among daughters and sons of alcoholics and their peers.

Alcohol is a factor in 90 percent of all child abuse cases.

Seventy-nine percent of Americans believe in angels.

Sources: National Association for Children of Alcoholics, National Center for Injury Prevention and Control, U.S. Advisory Board on Child Abuse and Neglect, Pennsylvania State University, and Fox News Poll

ACTIVITIES

1. Do you have any ongoing losses in your life? Do you have a support group that helps you deal with this and take care of yourself? It's easy to talk ourselves out of getting the support and help we deserve. We tell ourselves it won't make the problem go away, so why bother? And it's true—getting help may not solve the other person's problem, but it can help us feel better. Sometimes validating how we feel is all we need to come back to our center and get on with our lives. If you're living with an ongoing loss, how about being kind to yourself? At least get a journal and start writing about how you feel. There are so many support groups now. How about finding one for people going through a loss similar to yours? Sometimes doing something as part of "we" is easier than doing it alone.

2. Are you a child or an adult child of an alcoholic? Have you dealt with the issues that come with that experience? There are books and free support groups available in most cities and countries. If you have co-

dependency issues, you're probably skilled at taking care of others. It's time to take care of yourself. Contact numbers and Web addresses are as follows: Al-Anon Family Group Headquarters at 888-4AL-ANON (888-425-2666) or www.al-anon.alateen.org; Alcoholics Anonymous World Services at 212-870-3400 or www.aa.org; National Council on Alcoholism and Drug Dependence, Inc., at 212-269-7797 or www.ncadd.org; National Institute on Alcohol Abuse and Alcoholism at 301-443-3860 or www.niaaa.nih.gov; Co-Dependents Anonymous at 602-277-7991 or www.coda.org; Adult Children of Alcoholics at 310-534-1815 (leave message only) or www.adultchildren.org.

3. What's Left? In the introduction, I said there were two activities I encourage you to do. One is the Master List of Losses. The other is this one. It's so easy to look around and see what we don't have and what we didn't get. It's important to identify what we lost. But the inventory isn't finished until we know what we have left. This is an ongoing activity. Don't rush it. Take your time. Dedicate a notebook to writing down everything you have, everything you did get, everything you have left. No matter what your situation is—if you're in prison, in a hospital, in hospice—no matter who or where you are, you have something left and probably more than you know. Go on a treasure hunt in your life. What did you get? How were your needs met? How are they being met now? What resources do you have? What are your strengths? What did your losses mean to you—what did you learn from your losses and from what you endured? How did your losses shape you? What are your talents, abilities, gifts? Can you still see and hear? Do you have your senses of taste and smell? Can you walk? Run? Do you have a motorized chair if you're unable to walk on your own? Come on—let's get it all on the list. Ask friends or family for help making your list. What do they see you as having? What do they think you're lucky to have? What do they admire in you? What do you like about yourself? What have you been complimented on (even if you didn't accept the compliment)? What do you own? What are you good at? What are your accomplishments? Put everything on this list. Make it a goal to have your list of what's left be

longer than your Master List of Losses. The actor Christopher Reeve wrote in his book *Still Me* that he and other spinal-injury patients used to hear people who could walk, run, and move about complain about their lives, and they couldn't believe what they were hearing. Here people were—in perfect or almost-perfect health—coming around people who couldn't in some cases even breathe for themselves, and the healthy people were complaining and grumping about what they didn't have. Stanley "Tookie" Williams, the cofounder of the Crips, wrote nine books while he was on death row. He wasn't allowed to make any money from his writing; he did it because he realized he started life out on the wrong foot by leaving a legacy of violence. He wanted to change his legacy, so he wrote books teaching kids that violence, guns, and gangs weren't the way to gain self-esteem and respect. Williams did more on death row before his execution than many people who are free do their entire lives. Go ahead and scream about how unfair life is. Get it out—because it *is* unfair and unjust. When you're done hollering, can you have a little faith with the life you've been given, as unfair and disappointing as it might be? When you're ready to look at what's left, you'll find your destiny.

4. Go back to your Master List of Losses. Can you see any incidents in which you didn't get something you wanted—and deserved—from a source you expected it from, but life stepped in and took care of you some other way? For instance, maybe your mother wasn't nurturing and loving, but an older sister took care of you, and her love helped you survive. Maybe you don't have a strong connection with the family you were born into, but over the years you've created a family of choice. Or maybe you had a loss, but in some strange and unexpected way, you were taken care of—the Red Sea parted. Life made a way for you when it looked impossible for that to happen. It's important to honor our feelings of sadness, anger, and loss, especially when abuse is involved. It's also important to honor the good that happened, the ways we were taken care of, and the ways our needs were met. Most of us know clearly the people who didn't give us what we wanted and weren't there for us. How about writing a thank-you note to someone who was?

5. Chart your course. Have you been allowing other people's problems and pain to control your destiny and the choices you make? Maybe it's time to shake off their negative behaviors, realize they don't have to control you, and start choosing your own path. What would you like to have happen with your life? Get a notebook or journal. Make it your wish, goal, treasure, or dream book. Start thinking about what you'd like to have happen. Meditate on it. What are you passionate about? Let God show you what you can have. Put your ideas in your book. Cut out pictures. Write about it. You don't have to follow in others' footsteps. Go for your dreams. If those dreams die, life will give you some more. You survived. Now it's time to thrive. Give up the addiction to struggle. Be happy now.

6. Debrief from trauma. Are you a victim of abuse or any kind of trauma? You deserve to heal from whatever you've been through. Trauma can put us in flight or freeze mode. We become frozen in that moment when the trauma occurred. Experts agree that debriefing from trauma is key to healing it. Either on your own or with professional help, start surrendering to the traumatic experiences you went through, the ones locked inside. We're not going back to the past to wallow in it; we're going back long enough to unthaw and set ourselves free. In the bibliography at the end of the book, I list some books to read if you've experienced trauma.

EMDR (Eye Movement Desensitization and Reprocessing) therapy is an effective, fast way to heal. Often when we're traumatized, we disconnect from ourselves. That's when we begin to feel separate from God, others, and life. By surrendering to and healing trauma, we'll restore our partnership with life by restoring our partnership with ourselves. Survivor guilt, loneliness, fear of open or closed spaces, inability to make decisions, impulsive actions, physical illnesses, difficulty sleeping, and change in sexual desire are among the after-effects of traumatic events, writes Frank Parkinson in *Post-Trauma Stress*. The person being debriefed should discuss his or her expectations, what happened instead, thoughts, what he or she did or didn't do, why, how he or she felt originally and later on, how others reacted, the worst thing experienced, what he or she said, how the family reacted, and more. Remember, when you debrief from traumatic events you may feel worse for a while because you're bringing emotions to the surface instead of repressing or denying them. It doesn't mean you're getting worse. It's part of healing. Contact the EMDR Institute for more information at 831-761-1040 or www.emdr.org.

Be aware that when we suffer a severe loss, we may think that life doesn't matter and other things—like our health, home, savings—aren't important anymore. This is a phase we're going through. Please, get someone safe to monitor you; don't throw your life away. Life will come back into balance. In time you'll see things differently. You'll care about life again.

7. Have you given up because life isn't fair? Maybe you took a blow that wasn't just. You led a healthy life and got cancer; you were a good, loving, protective parent and your child died; you were a loving, faithful wife and your husband divorced you. It's easy to give up on doing the right thing if we do it and still get sucker-punched by life. But we still get the consequences from our behaviors. If we stop taking care of ourselves—playing by our rules—when life doesn't play by the rules, we're the ones who suffer the consequences. We may create more loss by what we're doing (or not doing) because we tell ourselves it doesn't matter. It's normal to feel like giving up for a while after a loss. But it can continue the pattern of loss and abuse. It's a signal that we're healing when we say, "Fair or not, I'm getting in the game again. I'm going to take care of myself; I'm going to show up. I'm living by my code, and I'm going to create the best life I can."

8. Set yourself free. Have you turned recovery from adult children of alcoholic issues, Al-Anon issues, or codependency issues into a heavy set of rules? We used to use the unhealthy family system rules to control ourselves. Now some people use the rule of recovery to keep themselves in line. The purpose, the heart, the goal of codependency recovery is to

set ourselves free. Trust yourself. Give if, when, and what you want. Be nurturing. Be loving. Be yourself. Be that way with others, but also be that way toward yourself.

9. Write your own legacy. It's easy to unconsciously accept a legacy of suffering and pain. Sit down with pen and paper. Write a legacy of all the positive attributes you claim from your ancestors. Give yourself what you deserve. You may want to write a list of the negative legacies that you *refuse* to accept.

CHAPTER 13

Restraining Change:
When Grief Makes Us Vulnerable

"He's horrible," the woman said, describing her soon-to-be ex-husband. "One minute I'll think we can still be friends. The next minute he's swearing at me and calling me names. He does it in front of the children too. Then when they get mad at me, they call me the same names. What am I going to do?" she asked. "I can't make him talk nice."

"You might not be able to make him talk nice to you, but you can make him stop swearing and calling you names. You can get a restraining order," I explained, "an injunction that specifically says he can't swear at you and call you names privately or in front of the children. I know because I had to get one when I divorced my children's dad."

When I'm interviewed about *Codependent No More*, people ask me for the rules for not being codependent. I change the subject or joke that the publisher should have called the book *Codependent Not As Much*, but the truth is there aren't any rules, and if there are, I don't know them. What helped me most wasn't rules. The heart of codependency recovery is being free to be and express who we are. How can there be rules for that? But people like rules. It makes them feel safe. Some people become frustrated when I won't give them rules, but I don't have any—except two.

Years ago, a reader began e-mailing me. He's a sweet man who fell in love with a troubled woman. A few months after they married, he came home from work one day to find the locks on the doors changed and his clothes piled in the driveway. He was shocked. He didn't know he and his wife were having problems. He wondered if she was seeing another man. He e-mailed me and told me he considered himself a good Christian, so why did God let this happen to him? Then he asked what he should do.

I suggested he go to Al-Anon, because his wife was drinking and using pills. "And keep feeling your feelings. In the meantime, there are only two rules," I said. "Don't hurt anyone else or hurt yourself."

He obsessed and obsessed. Finally his wife let him move back in. She became addicted to painkillers, and she is financially dependent on him. He feels trapped and can't remember being in love with her, but he still remembers the rules.

I give myself and others room to vacillate, make mistakes, and find our own way—except when it involves violence, harm, or abuse. The first time I realized how important these rules are, I had just started working as a family counselor at a treatment program in Minnesota. Many ideas that have since become common knowledge weren't popular yet. We were barely beginning to acknowledge domestic violence and abuse. I didn't know much about either topic, but I learned the rules the hard way and at a client's expense.

One of the addicts in the treatment center where I worked had finally earned a weekend pass to go home and stay with his wife and children from Friday evening through Sunday night. His wife was in my family group. She wasn't an addict; she was codependent (although we didn't have that word yet). Early Saturday afternoon she phoned me at home and said her husband had threatened to hit her. I talked to her. Then I talked to her husband's counselor, and he called the husband and talked to him. We all decided not to take the threat that seriously. We suggested they calm down and enjoy his weekend pass.

At eleven o'clock Saturday evening, a nurse called from the county hospital. My client had asked her to ask me to please come to the hospital right away. When I walked into her room, I almost passed out. Her face was so pulverized I barely recognized her. Her husband had beaten her while their children watched.

That's when I decided the rules are *don't hurt anyone else* and *don't hurt yourself.* That's when I decided that I would take even the slightest threat of physical violence as a violation of the rules.

I questioned whether to include the subject of violence in this book. Our culture has come a long way. Doesn't everybody know the rules? While I was wondering whether to continue with this chapter, I received a telephone call. It was a friend calling to tell me how upset he was because his friend's brother had committed suicide. The brother had left a note explaining the reason he killed himself was because he had been trying for years to get his business going and he couldn't get it off the ground. He had run out of hope. But when my friend's friend was going through his dead brother's mail, he discovered a signed contract and a check for $150,000 in his brother's mailbox. Now I don't think success can make us happy, but the man who killed himself did. He killed himself because he felt like a failure, but success was on the way to him—in the mail—when he pulled the trigger. Suicide is violence against ourselves, and it breaks the rules.

When I heard that story, I decided to write about the rules. Sometimes we forget the basics, and sometimes we can't help ourselves. We reach a breaking point, and we don't know what else to do. There are two more reasons I'm going to write about the rules. The first reason happened back in the seventies when I hired my first housekeeper. I hired her when I couldn't afford the $25 a week it cost. I hired her because I was a single parent who worked hard, and I didn't want to spend my time off cleaning the house or nagging my children to keep it clean.

One day, the woman I hired to do housekeeping showed up for work looking preoccupied, beaten down, and distressed.

"What's wrong?" I asked.

"My brother-in-law knocked on my sister's door Friday night," she said. "They're in the middle of a nasty divorce. When my sister opened the door, he shot her. He killed her with the children standing right there, watching."

That's one reason. The second reason I'm writing this chapter happened several years later. I hired a business professional to represent me. He appeared aggressive, sharp, and efficient when I contracted with him for his services. He had an impressive office in Beverly Hills. A few weeks later, when I went to his office for a consultation, he was stammering. He didn't make sense. His face looked puffy. A usually focused, hard-driving man, he couldn't make up his mind about how to proceed on my behalf.

"What's wrong?" I asked.

"My brother-in-law killed my sister," he said. "Then he shot and killed himself. He did it in front of the children. Now we're trying to figure out who will raise my niece and nephew. My wife and I are thinking we'll probably have them live with us."

The six degrees of separation theory says we're only six people away from any person or situation. Violence is closer than that. Sometimes people can't restrain themselves. They get so despondent they can't think of how to stop their pain other than to kill themselves. There are times people get so frustrated and enraged at life or other people they can't stop themselves from hurting someone else. That's when they need help. They need someone to tell them exactly what to do or what not to do. Freedom of action is no longer an option. They need to be restrained.

In another chapter, I've addressed suicide. This is a story about not allowing anyone to hurt us, threaten us, or hurt or threaten anyone else. If someone can't or won't stop themselves from hurting us—whether the abuse is verbal or physical—then we stop them. Some lessons we learn the hard way. We can get hit with it over and over until we learn. But all it takes is one bullet, and we don't get another chance. I know two women who would do it differently if they could, but they won't get that opportunity.

This story is for them. It's for everyone in all the Clubs. It's about not letting our grief make us vulnerable to abuse.

Sandy and her friend Carolyn were at the local mall when they spotted the sign: "Psychic Fair—Readings Five Dollars." The two women looked at each other. "Let's do it," they said in unison. This wasn't something either of them would ordinarily do, but five dollars? That's cheap entertainment. Eight tables had been set up in the area; booths offered crystals, incense, and sage. The psychics looked like ordinary people. Some of them were using tarot cards to do the readings. Most of the psychics were women. Sandy and Carolyn decided to go with the psychic who was a man. "He's not using tarot cards," Sandy joked. "Maybe this guy is for real."

Carolyn took the first turn. Sandy didn't listen that closely to what he told her friend; something about business improving and her mother getting sick, but don't worry, she wouldn't die. He asked Carolyn if she wanted to buy more psychic information. Carolyn said, "No, thanks." Then it was Sandy's turn. He asked Sandy to put her hands on the table. He touched her hands lightly with his. He sat quietly for a moment, then he scowled.

"I see you on the second or third floor of an apartment building. A man is hitting you. There's a lot of violence around the relationship." The psychic looked thoughtful, as if he was listening to someone Sandy couldn't see. "This isn't your karma," the psychic said. "You don't have to let it happen. You can avoid the violence if you want."

The psychic paused. "Do you want more information?" he asked.

"No, thanks," Sandy said. She was irritated she had to pay any money at all. *What a joke*, Sandy thought. Her? An abuse victim? Sandy had issues, but getting beat up wasn't one. No one had ever laid a hand on her. No one ever would. Sandy paid the man his money. "What can we expect for five dollars?" she said to Carolyn. The reading was so ridiculous Sandy immediately pushed it out of her mind.

The next year, both Sandy's and Carolyn's moms became ill. Carolyn's mom improved. Sandy's mom died. Sandy was brokenhearted. She loved her mom; she wasn't ready to let her go. When she ran into Phil that day at the grocery store, it was like destiny. She had known Phil casually for more than fifteen years. Since high school, they'd run into each other around town—at the movie theater, at restaurants, at the gym. Phil was now divorced. Sandy had been in one long-term relationship that ended a while back. This past year she hadn't dated anyone. Working and taking care of her mom consumed all her energy and time. Sandy had been attracted to Phil since high school, but she didn't think he was attracted to her. When he asked her out on a date at the grocery store, Sandy immediately said yes. It had been a long, dark year. Maybe Phil's gentle nature was exactly what she needed to come back to life again.

It was fun and it felt safe dating someone she'd known a long time. Phil wasn't like other guys she'd dated. He encouraged her to talk about her feelings. His dad had died when he was a teenager, so he understood Sandy's grief. He was tender and comforting. He could look her in the eyes and not be afraid of what he saw. He held her when she cried. He didn't try to fix her or make her better, but he did make her laugh. They had a lot in common.

Phil had a four-year-old son by his previous marriage. He was a sweet kid. There was a little tension between Phil's son and Sandy, but it wasn't anything out of the ordinary. She had the feeling that Phil's son was jealous of her and wanted his dad all to himself. Sandy didn't blame him. He only got to see his dad two weekends a month. Sandy encouraged Phil to have alone time with his son on his weekends, but Phil insisted on including her. Sandy wasn't living in a fairy-tale world; she expected some problems. From what she could see, she and Phil didn't have many. At the risk of sounding corny, Sandy told Carolyn she believed it was a relationship sent by God.

Sandy and Phil waited a while before becoming sexually intimate. It wasn't Sandy's idea to wait. Phil made it clear from the beginning that he wasn't interested in casual sex. It was either making love or nothing at all. Sandy liked that. Phil made her feel special, cared about. It felt good to be loved that deeply, especially now that her mother was gone. Her mom and dad had been divorced since Sandy was eight. Her dad had moved to another state. He had little contact with Sandy; Sandy was an only child. When Sandy lost her mom, she lost the only person who loved her besides Carolyn. She felt alone—until Phil.

The second time she made love to Phil, something happened that scared Sandy. They were lying in bed kissing when suddenly Phil pulled back. He held her face tightly between his hands and looked into her eyes. "If you cheat on me, if you're unfaithful to me, I'll kill you," he said. "Do you understand?"

Sandy didn't know what to do, think, or say. She knew Phil's ex-wife had cheated on him. *He probably feels insecure,* she thought. "I'm not going to hurt you," she said. "I promise." Phil relaxed. The incident haunted her, but Phil went right back to being sweet. She didn't mention the incident. It felt weird to bring it up. What would she say? She didn't tell Carolyn about it. Secretly, she felt it was romantic. The world was full of wishy-washy men who didn't know what they wanted—but Phil knew. He wanted Sandy all to himself.

"That was my first mistake," Sandy said later. "If I had it to do over, I would have left, gotten a restraining order, changed my phone number, and immediately stopped all contact with Phil. When someone says he's going to kill you, open your eyes. It's not romantic or sweet. It's not because he's a little insecure. You're dealing with an unbalanced man who's really insecure. He's acting crazy. He's threatening you. It's abuse. See it for what it is—a big red flag. Then run as fast as you can."

Six months later, Sandy and Phil became engaged. Sandy wanted to wait a year to get married. Phil didn't want to wait that long. "If we're going to do it, let's do it soon," he said. "We both know what we want. That way we can start building our lives together now." Two months later, they eloped to Vegas.

They walked around Vegas after the ceremony, through the casinos and by all the stores. Sandy was happy to be with Phil, grateful to be his wife. She cried when she said, "I do." It was so romantic. She loved Phil so much. She could see the love in his eyes when he looked at her. She had a hard time believing that any man and woman ever loved each other as much as she and Phil did. She loved their rings. Phil had picked them out. They had rented the honeymoon suite at a hotel. It was cheesy, but it was romantic too. "It was one of the happiest days of my life," Sandy said. "Then it became one of the most bizarre."

They walked around Vegas until Sandy was worn out. Phil didn't want to eat. He didn't want to go back to their room. He seemed removed, distant. After a while, Sandy said she was tired of walking. She pointed to a quarter slot machine. "Why don't we play the slots for a while?" she asked, sitting down on the stool. She pulled a ten-dollar bill out of her purse and fed it into the machine. Before she could start play-ing, Phil put his face right up to hers.

"I ought to knock you off that stool," Phil said.

Sandy reeled. Was he kidding? Was this a joke? Sandy looked at him—his face, his eyes. The only other time he'd gone wacko like this was that night more than half a year ago, when he threatened to kill her if she dated another man.

This wasn't the man she'd married, the man she knew. It was like there was somebody else inside him. Who was this monster? "When someone changes that fast, it doesn't register," Sandy said. "You think, *I'm not really seeing this. I'm not really hearing this.* It's too much to absorb. It's so bizarre all you can do is try to pretend it didn't happen. Otherwise, what are you going to do with it?"

Phil pressed the cash out button. Quarters spilled out of the machine. Sandy scooped them up and put them in a container. They walked back to their hotel room in silence. When they got there, Phil locked himself in the bathroom. She could hear him taking a shower. That night, they ordered room service, ate in silence, and went to bed. Phil didn't touch her. He lay as far away from her as he could. She knew he wasn't sleeping. They both lay awake late into the night not touching or talking. *I don't know him*, Sandy thought. *What have I done?* Finally Sandy fell asleep. The next morning, Phil seemed like his normal self. They went out for breakfast, then sat by the pool and sunned. The rest of the honeymoon was perfect. The man she loved and married was back.

"It was easy to push it out of my mind," Sandy said later. "It hap-pened so fast. It was so bizarre. Then it was over. We didn't talk about it. It's like it didn't happen at all. It didn't feel real. That was my second mistake. If I had it to do over, the second he said, 'I ought to knock you off that stool,' I should have started screaming 'Help!' at the top of my lungs. I should have screamed until the police came. Then I should have told the police he threatened me. I should have held him responsible for his behavior. I should have had him arrested and our marriage annulled. That's what I should have done.

"It was like little blips of insanity, flecks you see out of the corner of your eye," Sandy said. "You wonder: Did I see that or not? Was it real? If it would have been something big, horrendous—something that went on for more than one second, something I could have identified—maybe things would have been different." She says if the incidents would have lasted longer or been more frequent, she probably would have walked away. "I'd always judged women who stayed in relationships and let themselves get hit," Sandy said. "I'd think, *What's wrong with them that they're sticking around getting beaten? Why don't they take care of themselves, put the rat in jail?* Maybe sometimes it's simple like that, but it wasn't for me. Maybe part of it was because I was so beaten up and sad about losing my mom."

The next time it got crazy was three months later. Phil and Sandy had Phil's son for the weekend. They went to McDonald's for lunch. Sandy asked Phil's son what he wanted to eat. When it came time to order, she ordered for herself and for Phil's son. Phil ordered for himself. As soon as they left the restaurant, Phil started yelling in a low, threatening voice—his crazy voice—about how Sandy was trying to take over, trying to control everything, trying to run his life and his relationship with his son. When they got back to their apartment, Phil parked the car in the garage. The three of them got out of the car. His son ran out and into the courtyard. Sandy started to leave the garage, but before she could, Phil got in front of her. He slammed the door shut and stood there, blocking her exit.

"I'm going to kill you," he said.

Sandy looked at him. She didn't recognize him, the look in his eyes. She didn't know what to say. This was insane. It was like another personality had taken over. Her heart was racing.

"With what?" she asked.

Phil was silent. Sandy stood there. "I don't know if he didn't get the answer he expected or if he thought I'd be more frightened, but all of a sudden Phil burst out laughing," Sandy said. "Then we both walked out of the garage. Everything was fine, like it never happened."

Later that day, Phil went out for a while. When he returned, he had a dozen roses and a card. In the card, he wrote that he was sorry for scaring her, for yelling at her. He said he felt stressed when his son was there, and he felt guilty that he wasn't a full-time dad. He told her he loved her and he would forever. "The abuse crept in," Sandy said. "Looking back, I see all these opportunities I had to make my boundaries clear, to let Phil know exactly where I stood. But each time something happened, it was so strange it caught me off guard. I didn't know how to handle it. It was so freaky that I felt embarrassed and ashamed to talk to anyone about it. How could I tell Carolyn that the man I loved had threatened to kill me—twice now? I wasn't even admitting it to myself!

"Maybe I needed that intensity," Sandy said. "My therapist suggested later that because I was so numb from my mother's death, the danger and pain I felt from Phil made me feel real. How crazy is that, to need the threat of death to know that you're alive?"

The first time Phil's hand struck Sandy's face it was confusing. It could have been an accident. They were in the car and started arguing. "It was something stupid," Sandy said. "I don't recall what we were arguing about." Phil was driving. Suddenly he flung his hand over toward Sandy. He had his left hand on the steering wheel, and while he was using his right hand to express himself dramatically, to make a point, his hand accidentally struck Sandy in the eye. "I didn't mean to hit you, honey," he said, holding ice on her face later. "I'm so, so sorry."

Sandy says to this day she's still not certain if that was abuse or a legitimate accident. Sandy took vacation time until her black eye healed. She didn't tell anyone. No one would believe that it was an accident. She wasn't sure if she believed it either. After the first black eye, the incidents became more frequent. Each time something happened, there was less time until something happened again. Phil was always sorry the next day. "When I got my second black eye, I knew it wasn't an accident. That's when the lights came on. I'm not stupid," Sandy says. "This was domestic violence."

It had gotten so bad by the end of their first year of marriage, all it took was a look from Phil, and Sandy became afraid. She found herself planning and plotting about what she should or shouldn't do to keep from upsetting him. "It's crazy, but I felt ashamed," she said. "I'm the victim. I wasn't doing anything wrong! I kept thinking I must be doing something to attract this to myself. I'd always thought women who were battered must have wanted to be beaten, otherwise they would have left. Now I see how easy it is to get sucked into that crazy situation. You start reacting instead of taking action. It's so embarrassing. You don't want to tell anyone. It's hard enough to admit it to yourself.

"And I loved Phil," Sandy said. "That's the hardest part. It's not like this was some goofball off the streets. I'd known him for years. This was my husband, a man I genuinely loved."

After the second black eye, Sandy was out of sick leave from work. She had also moved out of denial. "I didn't care how much I loved him, this couldn't continue. I'm a career woman," she said. "I was going to jeopardize my job if I didn't do something. I couldn't go into work with a black eye, and I couldn't take any more time off."

Sandy made up her mind to leave. That's when she made her next mistake. "If anyone out there is being abused, please learn from me," she said. "There are some things you can do to protect yourself if you're in a situation like that. One is, don't tell him you're going to leave. Don't try to reason with him. You're not dealing with a rational situation. Your life, your safety is at stake." The most important thing Sandy said she learned—too late—is proximity. "If you don't let him get close to you, if you're not in a confined or closed area with him (or her if it's a woman doing the hitting), you won't get hit. Get yourself away to someplace safe, somewhere you cannot be reached."

Sandy came home early from work and started packing. When Phil came home, she was going to tell him she was leaving. She wasn't completely ready to think about divorce, but she knew they at least needed a separation. She couldn't walk out without an explanation. She couldn't just leave a note. She thought she owed it to him to tell him to his face, to treat him like a friend, and to treat their breakup with respect.

When Phil came home that night, Sandy was in the bedroom packing. She'd already carried some of her suitcases and boxes downstairs and loaded them in her car. Phil walked through the door in a rage. Sandy realized he must have seen her car loaded with boxes and suitcases and already knew she was leaving. Sandy told Phil she loved him, but she was gone. She said she didn't want to, but she'd probably end up getting a divorce. It happened in a second. Before she knew it, Sandy was lying flat on her back on the bed, pinned down, and Phil was on top of her. This time his fist slammed into her face once, then twice.

"I saw stars," Sandy said. "Later I learned it wasn't stars I saw. It was the light flashes that happen when your retina detaches."

Sandy pushed him off her. She ran across the room. She'd had it. She yanked his stereo off the shelf and threw it at him. They both watched while thousands of dollars of electronic equipment fell to the floor and shattered.

Sandy grabbed her purse, ran out the door, down two flights of steps, got into her car, and drove across town to a motel. As she signed into her room, she remembered what the psychic had warned her about two years earlier: a relationship surrounded with violence, getting hit on the second or third floor. "I hated to admit it," Sandy said. "That psychic was right."

Sandy says she knows what she did wrong at the next juncture too. This time, she didn't keep her new address or phone number from Phil, and she didn't get a restraining order. "Was I that vulnerable after my mom's death? I don't get why I kept going back for more other than I loved this guy and I had known him for so long. I kept thinking we were friends, so I didn't need to hide or protect myself. If that friendship thing hadn't been mixed up with our love and marriage, maybe I would have handled it differently from the beginning.

"It felt weird—wrong—to get a restraining order on someone I thought of as my friend. My thinking wasn't clear. For some reason, I thought getting a restraining order would make me look like a victim," Sandy said. "What I didn't realize is that it's the victims who don't get the restraining orders. It's easy to feel like we've done something wrong when we're the person being abused—like if we were healthy, we wouldn't be with an abuser, so we don't want to admit that we're being beaten. That's crazy thinking. The victim of assault isn't the person doing anything wrong."

It was the middle of the night, six weeks after Sandy left Phil. She had moved into her own apartment by then. Sandy was sound asleep. Something woke her up. She opened her eyes. Phil was standing over her. He had picked the lock on her door. Now his hands were coming down around her throat.

"I screamed the loudest, most bloodcurdling scream you'd ever heard," Sandy said. "The sheer volume of my voice pushed him back. I didn't know any human being could scream that loud. He started backing up. I screamed and screamed and screamed. Thank God he didn't have a knife or a gun," Sandy said. "I'd be dead."

Sandy doesn't know which neighbor dialed 911, but within minutes, the red lights were flashing outside her windows. The building was teeming with police officers. They arrested Phil. There's a small difference between victim and victor. It's all in how it ends.

Sandy got the restraining order. She stopped talking to Phil. From that day on, she didn't let him know where she lived. Phil knew she was serious. She never got near him or allowed him to get close to her again. The abuse ended. Sandy says if just one person learns from her story and gets out instead of going in deeper, putting her story in this book was worth it.

"All a restraining order does is say the police can arrest the abuser if he [or she] comes around you and violates the order," Sandy said. "But you've still got two or three or five or ten minutes until the police get there. If there is any chance of physical violence, go stay in a shelter. Don't let him know where you are. Protect yourself. Overreacting is better than underreacting; it's truly a case of better safe than sorry. This abuse story didn't just happen. At each juncture I had choices," she said. "I made the wrong decisions. Instead of getting out, I went in deeper. The psychic was right. All the violence could have been prevented if I had made different decisions from the beginning. The first time he threatened violence, it was abuse. Threatening someone is abuse; it's intimidating. I let the violence begin and continue. It's not my fault, but I could have prevented it by protecting myself."

Sandy is one of the lucky ones. She got out of her marriage alive.

Perpetrators of violence can be parents, a child, a sibling, a school-mate, an intimate, a co-worker, a stranger, a friend, or a spouse. Victims can be children, adult men, adult women, or seniors. Listen to your instincts. Don't give violence a chance or a foothold. If it feels crazy, it is. Don't make excuses for the abuser. Few incidents are isolated. They don't just happen; they're part of a cycle that unfolds and gets worse over time. If we don't make the choice to prevent, report, or restrain abuse, we decide to let it happen. Remember, we don't have to go through all the experiences on our path.

We should go around trouble whenever we can.

Every year, 1,510,455 women and 834,732 men are victims of physical violence by an intimate.

Every 20.9 seconds, somewhere in America a woman is bat-tered. Every 37.8 seconds a man is battered. (These statistics conflict slightly with statistics from the Family Violence Prevention Fund. It reports that every 9 seconds a woman is battered in the United States, and a Bureau of Justice Statistics special report states that 95 percent of all victims of domestic violence are women. This may be because domes-tic abuse among men is so highly underreported.)

On the average, more than three women are murdered by their husbands or boyfriends every day.

One in three women around the world has been beaten, coerced into sex, or otherwise abused during her lifetime.

Abused girls are significantly more likely to get involved in other risky behaviors. They are four to six times more likely to get pregnant and eight to nine times more likely to have tried to commit suicide.

Source: National Domestic Violence Hotline

ACTIVITIES

1. Have you been threatened or abused? Are you being threatened or abused? Do you have a friend or relative who's being abused? It's tempting to go into denial. We see someone we think we know turn into a monster, and we tell ourselves this can't be happening. If it's happening, no matter how far-fetched it seems, it's real. Don't take chances with your safety or your life. You don't deserve to be punished, hit, or threatened. Have you slipped into a pattern of believing you're causing it by something you're saying or doing? Maybe he (or she) does love you and maybe you love him. But the abuser has a serious problem, and if you're being abused, it's your problem too. Call your police department for phone numbers of shelters or domestic violence counseling services in your area, or call the National Domestic Violence Hotline at 800-799-SAFE (7233) or 800-787-3224 (TTY). If there's been abuse, but it's not happening at the moment or if it has been a pattern and it hasn't been dealt with, you've still got a problem. No matter what stage the violence has escalated to, you've got a chance to make the right choice right now. If we know a child or vulnerable adult who is being abused, it's our responsibility to report it, or we're in violation of the abuse laws too. Keep records with dates and witnesses or tape-record conversations. If you've been hit, go to the emergency room. Get the abuse documented. Abuse isn't an issue for forgiveness; it's something to be restrained. You can forgive in the privacy of your heart once you're safe—and you can forgive without forgetting what happened. The best way to protect yourself is proximity. Don't get into enclosed spaces with an abuser: a car, an apartment, a hotel room. Keep your distance. If a person can't reach you, he or she can't hurt you.

2. Have you talked to your children about reporting violence or threats of violence at school? If you haven't, do so. Report any threats of violence immediately to the police. If you're a teenager and reading this,

take all threats of violence by other students seriously. Report them immediately. Don't give violence a chance.

3. Take a self-defense course at a local martial arts center. It's good for every human being—child, man, woman, or senior—to know how to defend him- or herself. The more capable we are of protecting and defending ourselves, the less we need to use these skills. The way of the spiritual warrior is peace. Be confident in your ability to protect yourself and be clear about your boundaries.

4. Stalking is abuse. Stalking is not romantic; it's not love. Sometimes it's codependent, and it can be dangerous. There are stalking laws now. You don't have to put up with someone calling you, sending unwanted gifts (repeatedly), or tracking you while you're out—making phone calls, hunting you down. Keep a record of the stalking incidents with dates, any witnesses, and a record of what happened. Phone calls, unwanted visits to the house, even a deluge of e-mails can be stalking.

One woman shared this story: "I dated a man two or three times," she said. "He was extremely controlling. I felt uncomfortable with him, so I told him I didn't want to see him anymore. He started calling all the places he knew I went. I'd get there, and he'd have been there before me and left a present or a note. Sometimes he'd call me after I'd been out to eat. Then he'd tell me where I'd been and sometimes even who I'd gone with. I knew he was following me.

"One night I thought I heard someone at the door before I went to sleep, but I listened and didn't hear anyone knocking. The next morning I got up. There were twenty vases of flowers outside my door. Now some women might say, 'Oh, that's romantic.' It wasn't. It was creepy. I threw all the flowers away. I called him up. I was very clear. I told him I didn't want to talk to him, go out with him, receive gifts from him. I wanted him to stay away from me. I clearly set a boundary. He begged me to at least go out to lunch with him one more time to say good-bye. My mistake! He wasn't taking me to lunch to say good-bye, he was trying to talk me into going out with him again.

"When I clearly told him at lunch that I wasn't going to date him, I could see him becoming agitated. Stupidly, I had agreed to let him drive me. I had wanted to meet him there, drive my own car. When we got outside, I felt in my gut that it wasn't a good idea to get in his car with him. I could feel his anger. I told him I'd walk home. He begged me to let him drive me. I did. On the way home, he started taking verbal pokes at me, insulting me, calling me names. I should have kept my mouth shut, but I didn't. I said something back to him. That was all he needed. He slammed on the brakes, jumped over the gearshift counsel, and sat on top of me, choking me. I didn't resist. I stayed calm. Actually the guy is kind of a wimp. I told him he better be careful because I was going to get away, and when I did, I was going to put him in jail. When he calmed down and got back on his side of the car, I opened my door and ran away. I never let him near me again."

Make your boundaries clear. You deserve to be and feel safe.

5. Do you feel safe in your home? Make sure your windows lock securely. Put deadbolt safety locks on your doors. You don't have to build a fortress, but you can make your home safe. You can put long wooden sticks in the bottom of patio doors and sliding windows so no one can possibly slide them open. Security systems aren't that expensive. Many have panic buttons, so it's a simple matter of pushing a button on your key chain if you need to call for help. Be careful in dangerous situations, like walking alone at night in a dark parking lot. Don't leave your car unlocked and then get into it. Be careful at gas stations—even those minutes when you run inside to buy a bottle of water, make sure your doors are locked. Take the extra time to be safe; you're worth the investment.

Do an inventory of your regular routine. Are there any areas of your life where you're sloppy about safety? It's easy to get complacent. Be careful with things like passwords, credit cards, any areas where you're vulnerable. Don't leave that extra key hidden outside in case you lock yourself out. That's dangerous, and it's a trick everyone knows.

Whenever you feel unsafe, pay attention. Do whatever it takes to make yourself feel secure.

6. Know your boundaries. Boundaries are personal; they emerge from individual desires and dislikes, who we are, our culture, our personality—many influences. It's especially easy for people who grew up in homes where there was abuse to have foggy boundaries about violence. Even if you aren't an abuse victim, you might still want to make a one-month project of getting to know yourself and your boundaries better. Keep a small notebook in your pocket or purse. As you go through your day, be aware of all the situations where you wanted to say something and didn't. You don't have to do anything, just be aware. Also, having healthy boundaries doesn't mean we go around the world militantly shouting and demanding our due. The best boundaries can usually be set gently, quietly, from our hearts. We say what we want and what we need to do to take care of ourselves. The more sure we are of our right to be ourselves, the softer we can speak and the stronger our words are.

7. Take extra care when you're grieving. If you're going through a big loss, be aware that your normal boundaries may be weaker, not as clear.

You may feel guilty because of your loss, even believe you deserve to be punished. Like Sandy, if you've gone numb, you may need high drama to feel alive. That's common for people in deep grief or for people who come from backgrounds of abuse. You don't need abuse to feel alive. Also, be aware that in a perfect world, a grieving person would be protected by life and the world. It often works the opposite. Many times, when we're grieving and vulnerable, the vultures see us and come around pecking. We need to keep our guard up extra high when we're going through grief. Also, it's easy not to care as much when we're grieving, especially if we've lost someone or something important. We've already gone through a loss; we don't need more pain by allowing someone to abuse us. We need to keep up our guard.

CHAPTER 14

Time Changes:
The Empty Nest and Other Rites of Passage

I tried to avoid writing this chapter the way I'm writing it. First I disguised the story so it looked like someone else's. That didn't work. It lost its power—like soda pop without fizz. *I'll eliminate the subject matter from the book entirely*, I thought. *I can have a book about change and loss without covering this topic.* Some people say Boomers are so selfish we don't experience empty-nest syndrome anyway. They say we're so happy to have our lives back to our selfish selves again that we don't care when our children leave home.

While buying into that belief would have given me an out from writing this chapter, I don't buy it. I know too many parents, and whether they're Boomers, Generation X, or Generation Y (why?), the mere thought of having their children leave home makes their hearts ache and some of them have children just starting kindergarten now. I used to tell myself that the empty-nest blues were a crock. *It's something people make up to have another problem to write about*, I thought. *One more thing our mothers use to instill guilt.*

I've been through a lot of big loss. But the reason I didn't want to write this chapter using my own name is that while, yes, I acted out in my grieving periods over other losses (as many of us do), I don't remember being as insane, embarrassing myself as badly, I mean truly making an ass out of myself, the way I did when I joined the *My Children Grew*

Up and Left Home, and I Saw It Coming and I Know They Need to Be Living Their Own Lives, but Honest to God, I Don't Know What to Do with Myself Club.

If you're not a candidate for this club—if you don't have children, aren't interested, or if it doesn't fit whatsoever, you might want to stick around anyway. This story is about more than children growing up and leaving home. It's about honoring the sacred passages that come with the changes time brings to us all.

While there is the occasional parent who is unmoved by having a child, while there are parents who abandon, neglect, and abuse children, most parents agree that having a child is the one thing that universally opens their hearts and affects them like nothing else. (Some childless people say—and this is backed up by polls—that having a pet can open their hearts and activate this maternal or paternal spot too.) Having a child teaches us unconditional love, the absolute joy of giving to and loving someone while expecting nothing in return, the privilege of having a life utterly, naturally, healthily, and entirely dependent on us for its survival and well-being. We center our lives around this child. We sacrifice joyfully. We're glad to make the child first consideration in any choice—whether it's where we live (is it a safe neighborhood and are the schools good enough?), what job we take (will it allow us adequate time at home and to attend events at school?), how we dress (we don't want to embarrass our children, but that comes later when they're teens), or what kind of legacy we leave. More than ever, parents put their children first in every decision they make from the time they conceive until a few years after the child turns twenty-one. Sometimes it starts before conception, with Mom making certain she's in the best possible health and potential parents ensuring that the family finances are solid. With the current cost of living and the need to go to college or obtain some post–high school training, most people no longer consider eighteen the cutoff point. I figured somewhere between twenty-three and twenty-five it was time to cut the cord. It no longer felt appropriate for my daughter to have a fully furnished bedroom in my home. It became *my* house, not *our* house. It didn't feel right to be on call, give her needs top priority. I could say no, and it wasn't abandonment, neglect, or bad parenting. But I'm getting ahead of myself. That didn't happen easily or overnight.

I should have seen it coming. I wasn't a parent who said, "I'm going to keep my children living at home forever no matter what," and I know people who say that. I had a healthy attitude. I knew my job as a parent was to prepare my children to be independent, and that if I did my work well, I would someday be out of a job. But like most big changes, I wasn't prepared for it when it happened. I didn't see the day coming when being a mother wouldn't be a big part of my daily life and who I am.

In self-defense, I claim special circumstances. I closed the deal on the house where Nichole, Shane, and I planned to live out their teenage years the night before Shane died. I was cheated out of a huge chunk of family life. It was ripped away from me without an explanation or apology. I was looking forward to this time. Finally, I wouldn't have the exhausting physical tasks that accompany parenting toddlers and youngsters. My children would be young adults, real people. Fun, lively, interesting people. The end of our time living together as a family was in sight, and I wanted to make every moment count before it was done. Time was already passing faster each year. I savored the idea of living with teenagers. I wanted a swimming pool, a game room, an art room— space enough for us and their friends. Although we'd lived modestly until then, God had blessed me with the funds to do that.

I didn't love everything about teens. Once, I went in my closet to get a blouse I'd bought a few days earlier. I couldn't find the blouse anywhere. I looked for hours, until I thought I'd gone crazy. Had I really bought the blouse at all? Finally I allowed the missing blouse to be a mystery, stopped looking, and wore something else. Two weeks later, one of my daughter's friends strolled into the house wearing my new blouse. My daughter had borrowed it without asking, worn it to her friend's house, then had traded clothes with her friend (common teenage girl behavior)—only the blouse my daughter traded was mine, and I hadn't worn it yet. Yes, my children and I had our moments, but we stood toe to toe with each other in love. It was my commitment to be there for them no matter what.

I divorced their father when the children were six and eight. I never wanted my children to come from a broken home. It broke my heart the night their dad and I told them we were divorcing. Shane went through a year of deep grief. Nichole was older, stronger. She knew things between her dad and I weren't working. Then after Shane died, I was all Nichole had. We didn't have close extended family members. Her dad was still in the throes of alcoholism. Family meant two people: Nichole and me. Years after Shane's death, I wasn't there for Nichole the way I would have liked to have been. I wish I could have done better, but we can't shut off grief the way we shut off a faucet.

"Mom, aren't I enough?" Nichole asked once when I was crying about Shane's death. When she had children of her own, she understood. She also understands she got cheated. But when she was a child, she didn't understand what I was going through, and she shouldn't have had to. It's a parent's job to understand the child (most of the time)—not the other way around. Children despise seeing parents cry. Those years were hard on her. Nichole lost her brother to death, her dad to drinking, and me to grief. About the time I started coming out of my cave, Nichole (then nineteen) invited me to lunch for a talk. We hadn't been living together full-time for a while, but she still had her room at home. She was home more weekends than not. I was her primary emotional and financial support. Being Mom was still a huge part of my life.

That day we ordered lunch. She ate her food like a starving animal, then started in on mine. "I'm moving to New York," she said.

"No, you're not," I said pointing out why moving from L.A. to New York was an impulsive, irresponsible choice.

She interrupted me. "You taught me to live from my heart. You can't tell me to stop doing that now because my heart is telling me to do something you don't like."

This was a moment in time, but it was more than that. It had been coming for years—since she was born—but beginning officially the night of her fourteenth birthday, when I gave her a 35-millimeter camera and a Gucci purse. No more Barbie or Cabbage Patch dolls. She was becoming a young woman. I wasn't God to her. More often than not I was the opposite: "Mom, don't say that. Don't do that, you're embarrassing me!" Moving to New York was the end of a cycle of pushing me away so she could discover who she was. The process had been going on for years, and with that declaration—*I'm moving to New York*—the separation was complete.

If I were looking at anyone else's life, I would have seen the symptoms. I'd go out for dinner with someone, and when they'd ask how I felt, I'd tell them how my daughter felt. I'd talk about her all the time, as if talking about her would create her presence, which it did—for me. In retrospect, it's a classic case of Elisabeth Kübler-Ross's five stages of grief. I wallowed in shock, anger, bargaining, betrayal, and sadness drenched with the martyred *After all I've done to you, how can you do this to me?* I knew better than to say it, but that's how I felt.

"Oh, that's codependency!" I can hear people shouting. But much of codependency is grief—obsession, bestowing sainthood on the missing person, feeling like I lost part of myself. I didn't identify it as grief while it was occurring. I felt so ripped off that just when I was coming alive after living in the underbelly of grief, just when I had my spirit and spunk back, just when I could be a good—maybe great—parent again, it was too late. She was gone. Presto! Snap! That time in our lives was done. And she wasn't moving a block away; she was moving across the country.

Maybe I thought that compared to losing her brother to death, losing her to growing up wasn't a legitimate cause to grieve. For reasons I'm still unsure of, I didn't give grief its due. I didn't honor this passage, this loss. I wasn't conscious of my feelings, my behaviors, or my motivations. I was almost totally unaware of myself. And it's not like I didn't have the skills for self-awareness. I didn't associate the insanity or the volcanic kaleidoscope of emotions with traditional grief. I knew I was upset about her leaving, but I didn't recognize that her growing up and leaving home was a loss, the end to a part of my life that began the moment I knew I was pregnant. I'd told everyone I knew she was a girl, and that was before they had ultrasound photos that show an unborn child's sex. I could feel her the second she began growing in me, and I knew it was her.

It was the end to that gulp, that moment of claustrophobic panic coupled with performance anxiety that began when I brought her home from the hospital and stared into the eyes of this little stranger—who without any embarrassment screamed in outrage until she was fed to her satisfaction, not mine—and realized she was going to be right there by my side for the next twenty-one years. My life no longer belonged to me; it belonged to her, and I'd only met her a moment ago. Now I was spending the next two decades with her under my wing? I was so panicky, such a perfectionist. I'd boil her bottles and the nipples. If anything even touched the nipples while they were drying, I'd start the sanitization process over from step one.

By the time Shane was born, I was so relaxed that if I dropped his bottle, I'd wipe the nipple clean on my shirt. But having Nichole, then her brother, changed my life unalterably and permanently. You can't leave the house anymore to go to the store. You can't stay out late on Friday night. You can't take off on a whim. You can barely have a phone conversation because the second you do, the children start doing all the things they're not supposed to do because they know you'll either ignore them, scream in front of whomever you're talking to (which you probably won't do), or stop the conversation (which is what they want you to do). They gain control. Every decision, everything you do centers around this tiny stranger. And when you hold that child close, the first time she says "Mama" or smiles or says "I love you," you know you wouldn't want one second of your freedom back—not for anything in the world. Your life has irrevocably changed, but you wouldn't have it any other way. You are truly in love.

I couldn't get my bearings. I lost my center.

It started as a Web site. People were bugging me about how I needed one, how all authors should have one. I was living in a one-room castle at an artist's community in Rancho Palos Verdes, California. I had been renting a beach house in Malibu, but when my year lease was up, the landlord would only let me stay month to month. This after I'd painted the house, rewired it, had the house featured in *Elle Decor*, and substantially upgraded the property at my expense and with her approval. I hadn't caught on to California culture yet. It's different from Minnesota. A monthly lease felt too unstable, like I could be ousted in a moment if she decided to sell the house (which I'd heard she was going to do).

Then something told me to move immediately. It was a gut feeling. Months later, El Niño washed the entire cottage into the ocean. Gone. The house disappeared. For the first time, when I moved, I didn't have anyplace to go. For the first time in the twenty-some years since I'd gotten sober, it didn't matter where I lived. I didn't have children at home, didn't have to think about schools. My life, my future, was a big blank spot.

If someone had pointed out I was going through empty-nest syndrome and I should be careful—if someone had sat me down and said, "Melody, you're going insane with grief so protect yourself"—maybe things would have been different. But nobody did, and Miss Self-Help was about to turn into a loose cannon.

I didn't need more room than the one-room studio on the Rancho Palos Verdes estate. There was one of me now. There were peacocks wandering the grounds, screeching and pooping. It was eclectic and bohemian. The woman who owned it ran Friends of French Art. It was an odd time in my life. I traveled with a busload of eighty-year-olds around southern France and lived in my citadel that didn't have any heat, just a wood-burning fireplace in the middle of one room I called home. I didn't have connections in Rancho Palos Verdes, no real reason to be there. But then, I had no reason to be anywhere else.

Shortly before moving to Rancho Palos Verdes, I'd made a new friend in Malibu. Carl worked at a boutique there (but lived in West Hollywood). He was a new age product salesman at the boutique—crystals, oils, talismans—and he was an intuitive, a hypnotist, a clairvoyant. He also sold clothing at the boutique and had a knack for helping you choose the perfect outfit for any event. He'd drive to Rancho Palos Verdes to see me every week, but other than that, I felt isolated and alone. After I grew up and left home (I was the youngest in the family), I remember my mother talking about the years she drove around homeless (she actually owned three or four houses at the time) with her suitcases in the car, staying at one or the other of her children's homes and mumbling about how life wasn't worth living. She thought she was dying and repeatedly asked when was I coming back home after running away.

"I didn't run away, Mother. I got an apartment. I turned eighteen."

"You ran away."

"No, I moved out. There's a difference."

Actually, I waited until twelve hours after I turned eighteen, came home on my lunch hour from school, and took my belongings to an apartment I rented the month before. I owned a car (that I paid for myself). I had a good job even though I was still in high school and was an active alcoholic and addict. I was running, yes. I was running from home and myself. But that's another story, and I didn't run away from home. I legally left. My mother waited years for me to come back; she's ninety-two and she's still waiting. She was from the Great Depression generation. The Boomers discovered feelings—identified them (emotions have always been around). But we decided what to call them and we learned how important they are, although what exactly we do with them is something we're still trying to figure out. The point is my mother's generation didn't have a clue about feelings, which made grieving more difficult for them to do.

When Nichole moved out, I understood my mother. I wasn't homeless, but I felt like I was. That's how we feel when we don't have a center. I had no reason to call anyplace home. I didn't have a family anymore. I had only me. I didn't understand that when we lose someone we love, we lose part of our identity. Sure, I'd be Nichole's mom until I died, and then I'd still be her mom after that. But the part of my life that was dedicated to being her mom ended. She called once a week. We'd talk a few minutes. It wasn't like it used to be. She wasn't consulting me about her decisions. I wasn't her support system. She didn't need me anymore, and God that hurt.

Because I'm a writer, it doesn't matter where I live. All I need is electricity, a bed, and a table, which I had at the artist's estate. That's when I decided to construct a Web site. It would be a good project for me to work on since I wasn't writing a book at the time. While I was constructing the Web site, I got an idea: Instead of opening a bookstore online, which is what my Web site would have been, why didn't I open a bookstore for real?

From the day I started thinking about the bookstore, I started calling it my baby. I didn't associate it with the empty-nest syndrome. I didn't see that I was frantically and desperately trying to replace something I lost. All I knew was that if I started a bookstore, I would have someplace to be every day, something that needed me, a reason to live, and a reason to live somewhere. I'd have a center again. I didn't stop to consider things like leases, business plans, projections, what it would take to make a profit, employees. I asked Carl to help me. He said he would. We went to the owner of the boutique where he worked in Malibu. She had a second floor that was unused. How about if I sublet from the boutique and put a bookstore up there?

The Loose Cannon fired its first shot.

I'm not a merchant. Running my business as a writer means getting story ideas, negotiating contracts, researching, writing, editing. That's different from running a store. Carl didn't have a business background either. We were both in over our heads. Three hundred thousand dollars and two locations later, I closed the bookstore. My *baby* didn't survive. I had no training in how to manage employees, deal with things like shoplifting and theft. By the time I closed the store, according to the employees, the bookstore was taking in $300 a month and I was spending $5,000 a month to keep it alive. When landslides closed the main artery into Malibu and the Department of Transportation announced it would be a year before the road opened, I closed the store. A store isn't a baby. The owner needs to get something back: money. You need enough profits to know that the business is worthwhile, needed, breathing, surviving.

"Why didn't you stop me?" I asked Carl.

"I thought it was a good idea," he said, "at the time."

I thought closing the bookstore broke my heart, but my empty nest was what was causing the pain. There's a period of being lost, of floundering around in the unknown that we go through after any loss. The old is finished. The new hasn't formed. It took a week to close the bookstore. We worked fast. Carl helped me find someone to take over the lease. I lost a lot of money and time.

Grief goes on whether we're conscious of it or not. It's better to be aware. It still hurts. But if we're conscious, at least we know why we're doing some of the things we're doing. When we're not consciously grieving, instead of feeling our feelings, we begin acting them out. Going insane with grief is more than a cliché. It's something people do.

The Loose Cannon was about to fire its next shot.

I should have known better. I violated common sense. Someone should have been made temporary guardian of me. I should not have been allowed to make my own decisions. It cost more money, time, and pride.

I met Roger at a deli. A friend asked me to speak at a meeting in Santa Monica. After the speaking engagement, a group of us went out to eat. Mutual friends introduced us. He asked for a date and I said yes. Something about walking on the Santa Monica Pier with the Ferris wheel going 'round and the waves lapping and cotton candy and by the end of the day we decided, *We're in love. This was destiny. We were God's gift to each other for all the pain we'd been through.* Because of our ages, we didn't have time to waste. It was now or never, so it was *now*.

Carl got tears in his eyes when I tried on my wedding gown. Other than him, everyone knew I was making a mistake. Even C. J., the gossip columnist from the *Minneapolis Star Tribune*, knew I was self-destructing, and she was half a country away. I was shopping for honeymoon clothes in a boutique on Sunset Boulevard when my cell phone rang.

"It's C. J." she said. "I hear you're getting married."

I said yes. "How long have you known this guy?" she asked. "You can date someone for years and not know the person or if it's right." She talked about an article she'd read that said people could hide parts of themselves from each other for up to five years, and had I given myself enough time?

I tiptoed around the question. When you've done enough media interviews, you learn how to ignore the question you're asked and answer any question you want. Controlling the direction of the conversation, it's called.

My daughter was beside herself with annoyance. "You know you're making a mistake," she said. "Please, please don't do this."

"You aren't living with me. What difference does it make who I'm with or what I do? It doesn't affect your life. You moved out, moved on," I said sounding like my mother. "You just don't want me to be happy, have a life of my own. You want me sitting by the phone waiting for your call."

We got married in Larry Hagman's mansion (Larry was J. R. on *Dallas*). A rabbi presided. Nichole stood next to me the entire time, whispering loudly: "It's not too late. Don't do this. Stop yourself. Please." During the ceremony, the rabbi asked her if she wanted to say a few words. She glared at me and said no. My husband and I stomped on the glass wrapped in velvet to shouts of mazel tov. I wept tears of joy. The groom did too. Then we flew off in a private jet.

Before the jet landed, I was ill. I was dizzy, nauseated. The room was spinning. I couldn't get my bearings. *Dear God, what have I done?* I took to my bed the entire honeymoon, and not for the reason honeymooners do. A month later, the courts granted us an annulment.

"Why didn't you stop me?" I screamed at Carl.

"You looked so beautiful in your wedding dress," was his reply.

"I told you so," my daughter said.

I could say that anyone can open a business that goes belly-up. I could say any woman can get swept off her feet and get married. Then I could add that opening a bookstore was something I always wanted to do and I deserved one beautiful wedding. The truth is, it was all about me not wanting to let go.

I'd spent my whole life looking for a family. The family I was born into was a way to get to this planet, but that family didn't work. My mom says I came along late in life—unplanned, unwanted—and burdened her. She was already the single parent of three children whose father had died. Now my father left and she had to raise me alone? I felt bad that she had to be strapped with me when that wasn't what she wanted. Then I'd had my first son, John, when I was an addict and didn't know how to be a mother. All I could give him was life by not having him aborted, and peace by stopping the custody battle and giving custody up. When I married David, then Nichole and Shane came along, that was all I ever wanted. I had a family that loved and needed me, a family whose members could depend on each other no matter what. Our family was a safe, loving place to be. We were soulmates, kindred spirits. I was the luckiest woman in the world. I wasn't looking for my children to take care of and love me. From the day my children were born, I was happy to love and take care of them. To be their mom was a privilege and an honor.

Sure, we had problems with David's drinking, then a painful divorce. It took a few months to regroup after the divorce, but we did. We became a real family again. Then Shane died. It got dark with some iffy moments, but now when I finally come out of my darkness and can make our family work, family time is done?

I didn't want to let Nichole and this part of my life go.

I was talking to a friend. She had a tough time when her first marriage ended. She went downhill fast, and people didn't get it. Ultimately my friend survived, came through it. Now years have passed, and she's facing a possible separation in another relationship. "It's different this time," she said. "Back then when I got divorced, I felt like, who am I going to live my life for? Just me? That wasn't enough. This time I know if my fiancé and I don't get back together again, living life for me is enough."

I had Nichole three years after I got sober. Shane came along two years later. There wasn't that much of me when I first got sober and clean. The children became my reason to live, work, and make a good life. When the house burned down or David got drunk or we were dirt poor, I had those babies to keep me going. They depended on me and I gladly stepped up to the plate. I made a good life for them and a good life for me. After ten years of watching David botch our finances and thinking, *I can do better than that*, I did. One panic attack and three months of uncertainty later, I got my feet on the ground, and with God's help, made a great life for us. We were four, then three, then two. Now there was one. Me. Living alone. Like my friend said, what was I going to do—live life for myself?

That's when I started to see. I'd been running from the emptiness, the aloneness. Compared to the grief about Shane dying, this wasn't big. But it was grief and I'd been in it. I remembered the beginning when I had two babies in diapers and almost no help from my husband. It was like having three children. I was tired. My babies were good babies, but I was exhausted for years. My codependency complicated life, made it hurt. I loved those years, loved being a mom. But I seldom hired a sitter or left the house the first six years after my children were born. I could hardly go into the bathroom without one or both of them tagging along. As my life changed and I started earning more money, I hired a housekeeper and nanny, but even then when I traveled, I brought my children along whenever I could. Now, what I had done for them I was going to have to do for myself. No matter what *they* say—whoever *they* are—*that Boomers are so selfish we don't care when our children leave,* it was the second biggest heartbreak of my life when I realized family time as I'd known it was done.

Recognizing I was going through the empty-nest blues helped. When I surrendered to my sadness and let myself feel lost, the Loose Cannon stopped firing shots.

My daughter got married and had two children. She became a mom. Our relationship is better than ever. I see how important that apart time was. It let us each grow into our new selves. When I stopped clinging to Nichole, she enjoyed coming around me. Then she started begging me to move in with her. The thought was sweet, but that would be chasing our losses—something that rarely works. Nichole will always be my daughter. But I'm not a full-time mom anymore. I started living life for me. Once I started, I didn't want to stop. My center is where it belongs—in myself.

I began doing things I couldn't do when I had young children. I traveled around the United States, then the world—Paris, Algeria, Bali, Pakistan, the Sinai Peninsula, Israel, China, Tibet, the pyramids of Egypt. I studied martial arts, began hiking and skydiving. I learned to fly (but not land) a plane. One thing I'd never done was live with roommates, so I bought a cabin by the drop zone in Lake Elsinore—the Blue Sky Lodge—and filled it with roommate skydivers. We'd sit around campfires and have parties with parachutists training there from all over the world. It was one of the most fun times in my life. Just because a time in our lives that we loved ends doesn't mean all the fun is over.

That time eventually came to pass too. Everything has a beginning, middle, and end. Everything has its season. We can try to hang on, but when times change, it's not the same. When things fulfill their purpose, it's better to let them go. One day it was time to sell the Blue Sky Lodge. I cried when I packed up the last boxes. My roommate Andy wouldn't admit it, but I saw tears in his eyes too.

When we consciously grieve and honor these passages, we stop racing around trying to fill the empty spaces. We make better decisions. Replacing what we've lost before we face our feelings about the loss may not work out the way we planned. We may wake up one day and be horrified about something we've done.

Time brings changes to things, life, us. The first time we let go of Mom's hand and stay by ourselves at school. Graduation. Getting married or divorced. The one thing we have in common with everyone is we're all getting older. It comforts me to watch all the entertainers and musicians from my time aging. It feels like we're all in it together. We see some people desperately trying to hold on to youth; their smiles are pulled to their ears. Others handle it with grace.

On the other end, I see some people give up and completely stop taking care of themselves. Deep down, I think everyone in the *I'm*

Getting Older Club feels about the same. Although people talked openly about other losses for this book, people didn't want to talk about getting old. Maybe there's not that much to say. When we're young, we want to be older. Then we hit a peak, and from that day on, we want to be young. I used to envy the gorgeousness of youth. Now I see the beauty of age. There is a richness and depth that comes with maturity, and not just in the men—women have it too. It's like the difference between a bud and a fully opened rose. They're both beautiful in their own time. I was in my chiropractor's office one day when the receptionist asked us each if we wanted to draw a thought-for-the-day card. We did. The card she drew read: "I am exactly the age I'm meant to be."

Each decade has its own feel. Just when we feel like we've got things dialed in, times change again. In her book *New Passages*, Gail Sheehy talks about a second adulthood. When we were young, we thought about what we wanted to do when we grew up. Now with extended life expectancy, we face what we want to do when we grow up the second time. Many people need to have not one, but two careers. We can stop working in our fifties or sixties, but some people aren't fulfilled by retiring. Many need to continue earning money. Some people decide to start another family. We can fill our nest and lives any way we want.

When I went to Grandparents and Special Friends Day at my grandson's school, I looked around and thought, *This is a room full of old codgers*. Then I thought, *I'm one of them*. One day, I woke up and the first thought that crossed my mind was *In thirteen years I'm going to be seventy!* I didn't need coffee that morning; after that thought I was wide awake.

Something important happens when we realize we're not immortal. In Korea, when a person turns sixty, a party is thrown for him or her. The celebration is a reminder that this person has lived a full life, and from now on each day is a gift—it's time to make the most of what's left. One woman's theory is that when we hit our fifties, our bodies become like a used car with a lot of mileage. We either get it fixed and keep driving it—sometimes replacing big parts—or we total it and decide we're done. I spent much of my fifties getting the car repaired. My friend thinks we consciously choose how long we'll stick around.

One Thanksgiving, friends from Minnesota came out to Los Angeles to visit my daughter and me. One of the girls who lived on our block back in the seventies—who I babysat—now has a baby of her own. I held her baby and I felt this glow. I realized what it was. Babies just came from God. They've got God dust all over them. When we hold them, a little God rubs off on us. A woman was talking to me about her mom. Her mom is getting old now—in her eighties. She has Alzheimer's disease. My friend thinks her mom is getting ready to go soon because she doesn't recognize her daughter. But her mom keeps saying she sees her own mom, who's been dead a long time. My friend believes her mom really does see her mother. When we're first born, we've just come from God, and as we age, we move back toward Him. We start getting God dust on us again.

We give so much love and attention to children in our culture. Maybe we could take some of that love and give it to old people too.

A friend's mother is in her seventies. Her health is poor. She doesn't like to complain. It's not in her nature, but I know life is hard for her. During the winter she stays cooped up for months; she's too frail to be outdoors. She's on a limited budget and some months barely survives. She watches her pennies so she can leave a little something for her children when she dies.

"I think about dying a lot," she says. "Some days I wish death would come. I don't know why God wants to keep me around. I'm not doing anything with my life. I can't work anymore. Sometimes I can barely walk from the couch to my bed. I'm not sure what my purpose is or if I have one." This woman's mother was one of the first women to join Alcoholics Anonymous in the state where she lives. This woman herself is a recovering alcoholic and addict. Now she has several chronic physical problems and lives in a lot of pain. "I have to take pain medicine every day," she says. "For a long time, I felt guilty about it." She's not abusing the medication, but she comes from a fundamentalist recovery background. It was hard for her to give herself permission to take what she needs. Many aging recovering alcoholics and addicts are facing this issue. They need the drugs they used to take to get high to have any quality of life. We shouldn't have to suffer because we're old.

It's normal to feel lost when we go through a passage, when the old normal disappears and the new normal hasn't arrived. It's okay to walk around feeling uncomfortable. It helps us, being a little on edge.

A friend was talking about her daughter becoming a junior in high school and how they were starting the process of searching for a college. "We don't know where to begin. There's so much to choose from," she said. "I feel lost, overwhelmed. It's this whole new world and I don't know my way around it."

I told her what my friend's father said, "Just select one college and one major. If you don't like it, you can change. Once you start moving, you'll be guided. Besides," I said, "you're not there yet. We feel overwhelmed when we try to do tomorrow today because we don't have the grace for it yet."

"Oh, that's it," she said. "I've got to walk into the mystery. I've got to go into the unknown."

A man was telling me about his nephew—one of the first people to get AIDS back in the early eighties, before the medicine came out that turned AIDS from a death sentence into something that can be lived with. His nephew was in the hospital and probably not coming home. "Do you want me to get you some pills so you have control over this?" the uncle asked. "So you can choose when you're going to go if it gets too bad?"

"Thanks, but no thanks," his nephew said. "I don't want to miss one minute of this. It's the last experience I'm going to have."

Life is good to the last drop. The Jewish religion has many traditions to honor passages—from mourning to mitzvahs. Other cultures have festivals and rituals. We have a lot of holidays in the United States—two or three a month. Don't miss the true holy days—the rites of passage we all go through. Respect and honor your grief. Say good-bye to the old. Thank it for what it has given you. Remember it with fondness. Then open to the new.

When times change, it's time to do something else.

Baby Boomers are the 78 million people born when the U.S. population boomed after World War II—anyone born between 1946 and 1965.

Generation X (those born between 1966 and 1982) follows the Boomers.

X is followed by Y (Why?) (those born from 1983 to 2003).

Boomers compose more than one-third of the U.S. population.

The first Boomers began turning 60 in 2006.

Every 7.5 seconds, one Baby Boomer turns 50.

In the United States, almost 60 percent of 22- to 24-year-olds are living at home.

About 30 percent of 25- to 29-year-olds live at home.

Ninety percent of adult children living at home are single.

About twice as many young men as women live with their parents.

Most parents whose adult children (19 to 34) live at home are happy with the arrangement.

An adult child's unemployment or financial dependency on the parent increases chances of conflict.

If the adult child is divorced, separated, or has a baby with him or her, parents are less satisfied with the living arrangement.

In 2000, there were 600 million people 60 or older worldwide.

There will be 1.2 billion people 60 or older worldwide by 2025 and 2 billion people 60 or older by 2050.

In the developed world, people deemed "very old" (80 or older) belong to the fastest growing population group.

People who are elderly currently represent around 20 percent of the world's population and by 2020 will be 25 percent.

In North America, by 2020, the proportion of the population that is over age 60 is projected to reach 23 percent.

Sources: Boomers International; Armin Brott, author of *Father for Life* and host of *Positive Parenting*, a national weekly talk show; and the World Health Organization

ACTIVITIES

1. Celebrate your rites of passage. Are you going through a passage now? Take the time to recognize and honor it. Throw a party for yourself. Your normal is changing. It's common to feel lost for a while. Give yourself some slack, some room to wander about in the mystery and let your new life take shape and form. Have a private celebration. Go out to dinner with a friend and tell your friend the purpose of the dinner—that you want to honor this change in your life. Buy new clothes. Rearrange your home. Make a photograph album of pictures and remembrances from the time in your life that's passing. Or do some writing about that part of your life. Write a story. It doesn't have to be for publication—it can be just for you. Or it *can* be for publication—who knows? But tell the story about the chapter in your life that's coming to a close. Telling our story is a secret to getting through any change. We need to find a way to say good-bye to what we're leaving and hello to what's ahead. If you get stuck or find yourself having a difficult time

going through a change, ask for help. Talk to other people; find out how they're handling this time in their lives. It'll help validate how you feel, and you may be able to help someone else.

2. Help create the next part of your life. Although many things are out of our control, we can help create our lives by intention, desire, goals, and honoring the dreams in our heart. Life has an adventure in store for us. So you're in a passage. The old is passing away. What are some things you can do now that you couldn't before? Maybe there were limitations in the last part of your life that no longer apply—for instance, the limitations that come with having children. When they leave, we're free to do things that didn't fit before. Make a list of all the things you can do. Also, with every new circumstance come challenges and limitations. One of the ironies of life is that by the time we hit our fifties and sixties, we have wisdom, but our bodies may be banged and scuffed up. They're not twenty-year-old bodies. What are the limitations you have now, the things you need to work around? It's important to add our input into these times of transition. Living in the mystery—that time when the next part hasn't formed—is an important time to focus on what we want. Make a list of what you'd like to happen next.

3. Choose how you want to handle aging. We have the freedom to do many things that were taboo, impossible, or reserved for the elite before. Having plastic surgery or replacing knees, hips, discs—we can fix or replace many body parts that wear out. Some people give up when they age. They don't care if they put on weight. They don't care what they look like. They don't take care of their skin. They lose interest in working out. There are forms of physical exercise—even walking—that we can do our entire lives. Yoga and some martial arts such as tai chi are great ways to keep our energy vital. Make a commitment to take great care of yourself. You might want to get a few nips and tucks to reverse what gravity has done. There are noninvasive ways to smooth out the effects of time. Motorized indoor and outdoor chairs are available and in many cases paid for by Medicare for people losing their mobility.

Explore options. Decide what's right for you. We have the right to be as mobile and look and feel as good as we can.

4. Get a 500,000-mile checkup. Some people go to the doctor every year. Some get slack about checking in with the physician. When we hit our fifties, it's normal for parts to break. Stay on top of your physical health; know what's going on so you can catch problems as soon as—or before—they begin.

5. Make plans for your second adulthood. Some people are happy to retire. Others want to work. Is there a second career you're interested in pursuing now that your first career is done? Find out what you what to do after you grow up again.

6. Get your affairs in order. Have a will and a living will. We can use inexpensive home kits to make our last wishes known. There's a power that comes when we face our death. We realize the importance of today.

7. If you're young, begin preparing for your future now. I know many older people who wish they would have made plans for old age. They thought it would never get here, or they'd die before the day came. Now it's here, and they don't have enough. When we're young is the best time to create a nest egg to help with that time in life. Start putting money away and don't touch it until that day comes. Depending on Social Security alone is putting ourselves in a vulnerable, iffy predicament. It may not be enough to pay for survival expenses or even a minimal-quality life.

8. People are coming up with innovative options for living their later years. Some nonprofit organizations are creating co-ops in their neighborhoods, making services such as home nursing and help with cooking, transportation, shopping, and cleaning available and affordable so people can continue to live in their homes. Other elderly people are getting together and designing their own co-op retirement home with common

and private areas. They sold their homes, and together they're building their own retirement building. Members are designing the home and running it themselves.

9. Are you an empty nester? Are you hanging on to your children, trying to make them feel guilty for leaving home? Are you going through grief? I ran into a woman when I was out doing errands. She was working at a store I was shopping in, and we began talking about the empty-nest blues. She said she'd been home taking care of her children for the last twenty years, but now she was suddenly out in the world and she felt shaky and lost. She didn't know that much about computers, technology, how the world worked. She didn't recognize the world because it had changed so much. This was her second week on the job.

If you're going through empty-nest syndrome, be gentle with yourself, but let the birds go if they're not baby birds anymore. Begin to live life for yourself. This is a time when you can make what you want and need come first. There's a difference between being selfishly self-centered and having our centers in ourselves. Some people have the opposite problem. Their children are forty or fifty years old and still live at home. In some cases, that may be okay—we get to chose our normal and our rules—but if you're not okay with it, it may be time to get the scissors out and cut that cord. Decide on an appropriate cutting-off point. Give them notice in advance: After such and such a date, I'm not supporting you anymore. It's time for you to be on your own.

Take the time to consciously honor your grief when you go through the passage of your children growing up and leaving home. Write in a journal about it. I've heard women talk about how making a scrapbook helped when their children graduated and left home; my sister-in-law Pam did it. She enjoyed it, and it helped. Talk to someone who will listen and understand. Your feelings are valid—all of them, from anger to loneliness to feeling lost, desperate, panicky, or misunderstood. Remember not to expect your children to understand what you're going through. Many children feel guilty when their parents feel sad. Telling them about how you feel may cause them to respond defensively or with anger. They'll have plenty of time to learn about the empty nest when they go through it themselves. We're the parents, and it's our responsibility to take care of ourselves while we go through the sacred passages of life.

CHAPTER 15

Cheap Change:
When It Really Could Have Been Worse

I had a list of errands: acupuncturist in the Valley, back to town, then stop at the grocery store, the drugstore, and the post office. Oh, and stop by Coffee Bean too. Just as I pulled into my parking spot in back of the house, my car's *check tire pressure* warning light came on. I had concerns about one of the tires; I wasn't sure if it had a slow leak, but I'd taken it in, and the guys at the station said it was fine. I hoped it wasn't *that* again. I hated not knowing if I had a tire problem or not. What you don't want in L.A. is a flat on a freeway.

I checked the front driver's side tire, then worked my way around the car. By the time I got to the rear passenger side, I heard it. *Hissssssssssssss.* It sounded like a balloon losing air. That baby was going flat fast.

I lugged the sacks of groceries into the house. Erica, my house-keeper, was working in the kitchen. "I must have driven over a nail or something," I said. "Just when I pulled in the driveway, my tire went flat."

"*Te salio barato,*" Erica said.

"What?"

"*Te salio barato* means you had a cheap lesson." She fumbled for the right words so I'd understand. "You've been driving all over—on the freeways, the canyon road, right? You didn't get the flat tire until you were safe at home. *Te salio barato* means 'it could have been a lot worse.'"

Sometimes a loss is a mere irritation or annoyance. On other occasions, the universe is trying to grab our attention. Life gives us a warning, a reminder to be more careful in an area where we're becoming lax. We get a *heads-up* call. Other times, no matter what we say or how much we strive to maintain a positive attitude, we're going through a big loss. But when we're done going through our grief, we step back and see our experience in a different light. What follows is a series of vignettes from people who earned their membership in the *It Could Have Been a Worse Nightmare Than It Was* Club.

Claire doesn't date married men. It was a fluke when she got involved with Ben. He was legally separated from his wife when she met him. His wife was in treatment for drugs and alcohol. Ben and his wife had had several breakups, but this was their first legal separation. Ben was clear. The marriage was over. This was the fourth time his wife had gone into treatment. Even if she got sober, she'd probably relapse again, he said. And even if she didn't relapse, the damage had been done. His wife had been unfaithful.

Ben and Claire met at an art show in Santa Monica. They were introduced by a mutual friend. It wasn't love at first sight, at least not for Claire. She found Ben interesting and thought of him as a friend. They started seeing each other on easygoing, casual dates. In the beginning, Claire didn't consider the time she and Ben spent together to be dating. They would watch television together at his house or hers. Or they'd go for lunch. Some Saturdays, they'd go out for brunch, then walk around the Third Street Promenade. Ben had a great job as a cameraman—he was called a director's favorite by some. Claire wrote screenplays and was well-established in the industry.

Claire isn't sure when they slipped over the line from friendship to romance, but one night their relationship *definitely* changed. Claire suspected Ben felt more than friendship toward her from the beginning. Maybe she was too naive to see it. However or whenever it happened, their relationship turned into a steamy love affair.

Ben traveled frequently for work—four to six times a year, sometimes domestically, but often overseas. About six months after they met, Ben called Claire and said they needed to talk. Claire knew something was up by the tone in his voice. Ben calmly explained that his soon-to-be ex-wife had begged him, pleaded with him, to stop the divorce. She was sober for seven months, planned to stay that way, and wanted to work on their marriage.

"I hate to pull the rug out from under you—out from under us," Ben said. "But she's my wife. I brought her here from Savannah, Georgia. I owe her that much. If she's using, drinking, carrying on—well, then I have a right to walk away. But she's changed. This time it looks like it's for good. Please understand," Ben said. "It's not that I don't love you. I do. But I'm her husband. There's a commitment there, one I take seriously. I'm so sorry."

Claire was shocked, hurt, and angry. She could see that Ben was being controlled by guilt—not love. At least that's the way it looked to her. But there was nothing she could do. It broke her heart, losing Ben. She couldn't shut off her love just because he was done. In a strange way, she respected his decision. Marriage is a commitment. Ben was doing the honorable thing—even though it meant hurting her.

A year and a half passed. Claire dated other men, went on with her life, but she didn't stop loving and caring about Ben. Rarely did a day go by when thoughts of him didn't cross her mind. They talked on the phone a few times. They didn't have any clandestine meetings. Ben had made his choice clear. They talked as friends. Their friendship had been an important part of their love. When they talked, Ben said his marriage was up and down. Claire had the distinct impression that things weren't going great. But the last thing she wanted to do was talk to him about his wife.

Then one day, Ben called and announced that this time he and his wife were breaking up for good. He'd given it his best shot. Now he could walk away with a clear conscience. He still loved Claire, and if she'd give him another chance, he wanted—more than anything in the world—to be with her.

Claire didn't jump into Ben's arms, but after a while, she gave in. The only thing keeping her away was pride. But she went in with her eyes wide open and her foot on the brakes. She wasn't going head over heels this time. She didn't trust Ben not to jerk the rug out from under her again. But as weeks passed, then months, Claire slowly took the protective wrapping off her heart. She'd never been this happy in a relationship. There was something ultraintense about losing Ben, then getting him back again. Their love was gentle—quiet nights at home watching movies on TV, going for walks on the beach. Sometimes he'd read to Claire from a favorite book. Or they'd listen to their favorite music relaxing in each other's arms. They talked for hours about spirituality, philosophy, life experiences. They both enjoyed staying at home. Sometimes she'd cook for them, but just as often Ben would cook for her. Claire was in love.

Ben had been talking lately about moving in together, even hinting about getting married. Claire could tell he was testing the water, trying to see what her response would be. She had a feeling he was planning on buying her an engagement ring. His divorce would soon be final. Ben's was an uncomplicated divorce—no fault, nothing was contested, no children involved. Still, Claire wasn't ready for marriage. For now, living together was starting to sound good, like something she wanted. They were together most nights anyway. This driving back and forth was getting old. But it wasn't just that. It felt natural being together.

Her thirty-eighth birthday was coming up soon. Ben was going to be out of town on that date; he was going on location overseas. Claire decided that when Ben got back, she'd surprise him. She'd say yes, she was ready to move in.

Claire wasn't the jealous, snoopy, possessive type. But when Ben was on location this time, Claire got a feeling in her gut, and it didn't feel good. It wasn't just a feeling. There was something in Ben's voice. She could tell. *I don't know if he thinks he's smart or I'm stupid or both,* Claire thought, *but I know guilt when I hear it, and guilt is dripping from his voice.* Call it women's intuition, Claire knew Ben was fooling around with someone else. She didn't suspect. She knew.

Claire wasn't one of these young things who could be manipulated. She didn't judge those young, pliable women—she used to be one. In her younger years, she had been as codependent as they come. But she'd read the books, gone to meetings. There was a time when she was so blind she could walk in on a man who was with another woman, and she would let him talk her out of believing what she saw. It was the classic *What are you going to believe? What you see? Or me?* And she'd believe the man instead of her own eyes. She was that naive, easy to manipulate, and willing to avoid pain. But that was a long time ago. No more! She'd worked hard on herself over the years. Claire learned the art of trusting herself. She wasn't prone to jumping the gun either.

What Ben didn't know was that Claire knew one of the writers on location on this film. She was a friend of Claire's. Claire wasn't into playing detective, stalking, or that whole going-crazy-getting-information-in-a-codependent-way thing. But she had a right to know if there was something happening that directly affected her. Infidelity isn't only a matter of betrayal. STDs are serious business. Claire was fanatical about monogamy; today it was the only way to be. Claire didn't want to take the chance of being with someone who might be fooling around. It was too potentially damaging to her physical and emotional health.

Claire called the friend who was working on the movie location. She left a message on her voice mail at home. When Claire's friend called her back, Claire asked her straight-out if Ben was carrying on with anybody on the film. "This isn't a matter of being a tattletale," Claire said to her friend. "I don't want to sleep with this man if he's sleeping around. It's a matter of life and death. And don't worry. I won't say how I found out. I'm strong enough to say I believe it because I trust my instincts."

Her friend took a deep breath. From that sound alone, Claire knew the answer was yes. Ben had met a local woman one night when he and some of the guys went out on the town. They'd been having a little "thing" ever since. Sometimes the woman visited Ben at the set. There were times when Claire's friend bumped into Ben and the woman at the hotel downtown. Claire felt like someone had fired a bullet straight into her heart.

Happy birthday to me, Claire thought when she hung up the phone. *Great present: Finding out the love of my life, the man I'm on the verge of getting engaged to, is a dog.* She went out for dinner the next night with friends to celebrate her birthday. Halfway through eating, Claire burst into tears. She cried herself to sleep at night, she cried first thing in the morning. Before she started crying in the morning, her eyes felt wet, like she'd been crying in her sleep.

Ben denied it at first. Claire didn't feed into him, his indignation, his pledge of undying love. Claire knew better. She'd been through similar scenes too many times years ago. She knew how easy it was to give in and believe what you wanted to hear. Thank God she'd gone through her raving codependent days—well, *years*—already and had that lesson under her belt. She trusted the friend who gave her the information. Her friend wouldn't lie. She didn't have any reason or motive to break her and Ben up. Claire trusted herself.

Finally, in a roundabout, wishy-washy way, Ben *kind of* confessed. He didn't come out and say he did it, but he stopped acting indignant and stopped denying it happened. People with any sense at all know not to confess to cheating. There's nothing to be gained in most situations by telling that to a person you love.

Claire would have preferred it if Ben had come clean, but it didn't matter anyway. Claire was done. It took about eight months before Claire's heart healed from this betrayal. It went deep. Ben rubbed salt into the wound by having it happen on her birthday and right before she was going to move in and commit to him. But as the months passed, Claire began to see the situation differently. Yes, it hurt. She lost a relationship that was important to her. But what if she hadn't found out, had moved in, and then married him?

Claire knew a woman who was in the midst of a living nightmare. This woman had only slept with two men—her first husband, whom she divorced, then a boyfriend of six years. She'd left this relationship because she discovered her boyfriend was cheating on her. Now this woman had just tested positive for HIV. She knew where she got it— from her ex-boyfriend. HIV isn't an automatic death sentence anymore, but people would rather live without it than with it—especially if someone you love gave it to you as part of a betrayal.

"What I went through was heartbreaking. It was the most painful birthday of my life," Claire said. "I'll be leery of men for a while—maybe a long time." Claire started crying a little, the way people do when they tap into grief that still hurts. Then she stopped herself. "Honestly? I've never been that happy with a man before. The whole thing was an ordeal that I'd prefer to not have gone through. But what if I'd moved in, married him, and then this happened? What if I'd had a child and then he'd been unfaithful? Or what if I trusted him and, like my friend, got an STD? I'm not grateful it happened, but if it had to happen, I'm glad it happened when it did, and I'm grateful I trusted myself.

"Even though it was a nightmare, it could have been worse."

Roger smokes cigars. He knows he *shouldn't* smoke at all—secondhand smoke, not politically correct. Anyone who's alive knows what people say about smoking. "In defense of myself, Melody," he says, "it's the only vice I've got. People need to do *something*. It (doing something) is part of being human, part of being alive. I know people who eat sugar, overeat, do other things. I'm a good, decent guy. My one vice—and I intend to keep it—is smoking cigars."

Roger has a few favorite television shows. He owns his own business, a restaurant. He works hard, six days a week. He often works late into the night. He TiVo's (an electronic system that sets the television to automatically record) his favorite shows. After the restaurant closes, he likes to have a delicious meal to end the day. Then he likes to go home, get in bed, and watch his favorite shows until he falls asleep. That's when he enjoys smoking a cigar. He doesn't have much relaxing time in the morning—he does the paperwork part of his business then. The end of the day is his time. He's not married. Unless he's on a date, he has that time all to himself.

One morning when Roger woke up, there was a hole about six inches in diameter burned into the comforter and the duvet cover. He had fallen asleep. His cigar had dropped out of his hand. It had burned the bedding. By some miracle, the fire had gone out. "That's an expensive comforter. I bought the best. The duvet cover was expensive too. This little fiasco cost a lot of money," Roger said. "It also scared me— really scared me. I'm lucky to be alive."

Roger still enjoys smoking cigars. But life gave him an important warning. Compared to what it could have cost, the price was cheap: Don't smoke in bed.

Annie puts me to shame.

I was so angry when I learned I had hepatitis C. I wasn't just mad about having it. I was mad I had to walk around knowing I had it. It was one more thing to worry about. It took time taking supplements, and my medical insurance doesn't pay for them. Taking care of myself was eating away at my savings. And who wants to know they have a potentially fatal disease, even if chances are good they'll survive it? I stared at my liver for two years after hearing my diagnosis.

Annie doesn't go to doctors much. She's not big on annual physicals. But one day she felt like she should. The doctor examined her. "Annie, you have breast cancer," he said. "We have to operate right away."

The doctor performed a radical mastectomy. He took both Annie's breasts, then refused to do reconstructive surgery. "I won't do it because you're a smoker, and I don't approve of smoking. You likely wouldn't even heal right," he said. Now Annie can't have reconstructive surgery because insurance and Medicare won't pay for it as a separate procedure; they consider it elective.

"I don't need my breasts anyway," Annie says. "I'm getting old. Besides, I'm grateful. Yes, it was a shock. Finding out I had cancer was traumatic. The surgery was hard, and I'd just as soon not have had it. But if the doctor hadn't found that cancer, I'd be dead. That surgery saved my life. It was a nightmare, but it truly could have been worse.

"I think my surgery was harder on James than it was on me," Annie said. Annie and James have been married more than thirty years. "The night before surgery, in this quiet voice James said he had a favor to ask.

He wondered if it would be all right if he kissed my tee-tees good-bye because after tomorrow, he'd never get to see them again. He said they were a beautiful part of the beautiful woman he loved and would love all his life."

Recently James got rushed to the hospital with a heart attack. Annie was scared. "They put a stent in one artery. Then a week later, he went back with another heart attack and they put a stent in another artery that was blocked. James doesn't smoke. He leads a good, clean life, although sometimes he works too long and hard. I know this sounds silly, but we're both grateful he had his heart attacks. Many people aren't as lucky. They die. James caught it in time. The stents saved his life.

"James and I had a long talk," Annie said. "We didn't have wills or plans to handle final details—like burials. Now we've contacted AARP; we're looking into those inexpensive policies that cover the costs of dying. We're looking into getting insurance on the house so if something happens to one of us, the payments will be made for the one who survives. James is also going to shave off some of his long working hours— sleep in sometimes in the mornings and take off on weekends. We know we're going to die someday. But James's heart attacks were a gift. They pushed us to take care of final arrangements, and they gave him some extra time to live."

Annie's outlook got me to thinking. At first, when I learned I had HCV, I was furious. I took the supplements, but each handful I swallowed, I choked down with anger. I figured I'd had enough problems and losses. Why did I have to have this now? I'd finally gotten over the bulk of my grief about Shane. I was getting happy again. Then this—HCV! But John, a friend of mine, died from it. He didn't get a chance to drink milk-thistle and dandelion-root teas. They hadn't identified the disease yet. His stomach swelled up and his body shut down, and he was younger than me. I've seen people taking fifty to one hundred pills a day to keep from rejecting a transplanted liver because their livers were so damaged from hepatitis. Unless something changes or fate takes my life in another direction, I'm one lucky woman. What am I so angry about? Learning I have hepatitis C during a routine pre-op physical when I'm not sick and have no symptoms is fortunate. Life is giving me a chance to take care of my liver so I can live long enough to die from something else.

Oh, and what about this? One morning I wake up and go out to get in my SUV. It's less than one year old, and I really like this automobile. I look around. My car isn't where I left it. It's been pushed forty feet down the road, and it's scrunched like an accordion. My car was totaled while I slept! Then I notice that the three cars parked behind the garage next door have all been crashed too.

My neighbor comes outside and tells me the story. Teenagers were driving eighty-five miles an hour down the twenty-five-mile-an-hour road in a Jeep Wrangler. They decided to go for a thrill—pick up the pace and go fast over the bump—get that gravity lift like on the roller coaster when your stomach jumps up. What they didn't plan on was the tire popping, losing control, and slamming into all four vehicles. Their Jeep and three of the vehicles, including mine, were declared a total loss by our insurance companies. One vehicle was badly damaged but capable of being repaired. It took me more than a month to settle with the insurance company. It was a lot of hassling—two separate estimates, driving a rental car, then getting another new car when the one I had was fine. But what if someone had been in those cars when it happened? Or out behind the garages? And the teens walked away from the Wrangler. One had a scratch on his foot. Other than that they were fine.

Life can be inconvenient, annoying, and painful, but sometimes all we can say is *te salio barato*. It could have been a lot worse.

In one (recent) year, of the 42,643 fatalities on American roads,
- 25,321 were due to road departures (59 percent)
- 9,213 occurred at intersections
- 4,749 pedestrians were killed

Motor-vehicle crashes are the leading cause of death among Americans 1 to 34 years old.

Contributing to the death toll are alcohol, speed, and various other driver behaviors, plus the kinds of vehicles people drive and the roads on which they drive.

More than half of all people will have an STD at some point in their lifetime.

An estimated 65 million people in the United States are living with a viral STD.

Every year there are 15 million new cases of STDs, some of which are curable.

In a national survey of U.S. physicians, fewer than one-third routinely screened patients for STDs.

Each year, one in four teens contracts an STD.

One in four Americans have genital herpes, but up to 90 percent are unaware they have it.

As people age, their risk of injury or death in home fires caused by smoking increases.

More than a third of all fires caused by smoking (36 percent) were caused when the smoker fell asleep.

About 2.3 million women with a history of breast cancer were alive in January 2002. Some were cancer free, while others still had evidence of cancer and may have been undergoing treatment.

Survival rates for women diagnosed with breast cancer are
- 88 percent at 5 years after diagnosis
- 80 percent after 10 years
- 71 percent after 15 years
- 63 percent after 20 years

More than 80 percent of breast lumps are benign (not cancerous).

Acknowledging limitations in collecting honest statistics, at the time of President Clinton's intern "scandal,"

- 22 percent of men and 14 percent of women admitted to having sexual relations outside their marriage sometime in the past.
- 70 percent of married women and 54 percent of married men did not know of their spouses' extramarital activity.
- 17 percent of divorces in the United States were caused by infidelity.

More than one million Americans are living with HIV, and 24 to 27 percent of these people are unaware that they are infected.

Sources: U.S. Department of Transportation, Federal Highway Administration, American Social Health Association, Hartford Financial Services Group's *Fire Sense*, U.S. Fire Administration, National Fire Data Center, National Cancer Institute, American Cancer Society, Y-ME National Breast Cancer Organization, Associated Press, and the Centers for Disease Control and Prevention

---

ACTIVITIES

1. Are there times it really could have been worse? Review your Master List of Losses. Yes, we can almost always say it could have been worse because almost anything we go through could be worse than it is. But are there losses on your list that, once you grieved and felt your emotions, truly were a blessing? Maybe as in Annie's case, it saved your life?

Or as in my case with HCV, you're given a chance to take care of yourself so a problem doesn't have to become fatal? Other times, why waste your energy grieving? It's a minor annoyance at most. Saying *te salió barato* doesn't mean we trivialize our grief or how much it hurts. It *does* mean that there are times we need to put our loss in perspective. What we lived through was like a bad dream, but did we avoid a real nightmare? Know when it's time to mourn; know when it's time to say "thank you, God" too. Another tip: If you have a friend going through a big loss, don't lecture him or her about how it could have been worse. It's another one of those things that only works when we say it to ourselves. There are times we might want to remind a friend that they've been given a warning, and if they don't stop doing what they're doing, it will get worse.

2. Watch for warning shots being fired in your life. It's easy to get lax. A weakness of mine is I get clumsy—especially when I'm writing. When I'm working on a book, I tend to not stay present in my body. I'm up in my head. That's when I'm prone to falling down the steps, falling down (flat on the sidewalk walking through West Hollywood once—stone-cold sober too), poking a knife through my hand trying to cut off a safety cap, giving myself a concussion when I stood up after bending over to pick up my purse. I need to be reminded to slow down, stay centered. There are other warning signs. If we have people in our employ, we might get a red flag that we have an employee not doing his or her job or stealing from us; maybe we're getting a warning about our health. Sometimes we get sloppy about our driving habits—it starts by going five miles over the limit, then eight, then ten. Then we're in ticket territory. Watch out! Stay present and aware. Listen! Are warning shots being fired now?

CHAPTER 16

Changed by Love:
Making Peace with Adoption

I'm adopted. Those were the first words out of Amelia's mouth when we met. Amelia describes her parents as wealthy, successful in the world of academia, and emotionally reserved. Cold. "Do you mean your birth parents or . . ."

"When I say *parents* I mean adoptive parents," Amelia said. "I met my birth mother in my twenties. I was so excited. My birth mother got who I was instantly. It was the first time I didn't have to explain myself. She told me she was young when I was born. She didn't have a job. My father was a drunk. She had to place me for adoption. We stayed in touch for a while and even got together once. But she was such a victim. I couldn't stand it. I had to stop talking to her. Once she mailed me money—fifteen hundred dollars."

"Did you keep it?" I asked.

"What do you think?" she said.

Adoption is an ambiguous loss. Many losses fall into that category. We lose something, but we're not clear what that is or if we have a right to grieve. According to Pauline Boss, author of *Ambiguous Loss*, sometimes our grief is frozen.

"I'm supposed to feel grateful that this wonderful family adopted me," Amelia said. "I don't. Then I feel guilty about *that*. Other children have a sense of history. They're told their eyes look like their mother's, or this behavior came from Dad. Nobody told me things like that. I felt incomplete, searching for that missing piece. Something's not there that other people have. My hypnotist says my panic attacks likely began when I was taken from my mother at birth. She says I have emotional memory of separation even though I don't consciously remember it. What do you think?" Amelia asked.

"Could be," I said. "I've heard that part of us knows and remembers what happens during surgery when we're anesthetized. A part of us is aware all the time. They say we have memory of everything that happens from the time we're conceived."

Amelia left her East Coast home when she was eighteen and moved as far away as she could. From then on, family contact was rare. "They're as uncomfortable around me as I am with them," Amelia says. "When I was young, they told me I was adopted, but I knew before that. One of my earliest memories is looking at Mum, Dad, and my brothers thinking, *They smell funny, and I don't fit.*"

Once Amelia met a woman who was also adopted. They instantly clicked. "She understood my anger about being expected to feel grateful that my adoptive parents took in poor homeless me. It's this feeling that I don't belong," Amelia said. "It's difficult to understand if you've not been adopted yourself." Amelia met somebody else in the *My Birth Parents Didn't Raise Me and I'm Not Sure Who I Belong To* Club.

Since Amelia and I met, we've faded into and out of each other's lives. Years might pass before we see each other again. When I ran into her last time, something about her felt different. She was gentler. Her heart felt closer to the surface.

"What happened to you?" I asked.

Amelia was the only person who didn't want to tell me her story. Instead of talking, she handed me her diary. "I hope reading it helps you understand me," she said. "I hope it helps the book." This is Amelia's story about what changed her, told in her own words.

I promised my dear friend James that I would keep a journal of this journey, so here goes. The morning began by waking early next to Sam. Saying good-bye was sad, but it's good to know we have such a beautiful love. As the plane ascends and I leave the noise and bustle of L.A. behind, the sad task of going home to such deep pain finds its way to my senses. I wish myself strength and that I be guided with kindness and love. Let me be clear that I'm going home as a gift of happiness and hope to my dear Mum and Dad.

For a second I have a panic attack. I can't believe I'm doing this! After a glass of wine, I relax. I watch the sun disappear in a blaze. Three glasses of wine and I'm looking forward to seeing my parents. Interesting that it takes a terminal illness to dissipate anger. I hope this trip brings forgiveness. God knows they deserve it. Maybe I do too.

At my parents' home I find Mum in good shape, considering. Mum talks openly about her disease, multiple system atrophy, but doesn't want to know what stage it's at. I'll let her lead. Dad is clear about the implications, but he's busy—consumed with—trying to deal with today. Gradually the disease will attack Mum's central and autonomous nervous systems. She'll lose control of her bowels and bladder. She'll be unable to speak, see, eat, move. They'll insert a feeding tube or she'll starve. Then the illness will end in death.

Tomorrow is day seven of this trip. I'm halfway through and yes, I'm counting. It's not possible to write what I feel. This house does not permit the truth. I staggered back in after going outside for a quick puff on a joint. I can hardly see, I'm so stoned. This is insane. I've slept ten hours in the past six nights. My mind won't stop. I can't sleep, think, or shit. I can't face what's happening. I know I need to change my attitude in order to survive the week. I feel frozen in a bubble. No one can get near me. I've never been more uncomfortable except my entire childhood. My gift to myself is getting out of here and staying at a hotel tomorrow night.

I escape to the hotel. Soon I'm going to dinner with Elisabeth, my dear friend. Talking will be a comfort. Being trapped in silence at that house is such punishment. My ideas to bring love and happiness—how absurd! I can't stand who I've become. I must appear so cold and unkind. This is not what I envisioned. I must accept that I can't help.

The day I've been yearning for has arrived—I'm finally leaving. But the complete disappointment I feel! I behaved without warmth, kindness, or love. I was so angry. I wanted to leave the entire time. I saw Elisabeth again today. She's teaching me to come from love. Then Dad took Mum and me out for dinner. On my last night we have a friendly evening. By dinner I haven't said anything, but tonight feels like the right time.

Back at the house, standing on the sidewalk, I hug Mum. "I love you," I said. She pats me like a dog. "Good, good," she says. Then she bursts into tears. "I love you too," she says. Then she's hanging on to me, sobbing. I've never heard her say that my entire life. We both stand there crying in the cold. As I pull away I look into her eyes. Is this our last time? It hurts so much. I kiss her and say I have to go. Looking back, I see her standing there, sobbing. Why is it so hard to say what we feel? I say good-bye to Dad. It's that usual stiff, brisk hug but he has tears in his eyes. I can't say "I love you." I just look and cry. I know he can hardly manage what lies inevitably ahead. Neither can I.

Elisabeth drives me to the airport. We sit in the lounge and drink Bloody Marys. Slowly I realize two weeks' emotions in the safety of my friend. Thank God my last night was a happy one, that I said what I needed to say and Mum needed to hear.

Wow, time has passed. I'm on the plane going home again, this time to take care of Mum. Dad is taking a much-needed holiday while I and my brothers look after her. The disease has taken a critical hold. I've been back several times since I last wrote. We're near the end and there are more things I need to say. Mum, you have been a guiding light. You taught me to be a better person. I'm sad to see you like this. My love is with you always. Why did we create this barrier? I wish we had been closer.

When I arrive, Dad shows me the nightly routine. It's a slow process with many steps. I can't think of how hard this will be. I must go on autopilot. Please, God, give me the strength. Mum can no longer stand.

I spend the third night home alone with Mum. She goes to the bathroom every hour. I have to lift her out of the chair and onto the toilet. My emotional pain is oddly distant. Somehow I find the strength I need. As I sink into the tub I start to cry, but nothing comes out. I can hear that yelping sound she makes. My adrenaline is pumping. I feel no desire to sleep. I've been awake for sixty hours! There are no words for how hard this is. I can't take a sleeping pill, I might miss Mum's call. But if I could just sleep for five hours I know I could cope. Dad and I had a lovely day. I now understand how he does it—there isn't a choice. For all the hardship Mum faces, she's still happy to be alive.

Over the halfway mark. All the brothers are fighting. Mark thinks Stephen should be here more. Matt's got the depression excuse. He opted out. I use whatever it takes. I had a whiskey tonight. I hate whiskey! My poor mother pooped herself today. Thank God for Angelica, the nurse. She cleaned Mum up. This situation is out of control. They need to hire more help. It makes me want to scream and cry and kick and pray. While sitting on the toilet, Mum says, "Don't get teary. I don't want to cry because it makes a funny sound." Angelica tells Mum it's okay to cry. God knows she must want to—with humiliation and frustration. We all cry, cleaning the poop, but Mum soon stops herself. When did she learn to hide it all? This trip has been so important. I know she loves having me here. There's a beautiful exchange between us as we each say good-bye in our own way. The cheap buzzer Dad bought for Mum doesn't work, so I'm leaving our doors open. That snoring sounds like an animal yelping. No sleep tonight.

Time is slow here. I feel relaxed. All I can do is submit. My back is sore from lifting Mum on and off the toilet. It makes no difference. She pees on the floor or me anyway. Mum read *Final Exit*. She doesn't know if she'll have the strength to kill herself when that time comes. Odd as it sounds, things really are okay. Dad called. He sounds angry—I don't know. I've never understood him. I'm doing it and I think quite well. Mum is relaxed with me. Something is guiding us, a strength and serenity.

Mark and I walk along the seafront today. He's a good man. He takes care of everyone—not that they notice. They're too busy blaming and hating. This family is so negative. I've never seen such cheap people. Everything is saved—emotions, money, kindness. Mum has to drink from straws and Dad reuses them! It's actually quite funny.

Twenty-seven hours until I'm home. Mum and I looked at family photos today. I asked about her relationships. To my surprise she says she wasn't close to Granny. I believe Mum and I did the best we could. I asked about my adoption, if she felt different about me. She said yes, but because I was a girl, not because I was adopted. She said the agency offered her a set of Chinese girl twins first. I didn't want to hear any more.

My strength is back. I'm calm, clear, and feel an understanding of life's process and purpose. Most of this diary has been written coming and leaving. Tomorrow's another good-bye.

I'm at the airport after my good-bye to pot! It's gone, down the ceremonial drain! I had several last tokes before saying good-bye. For everyone's sake, it's time to be sober. I must face what lies ahead with clarity. I'm returning to see Mum for her birthday. I've been back there with Sam since I wrote last but didn't put pen to paper. I actually said "I'm an addict" to my therapist this week. She agreed and said I need a Twelve Step Program. Maybe at thirty-seven it's time to quit (note the maybe). A lot of things are leaving my life.

Can it get any worse? Today the nurses were giving Mum an enema. I walked past and saw the nurse pull on the rubber gloves and caught Mum's eyes. She looked terrified, humiliated, and helpless. Last week she broke down, saying, "I'm so unhappy." Each day her life force moves out of her, leaving her weaker and more despondent. Since Sam and I were here, she lost twenty pounds. She can no longer eat solids. Her voice is fading. Dad gave me a copy of her living will—no feeding tube. That's what she says she wants, and her wishes will be honored. She'll die of starvation. Tomorrow is her birthday and I'm sure the last time we'll all be together. I cannot imagine the stress Dad feels. His pain is deep and I understand why he keeps it in—if it came out he wouldn't be able to go on. God, please take care of Mum. She needs extra love.

Today is Mum's seventieth birthday. We went out for lunch. What chaos! The kids playing, Mum choking, everybody arguing, Dad panicking. Mum had a huge choke tonight; air gets trapped in her throat. She can't breathe. I can see terror in her eyes as she can in mine. I always said if something happened, I'd take care of Sam but observing this I see the horror of that. Dad's on call twenty-four hours a day, seven days a week, and Mum knows the stress he's under. He's so calm and she's struggling to stay alive to spend their last moments together. Does love always come with such a price?

Dad drives me to the airport. I nearly leap out of the car while it's moving. Sorry, Dad, but I need out! Brother Mark is now on Prozac. He hasn't worked for weeks. All my brothers' lives are plagued with depression. I told Mum and Mark about the magazine article I was in, "Twenty Women Changing Our World." "It's good, isn't it?" I pathetically asked Mark, hoping for some recognition. He said nothing, just walked out of the room. "Did you know someone at the magazine?" Mum asked. "Is that why they chose you? There must have been hundreds of others they could have picked instead." I spent my life feeling inadequate because I was adopted. Now I realize it's okay that I'm not of their genes! I must stop seeking their approval. It's not coming. I don't want to be like them. They don't know how to care. I deserve better. Thank God I've found it with Sam.

On the plane to see Mum again, we fly over the mountains. The sun disappears in a golden haze. When it reappears, I'll be in the midst of the nightmare that awaits.

I help put Mum to bed and hurt my back the first night home. She looks thinner and older, but she's sharp as a knife. The house is quiet, cold. Dad's going to New York for two nights and I'll be in charge. Mum can't move. Her hand can hardly press the emergency button. Time has its own pace here, slowed down in sync with Mum's life force. Mum's gasping for air. That strange yelping noise has been replaced by a choking sound. She hardly eats—a few pieces of goat's cheese washed down with chocolate milk. Feeding her, I realize the circle is complete. I'm now sustaining her life. Dad's lying in bed reading her a book. It's beautiful to see him caring for her every need. Their love is stronger than ever and I feel part of it. Mum is so protected by the love and care around her. I hope she feels safe to go.

Today the hell begins. Oh my God, where are You? Mum couldn't sleep last night. The machine that automatically moves her broke. We were up all night at 2:00, 3:00, 4:00 a.m. When the nurses arrived, Mum broke into tears, terrified she'll experience more pain today and tonight. This afternoon I baked Dad's birthday cake and sent him to nap. Mum kept calling—she's slipping, needs water, empty the catheter. Love is the only thing that stops me from snapping. Somehow the strength needed is given. It's day three, and I can barely keep it together. Dad must be at the end.

Mum was covered in poop today. I cleaned her. "Between one and ten, how comfortable are you?" I asked. She burst into tears and said, "Four." I can't contain myself. We lay together sobbing. Does the contract that gives us life include this kind of death? Everything in this house makes me want to scream—the smell, the anger, the sickness. I can't find peace. I'm losing my balance. I don't belong here. I never did.

Today's better. Last night I slept, so I'm less overwhelmed. Mum tells me a confession. She's sorry she made me wear short socks in middle school when she knew everyone else wore long socks and I was uncomfortable being different. I say I don't remember (lie) and she's the best Mum ever. She cries, then we laugh. Later she says if she can't die a natural death, she wants to end her own life. She says she's not scared to die and doesn't want Dad doing this much longer. "How will you do it?" I ask. "Liquid morphine," she says. She says no more about it. I have three days left. Between the slow and sad practical tasks we find time to talk. She knows what she wants to say. I would like the strength to listen and to say good-bye.

Dad returns so full of life he can't stop talking. Everything that happened is swimming in my head. Something changed today. I finally found my voice, and everything I wanted to say came out with ease. I thanked Mum for being a great mother. I said I'll miss her but it's okay to go. She said she thinks dying is like someone switching off the lights. I said I think it's like going home. She said when she gets there she'll send a message and let me know—an e-mail. We cried. I said when my friend died, he said, "Okay, I'm ready," then just went. She asked about his illness, was it like hers, did it get worse than hers, how much worse? She asked so many questions. I answered from my heart. I've spent my life concealing how I feel. That disappeared and we really talked. I asked who she wants with her when she dies. She said, "Just Dad."

I feel sad, tired but grateful I was blessed with the strength to say the things I wanted to say. I've changed. I'm not sure how, but it's okay. This has been quite a journey. I'm proud of myself. I can leave with a sense of peace. Maybe tonight I can finally sleep.

I'm sitting in the LAX airport lounge. Mum slipped into a coma today. I hope I'll reach her in time to say bon voyage. If not, Ma, I'll see you in my dreams. I feel sedated, calm, and sad. The journey has arrived that I've so desperately not wanted to take.

Mark meets me at the airport. Before he left, he whispered to Mum he was picking me up. When he said that, she immediately woke up from her coma. When I get to the house, I sit with her and rub her head. Her eyes are open. She tries to focus with her left eye for a second. I said, "I'm giving you a kitty rub," then I purr and rub her. That was our little childhood joke. She saw me and smiled. That's the last communication we had.

The brothers are here without wives or kids. It's like going back twenty-five years. If Mum wakes, Dad wants someone with her, so we're all doing shifts. Mine is 3:00 to 4:30 a.m. I hear Mark come in at 1:30, so I go sit with him. We sit for hours watching Mum. It's mesmerizing. Time has slowed but moves strangely fast. Mum's breathing is gurgled. She draws short little breaths. Sometimes there's silence. We glance to see if her chest is moving. Then she gasps and air forces its way out. Her body is drying up. Her mouth is sticking, and her catheter has been empty for some time. There are two strange incidents where we distinctly hear music. Mark gets up to look but finds nothing. I think it sounds like high piano notes. Mark thinks it's a piccolo. It's surreal.

Dad sits with Mum after Mark and I finish shifts. The rest of us sit in the kitchen drinking coffee. At 11:30, Dad walks in sobbing. "She's gone," he says. Mark goes upstairs. I follow. Mum's face is lifeless, white. She's still warm as I kiss her head. Mark and I grab each other and cry. At that moment I feel Mum with us. This is the sign she said she'd give me. I know she's okay.

After we all say good-bye to Mum, I see Dad in the room with her adjusting her blanket. "You won't mind which way I put this as you don't need it to keep you warm anymore," he says as if she's alive. I catch a glimpse of their private life and feel his sorrow. She died as she wanted—with him at her side. Dad said he was about to read the paper. She moved slightly to get his attention, then let out a long sigh and died. The most elegant death ever—so dignified, calm, and surrounded with love. You did us proud, Mum. Thank you for waiting for me and allowing us to say good-bye. We all received the gift of your life and love. I lovingly return you to the universe now.

Two undertakers arrive. They're women. I don't want Mum to leave the house. I hold Dad as he cries. "Here is a new chapter in my life," he says. Mum took care of us even as she was dying. The great suffering of her illness prepared us for her death. I hope you're okay, Mum. It feels horrible without you. I keep seeing her face as I rubbed her head and she mustered all her strength to smile. That face will stay with me forever. The gift of our love over the last months is the greatest achievement and feeling ever. In my sadness there is the most wonderful joy knowing we truly connected and our love will never die. As Dad says, this is a new chapter. Tonight I don't want to turn the page.

Today Mark and I make the funeral arrangements. They're removing organs for medical research. Do they know that tiny exhausted body is my mum? Then the thaw begins. It's the first time Dad cries since Sunday. He realizes she's gone. That hits me too. Denial only works if there's no reminder, and everywhere is traces of Mum. I tell Dad I'm leaving Monday and catch a glimpse of panic in his eyes. I don't want to leave him, but pain isn't transferable. I can't help him. I'm sorry, but I have to go.

Yesterday was the funeral. The day lasted for years. I couldn't cope. At 2:00 p.m. I took a Xanax. The family arrived, then came the hearse. Dad and I went behind it. The service was awful—I didn't feel a thing. Dad's tears were deep. I held him while he cried and gave him clean tissues. After the service, he went up to the coffin and touched it. "Get me out of here," he whispered. We sat outside in the rain while everyone else left. The others were all crying. I couldn't cry. It left me feeling empty and guilty. We all went to the house. After everybody left, the house was so quiet, an eerie silence that made me uneasy. It doesn't feel like home anymore. Will the family survive without Mum?

Today was strange. Dad and I went to a movie. He hopes I know how much I've done for him this week. I lie in the tub and realize I'm exhausted. Last night Mark could hardly make a coherent sentence—like me now. There's something so self-obsessed about depression. Everyone close to it becomes its slave. What strength I have left I will give to my father, whom I truly adore—even though he's crazy. Leaving the theater he decided to do back exercises in the aisle so everyone can see his backache! I wish him safe passage through his pain. Mum, I wish you were here. I'm sorry I shut down at your funeral. That's the scariest emotion. It removes me from myself. When I feel disconnected, it suspends the pain, and that feels good. On the way to the movies, Dad drives past the crematorium. Has Mum been fried or is she waiting in some cold box? I hate knowing they cut her up. I don't like being abandoned. Mum, why did you have to go?

It's midnight. The wind is howling and the rain is beating against the windows. I've been crying for an hour—so much for Xanax. I've forgotten how to sleep. I arrived with a mother, and tomorrow I leave without one. I thought tonight, the last night of my journey and the end of this journal, would be one of profound understanding, but there really is none. Whatever preconceived notion I had of how it might be or feel is not what it is. The journey can only be felt in the moment, and that moment always changes. I love you, Mum. I cannot believe you're not here and I won't be able to talk to you anymore. Or maybe I can. You just won't answer the same.

After a sad good-bye to Dad, Mark drives me to the airport. We hug and cry. Sometimes I feel unkind living so far away.

Last night Dad said, "Love often pulls people apart." I just took a Vicodin (sorry, therapist). I want to float out of here and suppress the sorrow. I caught a glimpse of my face as I left the bathroom. I look tired and old. I know it's going to be different now. Inside and out, the change is making itself known.

Amelia planned to go back to work immediately upon returning to L.A. She spent the next two years mourning instead. She barely worked. She underwent major surgery. Then she had an adverse reaction to a drug. It scared her so much she committed to sobriety. She went through a profound cycle of change; her mom's funeral was just the beginning. When I asked Amelia how she changed, she said, "I've become myself." Amelia came home to herself. Amelia's mum went home. They were both transformed by love.

When we have conflicted emotions about people important to us, their death is often a trigger for change. After her father's death, one woman went through a three-year confounding and chaotic transformation that she describes as *being insane with grief.* Her father was an alcoholic. She wasn't able to tap her emotions about him when he was alive. She went to therapy—worked hard—but the feelings were buried deeply. When he died, the emotions erupted, came gushing out. She couldn't stop them. Soon she was able to leave an abusive relationship. She became sober and stopped abusing drugs. The changes occurred naturally as part of a cycle that started with unthawing frozen grief.

I've heard this same story many times and lived it in my life. When we thaw frozen grief, we're freed to become ourselves. Until then, we walk around locked into dysfunctional behaviors, trapped in relationships—unable to change. We may think of getting sober or ending a relationship as isolated events that happen in a moment or singly, by themselves. But it can take years for transformations like that to take place, and often they're part of a cycle. It's not the old saying, "Loss comes in threes." We're going through a time of change.

We try to achieve spiritual growth by reading books, going to therapy, attending groups. These activities help. But the most profound changes can happen when we accept and surrender to the experiences in our life. This change is free. (Well, not entirely free; we pay an emotional price.) *Acceptance* doesn't mean "accept the entire situation at once." We only need to accept what's happening and what we're feeling now. We may feel angry, frightened, resistant, coolly detached. The next moment we're sobbing. Then we feel something else. If we look ahead, we panic. We only get Grace for now. Ironically, profound change doesn't always happen by taking action. It comes from simple awareness. We become aware. Then life naturally and organically changes us. That's why it's important to keep a journal. James extracting a promise from Amelia to write in a diary was extremely helpful. That we change by being aware of ourselves may sound overly simplistic—but it's truth.

Loss isn't about losing someone, feeling sad, then going back to the status quo. We may never be the same again. Mourning isn't wasted time. More is going on than just the grieving we feel and see. Life is transforming us—under, through, during, and because of the grief. The experiences we least want to go through are often the ones that change us the most. These cycles may feel crazy and confusing when we're in them, but we can trust what's taking place. When we're raw with grief, we're like putty in life's hands. We're being changed by love.

Amelia's journal was significantly edited for purposes of this story and ease of reading. I usually don't recommend that writers use diary entries as an article or book, but I decided to break that rule. The story in this chapter is the change taking place inside Amelia's heart, and that isn't a story that can be narrated by me. Telling the story any other way reduced its power; it then became the story of an adopted child making peace with her mother, which is a good story, but not the one I wanted to tell. This story is the raw, honest, and occasionally ugly truth about how Amelia felt. It's a story about things we often only reveal to ourselves, and how important those revelations are. The reason we have journals is to say things we can't say to anyone else. A diary is a safe place to reveal all the parts of who we are. I thank Amelia for being vulnerable. Letting us read her diary was a brave thing to do.

In the United States, 2.1 million children live with adoptive parents (not including stepchildren).

Six in ten Americans have had personal experience with adoption: either they themselves, a family member, or a close friend was adopted or placed a child.

There are 1.5 million children in out-of-home care in Central and Eastern Europe and the Commonwealth of Independent States (composed of several countries in the former Soviet Union) alone—a 150,000-child increase in the last decade, according to a recent UNICEF report.

U.S. citizens adopted more than a quarter million children from other countries in the three decades between 1971 and 2001, and international adoptions have more than doubled in the past eleven years.

Hospice and palliative care is an expert team approach to helping people die without pain and with dignity, mostly in their own homes.

In 2002, more than 885,000 people living with life-limiting illnesses received services from one of the 3,200 hospice providers in the United States. In 2004, more than 1 million Americans received services.

An estimated 100 million people worldwide could benefit from basic hospice and palliative care annually including the 33 million people dying annually (60 percent of the total deaths) and their 66 million family members, companions, and caregivers.

Sources: Evan B. Donaldson Adoption Institute and the National Hospice and Palliative Care Organization

ACTIVITIES

1. Are you going through a significant change? Amelia promised a friend she would keep a journal of her journey. How about promising that you'll do the same? The feelings are so intense, we think we'll never forget. But loss can and does interfere with short-term memory and pain fades with time. Writing in a journal can feel like an extra job when we already feel overworked. We might groan at the thought of it. But keeping a diary is a way to document and honor these tragically beautiful events. It's an excellent way to observe the transformation taking place, and it helps us surrender too. It shows us the beauty of staying in each moment and expressing how we feel. (Other options include keeping a file in our computer, making a scrapbook, or recording the experience on video- or audiotape.) A journal is a beautiful gift to give to someone else or ourselves.

2. Take care of your health. It's common when we're grieving to have compounded losses. We get loss piled upon loss, then another one layered on those. Our immune system may be shot. Chronic or acute illnesses frequently begin during grief. Carefully watch your health. Get the medical care you need. Seek a doctor's assistance for short-term medication for trauma (trauma can make heart rate and blood pressure rise). Be aware that later on, you may need to go back and do emotional trauma healing work. It's a huge blow to the psyche when people we love get ripped from our lives. See an understanding doctor with an awareness of addictions. Don't prescribe for yourself.

3. Were you adopted? Have you placed a child for adoption? Have you consciously tackled that grief? Have you made a decision whether or not to contact your birth parents or the child you placed? If you haven't faced these questions or your emotions about the adoption, maybe it's time. Meditate and ask for guidance about what to do and when. If the

feelings are too intense to face alone, get professional help. Is it time to release any anger, guilt, or other feelings and set everyone free? Remember that, just like in Amelia's situation, life will bring us the experiences and opportunities we need to make peace. It's up to us to say yes.

4. For hospice care assistance, contact the National Hospice and Palliative Care Organization at www.nhpco.org or 703-837-1500 or the International Association for Hospice and Palliative Care at www.hospicecare.com, 713-880-2940, or 866-374-2472 (toll-free). For free information about end-of-life care, contact Caring Connections at www.caringinfo.org or 800-658-8898 (toll-free).

5. Deal with your ambiguous losses and your frozen grief. Go over your Master List of Losses. Are there any losses you actually experienced, but because the losses weren't clear, you didn't give yourself permission to grieve? We might have had a parent at home who was an alcoholic (or codependent). Maybe our parent had another problem or illness. Our parent's body was there, but our parent wasn't emotionally present. That can happen when a sibling dies; our parents are there, but they're not able to be present for us because they're grieving. Maybe one parent left when we were an infant. We didn't have that parent around, so we weren't consciously aware of our loss, but our hearts know what we didn't get. Another ambiguous loss is relocating from another country. We gain a new homeland, but we lose our roots, traditions, and sometimes our extended family and our culture. Living in our own country but watching familiar culture disappear as the world evolves and changes can also be ambiguous and confusing. I included as many ambiguous losses as I could think of in the Master List of Losses, but there are some I may have overlooked. Ask God, ask life, ask your guardian angels to show you any ambiguous losses you've experienced or may be going through now. Start the healing process by becoming aware.

CHAPTER 17

Ex-Changes:
Making Peace with the Past

I try to figure out where the story in this chapter starts. At St. Paul–Ramsey Medical Center with Shane's death, when my *initiation* begins? When I get the phone call telling me I have hepatitis C? I can't tell the story of hepatitis C without talking about the journey that begins when I learn I have it—a journey that takes me back to my drug-using days, my high school years, then all the way back to my ancestry—a story I'd rather forget. I can't tell that story without talking about the experience immediately following in Munich when I get a new spine—a trip that metaphorically and literally shapes my life and who I am now. I can't tell you what it means to learn I have hepatitis C thirty years after becoming sober without explaining that I had barely become happy after losing my son when life as I know it got upended *again*. You wouldn't understand how broken I felt. It all entwines.

Some stories aren't straight lines. In Tibet, when devotees go on pilgrimages, they go in circles. Life does too. We circle back to the beginning. That beginning leads to an experience with an ending that leads to another beginning—circles within circles that all connect. So much of my life has been spent running away from pain only to discover that the line curves and takes me back to what I'm running from. "Sometimes life feels like one long series of losses," I said to a friend. She understands.

This book started as a simple grief book to comfort people during loss. It turned into a book about enlightenment—but it's not about yogis and maharajas. It's about people like the woman who commits to her grief after her brother kills himself and learns that feeling emotions makes her strong not weak, another woman who bravely takes small steps to change the status quo after becoming homeless, and beautiful Kate Somerville who shows us it doesn't matter who did what to us, what matters is what we do now with what we have left. It's about Faith learning that true love is tending to her husband during his last years when Alzheimer's corrodes his mind so much he can't remember who she is, Lori learning that embracing the part of her life she stubbornly rejects as a mistake transforms it into destiny, Mark seeing his years of agony as boot-camp training to help others. It's me learning that the coolest changes happen when we humbly ask for God's help. These are real-life stories about what enlightenment is.

It's a book about the journey life is inviting each of us to take. Enlightenment isn't waiting in the mountains of Tibet. It's in the experiences we're facing—and often resisting—in our lives today. It's in the changes we didn't expect, ask for, or want. We can fantasize about the perfect life. It takes courage to have faith with the life we've been given and show up for it each day.

I was walking down Ventura Boulevard when a stranger wearing a turban approached. He started prophesying in a thick dialect. I backed away. Shirley MacLaine said it: "Los Angeles is like a box of cereal—full of flakes, fruits, and nuts."

"Soon you're going to be happy for the first time in your life," the stranger said.

Yeah, whatever, I think.

"People think you're happy, but underneath your strong exterior you hurt."

Me and the rest of the world, I think. *It doesn't take a psychic to know that.*

"It started when you were a teenager, with the abortion," he says. "You need to find forgiveness. That's how you'll find happiness."

Now he has my attention. Yes, he wants money. I give him some. Yes, he probably hustled me. But his prophecy comes true. I do find happiness. It doesn't come in the shape I expect. It comes at the end of changes I don't want.

"I know God wants me to be happy," a woman screamed one day. "God didn't promise happiness," I said. "God promises peace."

This is a story about circles. It's for people in the *It's Time to Make Peace with My Past So I Can Be Happy Now* Club. It's for people who want to learn the art of making every moment count. It's for people who give up the illusion of control and are living in the mystery and loving it—*most of the time*. It's for ordinary yogis and maharajas like you and me.

"Guilt—the gift that keeps on giving." That's what Marge says. Marge is my friend who calls big loss *initiation*. Like me, she comes from a fundamentalist background filled with right and wrong, sin and good works, and rules. Many rules. People like rules. Rules keep them safe—at least that's what they think.

Fundamentalism can crop up in religious groups, recovery and new age groups, institutions, treatment centers, government organizations, schools, corporations, cultures, and families—wherever people gather. Fundamentalism is the absolute thinking that leaves no room for being guided by intuition, awareness, evolution, and what's right for us. There's no heart, no compassion. Fundamentalism breeds rules, and rules breed guilt.

I like to think I don't have any guilt, but when Shane was on his deathbed, I prayed so hard. *Please don't let Shane die, God,* I begged. *I'm sorry I divorced his dad. I promise I'll get back together with him if You let Shane live.* Shane didn't live, and I didn't remarry Shane's dad, but praying that way shows how guilty I felt about getting divorced. Getting divorced broke a rule. I still felt guilty about divorcing the father of my first child, John, and for not raising him. I have traces of those core beliefs that say, *Who I am isn't okay; I can't trust myself; whatever I think, feel, and do is wrong.* I still have a tendency to blame myself. Sometimes I still feel crazy when it's the people around me who are acting insane.

I hate feeling guilty. It's easier to walk away from whatever I did that created the guilt—cut off that part of me and leave it behind.

I'm twelve years old. My mom finds a package of cigarettes in my jacket pocket. "You're no good, just like your father," she screams. "I ought to take you in the basement and beat you." Later that night I ask for her forgiveness. "No," she says. "You don't deserve it."

"Many people believe they're unforgivable," Marge says. I believed that most of my life. In fairness to her, Mom rarely struck me. Once, when I was seventeen and started to openly rebel, she smacked me across the face for smart-mouthing. I had it coming. But I watched her hold my brother by his hair and beat him across the face with a paddle. I heard the story about how she held his head in the washing machine (when it was sloshing on the wash cycle) and didn't let him up for air until she heard bubbles. Once my oldest sister was supposed to be home by ten. When she was two minutes late, my mom told my father to take her down to the basement and beat her with a garden hose. He did. Another time, my mother broke a glass bleach bottle over my sister's head because my sister bleached her hair blond. I didn't have to go down to the basement. The other kids had been there. That was enough to scare me.

My mom isn't a bad woman. She did better than her parents. Each generation usually does. She says my grandpa used to make my grandmother prostitute herself to earn money for the family. She says Grandpa tortured her (my mom) and all my mom's brothers. I only saw my maternal grandmother and grandfather a few times. I never met my paternal grandparents. I heard that my dad's mother died when she was twenty. She fell out of a boat in a lake and drowned. There were whispers of suicide and alcoholism. I didn't know anything more than that about my ancestry, and I didn't care. The further away I got from all of them, the better. They could scream and threaten, but they couldn't conquer me. Winning meant not giving in to the pain. Control kept me safe—my control. Rebellion made my mark. What I didn't get was that when I rebelled, I *was* controlled by them. I ran straight into more guilt and pain.

My mom gave me what she could. She gave me strength, made me fiercely independent. She sent me to a private school. I hated that academy. I had to ride the bus two hours each way. It was dark when I left the house in the morning and dark when I got home. I had one friend at school—Carlene. We didn't have dances and proms—we had senior banquets and chapel in the morning. I was raised with that fundamentalist guilt that says I was born bad, I'd always be bad, God is love, and Jesus saves. The only time I felt saved was when I drank that first shot of whiskey when I was twelve.

Atonement is being cleansed from what we've done wrong. If we break that word down, we get *at-one-ment*. There are two ways to interpret at-one-ment. One is the codependent way. We glob onto people, try to become one with them. We want someone or something to take away our pain and guilt, make us feel better. The other at-one-ment is where the initiation leads. We remember our oneness with God and life. That's when we learn what true forgiveness is.

My friend Marge's initiation began when she gave birth to her second child. The doctor stood at the foot of her hospital bed saying something about genetic abnormality. "I didn't know what he meant, but I knew something was wrong with my baby," Marge said. "I was flat on my back in bed, but it felt like I was falling backward in space."

When I learned I had hepatitis C, I didn't *fall* backward. I was pulled back in time.

It started with the phone calls from my oldest son, John. "Dad asked me to call you. He's sick with hepatitis C and thinks you should get tested."

"I just got tested," I said. "I have it."

A week later he called again. "Dad's in the hospital. He used interferon and went into respiratory failure. They gave him that paralysis medication so they could put the breathing tubes into his lungs. Now he's in a coma," my son said. "I have power of attorney—control over his life. I'm scared. I don't want Dad to die."

I hadn't seen John's dad in years, but when that second phone call came, I knew I was going to be back in his life.

Jake looked like Jack Nicholson when I met him—that twinkle in his eyes, that crazy laugh. Thirty-five years later, lying in the hospital bed with an oxygen mask on his face, he still looked like Jack Nicholson. We were married for a minute. He was a rich boy who promised to take me on a magic carpet ride. He got me pregnant, then took away the child. He taught me to shoot dope, then gave me hepatitis C. Some ride.

Running. That's how Jake described me. When I was twelve, I started counting the days until I turned eighteen. They say children of alcoholics don't drink or use drugs to get high; they drink to feel normal. That's what I did. By age thirteen, I was blacking out from alcoholism. Being an alcoholic was in my genes. When an alcoholic girl has blackouts, it's better that way. The things you do, you don't want to remember. The hard part is that the things you do show in other people's eyes. You see how bad you are when you look at them. So you fix it by drinking or taking more pills. It got real bad after the abortion. One day my mom said, "You're pregnant." The next thing I knew, I was lying on a doctor's table in L.A. with an eight-inch needle piercing my stomach. I was never right after that, but I wasn't right before that either. What I didn't tell Mom was that I tried to get an abortion myself. It didn't work.

I sat on a chair next to Jake's bed and rested my hand on his leg. He took off the oxygen mask. "You didn't have a floor," he said. "You just kept stepping on the gas. No matter how high you got, you used more. You didn't have any veins left. You didn't care. You just kept stabbing at your arm with the needle. It was disgusting," he said. "I was a scumbag, but all I had to do to take John away was prove you were a worse scumbag than me. That was easy. I had a better attorney than you."

Jake took a whiff of oxygen. "You brought John into my life. Then you got me into treatment. Whenever you come into my life, I get transformed. You're like an angel, my junkie angel," he said. "One day when we were still married, you were screaming I had my parents and didn't need you for anything. Well, junkie angel, I need you now."

Eight years ago, Jake was on vacation with his now ex-wife when he ran out of steam. After he sobered up, he'd been a marathon runner, but suddenly he couldn't walk a block. He knew he had hepatitis C, but he didn't connect it with the fatigue. Then he started talking crazy—something about aliens telling him what to do. Hepatitis attacks the liver. When the liver stops cleaning the blood, toxins go to the brain. You get delusional. Jake's wife was scared. She thought he'd gone crazy. That's what broke them up.

After visiting Jake in the hospital, I returned to California. Jake wouldn't get out of bed. The doctors didn't know what to do. "I can't breathe," Jake said. "How can I get up?" After weeks of phone calls, the doctors let me bring the teas and supplements I'm taking for hepatitis C into the hospital for Jake. They didn't think it would help, but they decided it wouldn't hurt.

"Don't get your hopes up. Jake sounds pretty far gone," Lloyd said. Lloyd runs the Hepatitis C Free program where I bought the supplements.

I ignored him. "Just tell me what to do to help this guy get well," I said.

A month later, when I was back in California again, Jake called. The hospital was releasing him; he was going back to his mother's house. He had lived in a small apartment in the back of her house since his divorce. I was excited. This meant he was getting better. Then my son called. "Dad's home, but I don't know how to take care of him. Please come, Mom. I need your help."

I walked into that sprawling house I hadn't been in for so many years. I started at one end of Jake's apartment and cleaned and scrubbed my way to the other. I set up a small fridge, a microwave, everything Jake needed to take care of himself from bed. I met with Jake's other ex-wife and their children. We'd work as a team to help Jake get well. I'd come back one week a month; they'd help the rest of the time. "Be optimistic," I said. "Don't look at him with fear. I'm taking the same supplements. Never felt better in my life."

As the months passed, Jake's face filled out. His hair grew back. He still needed oxygen to breathe, but he looked alive. Even his diabetes was under control. He fired his home-care nurse. Soon I remembered why I felt attracted to him in the first place. I was grateful that after all these years, our son finally got to see us getting along—got to see how his dad and I were together when we first met. Children should know they were conceived in love.

In the afternoons, Jake liked to talk about the old days. "Remember Jimmy Fox and that dope deal with Art?" he asked.

Every junkie in Minnesota knew Jimmy. Jimmy and Art lived in the same building. Jimmy was a junkie. He'd shoot up in his neck, anywhere he could stick a needle. When he ran out of drugs, he'd drive to the nearest pharmacy, stick a pistol in the pharmacist's face, and tell him what he wanted. He'd get it. Art was a whiny rich brat. His dad was supporting him while Art went to college. Art didn't think he was an addict. He saw himself as a student who needed to get high because it helped him study. Every day when Jimmy left, Art would sneak up to Jimmy's, pick the lock, and steal dope from Jimmy's stash. Jimmy knew what Art was doing. He kept telling Art to stop, but Art denied doing it. He thought he was better than anyone else, especially junkies like Jimmy.

One day Art stole Jimmy's last hit of dope. In the drug world, you don't do that. You can steal from the pharmacies but not from a fellow addict and especially not his last hit. It's part of the code. Addicts plan their lives around their stash—how long it will last and when it's time to get more. All that stands between an addict and getting sick is that one last hit. When Jimmy got home and went to shoot up, he was livid. He went to Art's apartment and told Art to come with him. Art asked where they were going. "We're going to score" is all Jimmy said. Jimmy drove to a pharmacy, parked the car, left the engine running. Minutes later, he got back in the car, handed Art a gun, and told him to put it in the glove box. Then Jimmy threw a bag of drugs in Art's lap. "Your fingerprints are on the gun. You're holding the bag. That makes you an accomplice to the crime. You're a thieving dope fiend just like me. If you want drugs, buy them or rob a pharmacy but stay out of my stash. You don't steal from friends. Get it?" Jimmy asked.

These were the years before the recovery revolution. We didn't know about treatment, AIDS, hepatitis C, or that we could even get straight. It was Minnesota 1970. We thought it was our God-given right to stay high. There were two federal institutions where they sent addicts to detoxify. Most

addicts went to Lexington. When Jimmy got sent there, he held up the phar-
macy in the facility. They found him stoned, with the pharmacy drugs under
his bed. After that, Lexington wouldn't take Minnesota addicts. They had to
go to Forth Worth. The last I heard about Jimmy, he was in a state prison
in Wisconsin writing "Jesus Saves" on the wall. Word had it he died from
hepatitis C.

"There's a hierarchy in the drug world," Jake said. "At the bottom level were the hippies who smoked pot and talked about love and peace. The next level took pills. The next level snorted drugs. The next shot dope. At the top were the drugstore burglars. They got first choice out of the bag. My favorite were the art school students," Jake said. "They'd take anything—even birth control pills—if they thought they'd get a buzz. Jake apologized for standing me up the first time we were going to get married. "I couldn't get any drugs that day," he said. "I was in withdrawal, too sick to get out of bed."

Jake's parents had been married for thirty years; he believed our marriage would work. In my family, men came and went. I thought marriage was something you did for a year. "Our paths crossed but just for a minute," Jake said. "I'm finally starting to see that. You were running into the drug world. I was trying to get out."

I drank, smoked pot, and took pills until I met Jake. Jake taught me about shooting drugs. I was a stripper then. They called us exotic dancers, but there was nothing exotic about it. We worked in grimy clubs for grimy men, so more grimy men could gape at us. I danced because it was the only way I could make five hundred dollars a week.

I was twenty and an addict when I became pregnant with John. I didn't know about recovery. I didn't know how to be a mom. When I found out I was pregnant, all I knew was that I wasn't having another abortion. This child was going to be born. I was already on probation for possession of drugs. Jake's family had connections with the probation department. Even though Jake was getting high and supplying me with dope, he reported me to my probation officer for getting high when I was pregnant. My probation officer sent me to live with my mom until John was born. It forced me to be sober—like being in prison. I was angry with Jake but now I'm glad he protected our unborn child. I didn't know how to stop using. After John was born, I moved back to Minneapolis and lived with Jake and his parents. The day John was born, Jake gave me a present: the biggest bottle of drugs I ever saw. I started using again right away. I knew way back then I wasn't going to keep this child. It was my destiny to lose him. I couldn't stop it from happening.

After we got married, Jake and I lived in a small apartment. Jake got a job in a shipping department. I worked as a legal secretary. As screwed up as I was, I had gone to an excellent school. I could take shorthand and typed 130 words a minute. Our son, John, lived with Jake's mom or my mom. At work on coffee breaks, I went in the bathroom and shot dope. The firm I worked for represented the methadone program. The waiting list to get on the program was a year long. Methadone is a synthetic opiate. If you take it, you don't get sick. You get kind of normal. The thought behind it is, if junkies take methadone, they won't take street drugs or do crimes. It's a form of rehabilitation. One day I walked into my boss's office. "I'm a drug addict," I said. "So is my husband. We need to get on the methadone program right away." The attorney got us on the program, but I lost my job.

Jake was happy to take methadone; he had a floor. All it did was make me want to use drugs more. One night when I was playing the organ in the living room, Jake pried off the bedroom window, crawled out, and ran home to his parents. John was already there. Now I was alone. After Jake left, I fell hard. One afternoon I went to the store. When I came back, the firemen had come and gone. My apartment burned down. I blacked out. The next thing I knew, it was six months later and my mom was helping me move into an apartment near downtown Minneapolis. I enrolled in college. I was still on the methadone program, but I got high on whatever else I could. I wasn't done in the drug world.

On July 8, 1972, I took a shower, put on new clothes, and walked to the park by the Art Institute. I laid in the sun all afternoon reading a book about how a cocaine addict climbed a mountain and found God at the top. That night I met David Zempel, the best drugstore burglar in town. I loved him, and he loved me. We drove around the state burglarizing drugstores. Someday we'd get married and have a little girl and a little boy, we said. We just didn't know how to stop shooting drugs. That's what our normal was.

I went to a friend's house one afternoon. He did burglaries with David too—ear, nose, and throat doctor's offices for liquid cocaine. That day, I had two syringes of coke prepared and in my boots. When I knocked on our friend's door, a stranger opened it. My friend was on the couch sleeping, his hands behind him. I didn't know he was handcuffed. I went upstairs to the bathroom to shoot some coke. I didn't have many veins left. Shooting drugs was like throwing darts. When the bathroom door flew open, I was sitting on the floor trying to shoot up. Policemen shoved guns in my face—the stranger who answered the door was an undercover cop. "Put your hands up or we'll shoot!" they yelled.

"Are you kidding?" I said. "I just found a vein."

They arrested us, then they sent David to prison and me to live with Mom (like that was a cure). I didn't know how to live without drugs. One night I was on the roof of the drugstore in the small town where she lived, trying to get into the ventilation system, when the police surrounded me with rifles and spotlights. I had decided it would be better to be stoned or in jail than to be where I was—lost without David and drugs in small-town purgatory.

By then the revolution had begun. A judge finally sent me to treatment instead of sending me to live with my mother. He said "for as long as it takes to get sober, or you go to prison." It took eight months. It was a cool change. I asked for God's help. To my surprise, I got it. I became transformed into a sober human being.

When I called Jake to ask if I could have my son back, he and his parents said no. I stopped the custody battle. I didn't know Jake was still using. I had so much guilt, all I could see was what I did wrong. After I got out of treatment, I moved back to Minneapolis. Each weekend I'd visit my son. I'd clean house, help Jake's mom. Jake and I started dating again. I took him to a few recovery meetings. One night he stopped by my apartment and threw a bottle of pills on my sofa. I screamed at him to take the drugs and get out. I still didn't get it that Jake wasn't sober.

Then a counselor from a treatment center called. He warned me that David, the drugstore burglar, was released from prison to their program but had run away. "He's obsessed with you," the counselor said. "Watch out." I had written David a letter from treatment saying only "good-bye." I knew he wouldn't understand who I was becoming. I didn't understand myself. Plus it was a violation of my probation to have contact with David. I loved him, but I had a new normal. I didn't want to see him if he wasn't sober. I didn't want to get high, and I didn't want to go to jail.

The counselor who called was David Beattie. I didn't know I would marry him a year later (I was planning on remarrying Jake). The program he was calling from was Eden House—the program where I'd get my first job as a codependency counselor, even though I (and the world) didn't know what that word meant yet. Then the counselor called again. They found David in a hotel room, dead from a drug overdose.

A few days later, after work on Friday (I was working as a legal secretary again), I went to Jake's house like I did every weekend. His mother had gone on vacation. Jake and I had been talking about remarrying. Jake said I could live by myself in the small apartment in back of the house (where Jake lived now). I could help his mother with housework and take care of John. Jake and his father were sitting in the living room. They were hungry and were waiting for me. I looked at Jake, and something clicked. It was a moment of truth. The only reason I was considering remarrying him was because I couldn't stand the guilt from being divorced and not having custody of John.

I was done being held hostage. I grabbed my purse and walked out the door. Two months later, Jake called in the middle of the night. "I overdosed and almost died. I'm scared. I never stopped shooting drugs. Please help me," Jake begged. I helped him get into treatment. But when he called and asked if I'd go to family group, I told him to go to hell.

"After you went to treatment, I didn't believe you were sober. But when I brought you that dope and you threw it at me and told me to get out, I knew you were for real," Jake told me now, thirty-five years later. "You were my inspiration. I figured if you could stop using, anyone could. It doesn't seem strange that you're back in my life," Jake said. "Junkie angel, you always help me get to the next place."

In April, I flew back to Minnesota to spend the week with Jake. He didn't want to talk much this trip. We'd run out of things to say. He lost his appetite. He moaned from pain. He was too tired to take supplements. His urine turned dark, almost black. His ex-wife and I had a conference, then we called the home-care nurse. She showed up on my last day in town and congratulated us. "You've been doing an excellent job of hospice care," she said. "I couldn't have done better myself."

Hospice care? Jake was going through a transformation, but not the one I thought. This was the big one: death. I looked at Jake. He'd known all along! I couldn't believe he was dying. I thought he was getting well. Jake begged me not to leave. "I'll be back in three weeks to take care of you," I said.

"No," he said with that twinkle in his eyes. "I'll see you in ten days."

Jake was right. Ten days later, I returned to Minnesota. Nichole, my daughter, came with me to support John and me. By then Jake was in the hospital, in a coma. Machines were all that was keeping him alive. My son had met with the doctors and the minister. John had decided to take his father off life support. It was time to let his dad go.

The night before John planned to shut off the machines, I got a call at the hotel. Nichole's dad (who also lived in Minneapolis) fell down the stairs. He fractured his skull. They found *him* dead. Both my children's fathers died at the same time.

The next day, John shut off the machines. We said the Lord's Prayer, but Jake was still breathing when we said, "Amen." John looked confused, like *what should we do?* He suggested saying the prayer again. When we finished, Jake exhaled his last breath. I'd heard a last breath before in Shane's ICU room. The last breath sounds unlike any other.

Nichole made the arrangements for her father. John, Jake's other ex, and his family planned his. Both men were cremated. David Beattie's memorial service was one day, Jake's the next. Both services took place in the same chapel where we held Shane's. I think I set a record that week. My name appeared in two obituaries on the same page of the same paper on the same day in the same way: *survived by Melody Beattie, ex-wife and dear friend.*

"I promised Jake's family he'd get better," I told a friend. "I feel like such an ass."

"Maybe you needed to believe that," my friend said. "At least you had a chance to forgive each other and make peace."

I forgave Jake a long time ago. What happened is I finally stopped hating myself. I thought I was back in Jake's life to help him get well, but I was back there to heal me. We think we know what's happening, what we're doing, and why. Sometimes we do. But more often than not, we don't know what's happening until the experience ends. That's what *living in the mystery means.* We let go of our need to control and let life teach us what it wants. We stop trying to figure it out.

I called my remaining ex-husband. "Be careful," I said. "It's not a good time to have been married to me."

"No worry," he said. "I'm fine." But within fourteen months, he would die too. There's another piece to this story about the changes with my exes; it's another one of those circles within a circle. David's sister (David the drugstore burglar) tracked me down shortly after I learned I had hepatitis C. On one of my trips to Minnesota, I met her for dinner. It's the first time we'd talked in thirty years.

"David called me when he ran away from treatment," she said. "He knew where you lived. He watched you visiting your son every weekend. He knew you were straight—not using drugs. He said the most loving thing he could do was let you go and leave you alone. That was right before he died. From the minute David met you, he told me there was something different about you. He knew someday you'd be a writer." David's sister said nobody told her he was dead until a month after they buried him. She still hadn't been to his grave. We went together. She gave me the Mother Mary medallion he was wearing when he died.

"He'd want you to have it," she said.

I bought a silver chain and put the medallion on it. When I wear it, the medallion sits right over my heart—another missing piece. After Jake died, I went back to David's grave. I brought flowers, cleaned the marker, and thanked him for being in my life. Our relationship was crazy, but it was what I needed at the time. My entire sobriety, I didn't think anything that happened before I got sober counted—especially my drug-using days. *All of my life before I got sober was one big mistake*, I thought. I felt guilty about everything I'd done and who I was until I got clean. After I made peace with that part of my life—for the first time in all those years—I was able to go back to the park by the Art Institute, the one I went to the day I met David. That circle was complete.

I watched a movie about a husband and wife who were wrongfully convicted and spend fourteen years in prison. When their sons grew up, they freed their parents. It was a true story. I cried so hard watching it. I didn't spend a lifetime in prison, but I know what it feels like to be imprisoned by guilt. It dominates you, runs and ruins your life. Like Marge said, "Guilt is the gift that keeps on giving." It feels like it lasts forever. If you even start to feel happy, you wreck your joy. You don't stand up for yourself. You let people walk over you. *Who am I to say what I want?* you think. You don't believe you deserve peace. *That's my punishment*, you think when anything bad happens. *God doesn't love me.* You not only have pain from the loss, you have pain from believing you deserve to lose what you don't have. It takes courage to forgive ourselves.

After the funerals of my ex-husbands, I still didn't understand why I was being pulled back to my past, not completely yet. The doors to my guilt prison were swinging open. I was becoming free. But there were more circles to travel in my pilgrimage, more pieces to find. Sometimes life is a series of losses. To complete the grieving process—to heal our hearts—we need to go back and make peace with each one.

"God has forgiven you," my therapist, Sonja Ray, said. "But that doesn't do any good unless you accept God's forgiveness."

"What am I supposed to do? Stand in front of the mirror and say one hundred times a day, 'I forgive you'?"

She said, "That'd be a start. You have to go all the way back. The sins of the father, the sins of the grandfather, the great-grandfather, the great-great-grandfather, and his father and mother too. Their guilt is in your

DNA. Hate them, and you hate yourself. Forgive them, and you're forgiven. Do a family tree," she said. "Something will happen. It always does. When you honor and forgive your parents and ancestors, you forgive yourself. People need to know it matters that they were here, that their lives have value and meaning. What you do unto others is done to you."

I found the names of as many of my ancestors as I could—five levels up on each side for my mother and father. At first I groaned about this assignment. It was hard work; it took time. Then it became interesting, fun. "Pray for forgiveness for and from them," Sonja said. "Do something to honor their lives." I planted a tree in Jerusalem for one ancestor, donated to a charity in the name of another. I planted more trees in parks around the United States for others. I put a beautiful bench in one national park to honor my mom. It has her name and birth date on it. I called and told her what I'd done and that I love her. I thanked her for being my mother. I did my family of origin work—but not the kind where we say what monsters they are. I began to understand how their lives positively contributed to mine. We're all links in a chain. We really are one with each other and life.

The turning point that Sonja promised would happen occurred when I was digging around at www.ancestry.com. I pulled up a photocopy of the original census sheet signed by Annie Vaillancourt, my dad's grandmother. It happened when I saw Annie's handwriting. She became a real person. Dependents: two grandchildren, my dad and his sister. The story ran through my mind—the one I'd heard whispered about all those years. When Annie's daughter was twenty, she fell out of a boat and drowned. My dad and his sister were babies when they lost their mom. Annie was single. Did her husband walk out on her? Did he die? *Her heart must have broken when her daughter died,* I thought. *What a tough life Annie had losing her daughter, then raising her grandchildren by herself back when women could barely find work.* I could almost hear life saying it: "Melody, meet your great-grandmother Annie. Annie, meet Melody." I felt overcome with gratitude and started to cry. I finally had a grandma I loved. What happened from this family of origin work is my heart healed. Then I found peace and joy.

People say you can't change the past. Not true. You can change it from a big ugly mistake into a history with value and worth—even the things we judge as wrong.

About then, I got an e-mail from one of my daughter's friends in Minnesota, telling me a story. She's a substitute teacher now. One day when she was teaching, she called a student up to her desk. "Do you know where you got your name?" she asked the boy. "Yes," he said. "When my mom was pregnant with me, my aunt babysat for a boy and girl who went to this school. One day the boy went skiing. He hit his head and died. I was named after Shane Beattie," the boy—Shane—said.

My therapist said I didn't need to plant a tree for my son. His memory is alive.

Years ago I had a dream. *I'm an alchemist, a wizard who transforms dross into gold. My experiments had gone bad. I chopped off so much of myself with an ax that there was only a little of me left—a torso and a head. I hid in bed covered with a quilt, ashamed of what I'd done.* I understood part of the dream. Since I got sober in 1973, I've devoted my life to helping myself and others turn mistakes into lives with meaning. I'm like an alchemist. But the cutting off of so much of myself? I didn't get it—until now. I had cut off the part of me that was married to Jake. Then I cut off the part of me that was a junkie mother. I cut off the part of me that was with David, the drugstore burglar. I wouldn't even drive by the park by the Art Institute—the one I went to the day I met him—much less go in it. I cut off my childhood, the abortion, my ancestry. Chop. Chop. Chop. I cut off everything that caused guilt. How much farther back could I go?

There was one more piece I'd left behind.

I set the alarm early—6:30 a.m. I've done hundreds of speaking engagements. I don't remember being this anxious even when I've been on *Oprah*. It wasn't just that I'd be talking to teens. I was going back to the fundamentalist religious academy I attended when I was drinking and using drugs. That was back when we didn't know teenagers could be alcoholics and addicts—especially the ones who get straight A's.

I drank my coffee, took a shower, tried to get dressed. Fifteen minutes later, half the clothes in my closet were piled on my bed. Nothing looked right. Just once I wanted to walk through the doors of that school liking how I looked. I'd been at a book signing when a man said, "Do you remember me? We used to ride the bus together to and from the Academy." Then he asked if I'd speak at the school. Something pushed me to say yes. This was about more than giving a talk on drugs or a school reunion. It wasn't a coincidence it was happening now. It's part of healing my past.

I walked up to the stage. The principal had a surprise. He found one of the only pictures of me that exists from that time. On the wall behind me—bigger than life—he projected the picture. There she was—the girl I left behind. The students giggled. I looked so ugly. One girl said, "Wow, you're so pretty now." I talked about how badly I felt about myself when I went to that school. I told the students that when we and our lives are different from others, it's because God made us that way. God has a plan for us and can use all the parts of our lives and everything we do—even our mistakes—for good. We have a place in the world and sometimes a special job to do. We each have a path. And we're not as different or as separate as we think. We look at other people and think they've got it together or have something we don't. But we don't know how they feel inside. Everyone has something he or she is dealing with. Afterward, a girl from the audience came up and thanked me for what I said. I looked at her and knew I was looking at me. *She's just a kid*, I thought. *So was I. I didn't hate the school. I hated myself. I wasn't a monster. I was doing the best I could.* Another circle was complete.

For the next four months, I sank into depression. It wasn't grief like I felt after Shane died. It was every feeling from my childhood I didn't know how to feel back then. Then a new feeling emerged: compassion for myself. *If I felt like this back then, it's a miracle I didn't kill myself,* I thought. *I was drinking to self-medicate the loss and pain. I used drugs to survive. Then the cure became a disease.*

There's a reason for everything that happens. That includes the things we do—not just the things that happen to us. There was a reason I got into each relationship. There was a reason I got out. *If I knew then what I know now, I wouldn't have made all those mistakes.* But the reason I am who I am now is because of all the things I've done—including the things I've done wrong. Every moment counts.

I didn't think the pain I was feeling would ever end. "You don't have to feel all that sadness," a friend said when I told her about the depression. "I take antidepressants," she said. "I feel happy all the time."

"Maybe sometimes we're not meant to feel happy," I said. "Our bad feelings count too. It's just that I'm not sure what I'm supposed to do." We saw it at the same time written on the vanity license plate on the car in front of us. It read: CRY. So that's what I did. Sometimes life answers our questions in funny ways.

I was at my chiropractor's office days later, talking to the receptionist. "I don't want to take antidepressants," I said. "It's my life and my pain and I like it." I must have been talking too loudly because when I finished, the people in the room applauded.

Some people need help managing depression. They want to feel normal, feel like themselves. Sometimes depression is caused by a chemical imbalance in the brain. Some people are depressed because they're stuck in jobs or relationships they hate. Other times, depression and anxiety are created by all the feelings we've buried, and those feelings create an imbalance in us. Those old feelings are trying to come out so our hearts can heal and we can feel peace. For many years I thought drugs would make me feel good or a relationship would make me happy. Feeling happy and normal aren't out there. They're inside, underneath all those emotions we try so hard not to feel.

When life is changing, we need to be willing not to feel like ourselves for a while. Chemical therapy may help and be necessary after a loss. But are we willing to feel some discomfort until our new normal begins? That's how we evolve and become who we are.

I trudged through the feelings—thick, heavy sludge. Finally they lifted. I found me underneath, and a new normal began. I surrendered to the hepatitis C. So what if I have it? Millions of other people do too. I contracted a disease as a consequence of a behavior. It's not punishment. If I hadn't been an addict, I wouldn't have done the writing I did. It's all part of destiny. I'm happy. I feel better physically and emotionally then ever. For the first time I'm whole—not fragmented. Even with hepatitis C, I'm complete.

Four days after this awakening, the trouble with my spine surfaced. I was going through a passage.

"Be grateful," a friend said. "People in their fifties either fix their bodies and stick around, or they give up and leave." Howard Wills said it like this: "By the time people get to their fifties, they've got so much negativity accumulated that chronic illness often begins. If people don't forgive other people and themselves, they can't get well."

That doesn't mean we're to blame if we're sick. We may need holistic or medical help. Sometimes our number is up. But the real miracle comes with forgiveness. Even Jesus didn't say, "Your liver or back is healed." He said, "Your sins are forgiven."

People say I've changed. I'm more comfortable in my body. My no's are quiet but have more power. My yes's do too. I speak my truth because I trust who I am. I surrender more quickly to each moment and whatever it brings. Then I'm guided into what to do next. More quickly and easily, I make peace with what is. I don't always like what's happening, but when I surrender to how I feel, I'm happy even if I'm feeling sad. It doesn't get much better than that. Toxic guilt is the worst feeling there is. It's hard to feel your way through it. But I'm learning to accept forgiveness and to forgive others and myself. Blessed are those who mourn; they'll find comfort. Blessed are the meek; they inherit the earth. The biggest paradox: To be happy, surrender to what hurts. Forgiveness isn't a one-time deal. The need to make peace is ongoing. The way to be happy is to be present for each moment, be aware. That's what love is. I used to think love was getting people to be and do what I want. True love wants people to be who they are.

The biggest change is I don't feel separate. That's where my initiation led. I'm one with life. I used to believe that support always failed me. Now

I know support is always there. How can it not be when we're one with life? I don't *hope* it's going to be okay. It's okay now—no matter what's taking place. When life is in upheaval, it's part of a change. We can trust life. After everything I've been through, that's a bold statement to make. I don't mean we can trust life to give us what we want. We can trust life to take us where we're meant to go. That place is always right here, right now. That's the peace we've been promised. It surpasses all understanding. I'm no longer surviving. I'm present for myself, others, this moment. I'm thriving. I love living this way. I like who and how I am.

At times I don't recognize the world. "What happened?" I asked a friend, one I consider a master. "The revolution in the sixties started so good. What went wrong?"

"Every revolution becomes an institution," he said. "And there's that yin-yang thing. Life is constantly evolving."

I'm not naive. Bad things happen. I was raging one day about how God wants us to trust Him, then He smites us by raining disaster on us. "How can God expect us to trust Him when He does that?" I asked.

"Make the container bigger," my friend Marge said. "Stretch it until it contains disaster *and* trust." Life isn't black and white, good or bad, right or wrong. It's not either/or. It's both at the same time. Life is what it is.

You think you know the shape of your life, how it's going to go, then you wake up one day and that shape changes. As much as you want to go back to that moment in time—that second before it changed—you can't. "It's not that things change," I said to my friend. Then we said it together: "It's that we expect them to stay the same."

Welcome to the Club.

———

Children of alcoholics are about four times more likely than the general population to develop alcohol problems. Children of alcoholics also have a higher risk for many other behavioral and emotional problems.

One in ten American women takes an antidepressant drug such as Prozac, Paxil, or Zoloft, and the use of these drugs by all adults has nearly tripled in the last decade.

Depressive disorders affect approximately 19 million American adults.

Depression will be the second-leading cause of disability in the world by 2020, trailing heart disease.

Every 78 seconds a teen attempts suicide; every 90 seconds one succeeds.

Sources: National Institutes of Health, *Washington Post*, National Institute of Mental Health, World Health Organization, and National Center for Health Statistics

Activities

1. Make peace. Review your Master List of Losses. Are you willing to be at peace with all the ups and downs of your life? Which losses haven't you made peace with yet? What do you have the most guilt about? Are there any people from your life you believe you will never forgive? Do you believe you're unforgivable? These are heavy questions. This isn't an activity to be accomplished in a week, month, or year. This is a long journey—your pilgrimage. Are you willing to forgive others and yourself? Are you willing to receive forgiveness? Are you willing to become willing? Healer Howard Wills suggests the following prayer: "God, please help me forgive them, help them forgive me, and help us all forgive ourselves. Please God. Thank you God." (© Howard Wills) I've heard it said that we know we're at peace when everyone we know and everything we've done has clear and peaceful passage through our mind. What that means is, we can think of an event or person and we don't become riled, angry, guilty, or upset. What events and which people don't have clear passage through your

mind? Use Howard's prayer until they do. (The complete forgiveness prayer can be found at www.howardwills.org.)

When I began recovery, I was told to use the following prayer for anyone I resented: "God bless them, God bless them, God bless them." I was told to keep praying it until I meant it. It sounds simplistic, but it works. It might take months or years, but if we're serious about forgiveness, we can achieve it. Willingness is the first step. On your road to forgiveness, become aware of any feelings you have. Don't use forgiveness as denial. But don't let bitterness and grudges become a way of life. At the end of the day, we want to be at peace with everyone we've met, everything we've experienced, whatever we've done, and who we are right now. Remember, forgiveness isn't something we do just once. It's easy to let new grudges pile up. At the end of each year, before the new year begins, look through your day planner and personal directory. Are there any people you have something against from the year passing? Ring in the New Year with peace.

2. Do your ancestral family of origin work. Go back five generations. Make peace with and for your ancestors. Clear the energy from your bloodline, your family tree. Go up five levels on each side—your mother's and your father's side. Find out the first and last names of each person in each generation. It helps to draw the family tree and fill in the blanks. There are free downloads available online, or you can draw a simple chart with blank lines. To get information, dig. Call relatives. Ask to go through old photos. Visit www.ancestry.com—it's a helpful Web site, although it costs money to use its resources. If you've diligently tried to find the names of your ancestors and can't, fill in the blanks with a generic "father's grandfather's father," but give it your best shot. The willingness to do the work is part of honoring our ancestors and parents. Once you have your family tree made, pray for forgiveness for each person. Ask that they be forgiven by God and by anyone they've hurt or anyone who thinks they've hurt them; ask that they forgive anyone who hurt them or whom they think hurt them. Ask that they forgive themselves and receive forgiveness by God. You forgive them too—for

anything they may have passed along in the bloodline to you.

Tell all the people in your family tree (individually) that you honor and respect them, that their lives had value and meaning, and thank them for living. If it hadn't been for them, there wouldn't be a you. Thank them for the unique contribution they made to your life and your DNA. It would be a lot to do a memorial for each person—but choose five to ten of your ancestors to honor by planting a tree, making a donation to a charity, or having his or her name engraved on a bench in a park. If funds are low, get creative. Make a scrapbook and donate several pages to each person. Find out details about his or her life. Write something about the person or find pictures. Sonja, the counselor who suggested this work, insists that if this activity is tackled with an open mind and willing heart, it works every time. Howard Wills says you'll see miracles in your family and in your life once the ancestral negativity is cleared. You may even see changes in family members who are alive and don't know you're doing the work. I did. Open your heart to your ancestry, to what they contributed to your life. Meet the people whose lives linked and helped form you.

3. Make a scrapbook of your life. A television interviewer asked me to make a scrapbook of my life as a prop and guide for the show. Again, I groaned at first. Then it became fun. I bought a big scrapbook. I started gathering, cutting, pasting pictures, writing about different memories from my life. Sometimes I'd write a little story about an experience. Or I'd cut and paste different symbols or pictures that represented something and had meaning for me. You'll get ideas as you go along. Cut out pictures and words from magazines. Get as creative as you can. Make a book that talks about the highs and lows—the story of your life. You may find that not only will you enjoy this book, your relatives will get a kick out of it too.

4. Is there any part of yourself or your life that you think is so horrible that you've cut it off and left it behind? It might be a town, a school, a restaurant—some place that reminds you of something in your life that

you're still in turmoil about? Sometimes we physically need to go back and get that piece—travel to the town or the place where it happened, take a trip down memory lane. Are there any places you refuse to go because you feel so much guilt or pain about that part of your life? The park I went to the afternoon before I met David was a place like that for me. For thirty years I drove around that park. After I did the forgiveness work, I was drawn to that park. I came full circle to find peace. Maybe you need to take a trip to yesterday too. When we do, we're more present for now.

Master Loss Checklist

Following is a list of possible losses, changes, and passages. Scan it. Put a check mark by any losses or changes that apply to your life. Mark losses that happened in the past and changes or losses occurring now.

If you've experienced a loss but feel at peace with it, put a "P" by that loss.

Some losses, such as a serious physical impairment or the death of a child, will stay with us all our lives. Put an "O" by any loss you feel is ongoing. Only you can decide if a particular loss will affect you and for how long. (You may be marking your losses with more than one letter. Use as many letters as you need to accurately describe your grief.)

Put an "H" by any loss that currently hurts. If you want, use the same rating scale that doctors use to assess physical pain. On a scale from 1 to 10, with 1 being the least and 10 being the most severe, mark how much that loss hurts on your best days and how much it hurts on your worst. Do you have any days that are pain free? How many each month?

If you see losses on the list that you haven't dealt with, mark those with an "F" for frozen.

If a loss has caused you trauma, mark it with a "T." Remember, only you can decide what's a loss and how traumatic it is.

We can lose tangible things like a person or a home, and intangible things like self-esteem, innocence, and having a sense of safety in the world. There are unclear or ambiguous losses, as psychotherapist Pauline Boss calls them in her book *Ambiguous Loss*. Those losses can be confusing. Mommy comes home every night, but she isn't really there because she's drunk. Or we're immigrants to a new country. We have all the gains the move to a new country brings, but we've lost the traditions, values, culture, and family contact that we had in our homeland. Because we've gained something, what we've lost may not be clear, or we may think we're complaining unnecessarily for having feelings about what's gone. We need to give ourselves permission to grieve and to feel.

Losses can accompany welcomed change, such as the loss of freedom—even the loss of a good night's sleep—that happens when our children are born. "I haven't been able to watch a football game from start to finish for five years," one father said. "I love my children. But I miss watching sports on Sunday afternoons." We may go through grief when there are changes at work, even if the reorganization is good. Most people agree that all change brings loss. That's how life works. There are losses involved with expected life passages such as moving from childhood into adulthood, marriage, old age, and death.

A woman who is more in love with her husband than anyone I've met pulled me aside a few months after her wedding. She married later in life; she was in her mid-thirties at the time. "If I get up to go to the bathroom, he asks where I'm going. He expects me to go to bed at the same time he does. I've been a single woman for a long time. I love him, but I feel like I've lost my freedom. I can't even sit, space out, and watch my favorite shows on television or come home after a hard day's work and not talk for a while. He's waiting for me to visit with him, tell him about my day. Nobody told me it was going to be like this. I love him," she said, "but losing my freedom is driving me crazy. Somebody ought to write a book." She's hoping to find a way to balance her need to take care of herself with her need to respond lovingly to her husband. There are normal expectations for people in a live-in relationship—calling if we're going to be late or sharing the remote control—things that don't happen when we live alone. Sometimes awareness is all we need to ease our passage through the change. There are advantages—blessings and gifts—and limitations that accompany each stage of life.

A loss may be personal and affect only one person—us. Sometimes other people are involved. When a child dies, that child's family, friends, and neighbors are affected—each in his or her own way. Some losses affect an entire community. Sometimes a country or the globe is affected by a natural disaster or by war. En masse, we grieved over Mother Teresa's, Princess Diana's, and President John F. Kennedy's deaths. We each had our feelings, but we went through the grief together. It was a personal and cultural loss. Sometimes the passing of one person is symbolic of the passing of an era (as when Johnny Carson died). Another category of loss is the natural evolution and the changes that take place in cultures, our country, and the world as times, ways, music, fashion, entertainers, and art change.

Each person grieves in his or her way, pace, and time. We each find our path to peace. Losses that might be minor to an adult can impact a teenager or child more or differently. Losses that cause minor distress to one person can be major for someone else. We are the only ones who know how we feel.

Some losses cause more pain than others. But even if we've gone through the worst loss, other losses still hurt, and it doesn't help to compare pain. Experiencing a catastrophic loss may make additional losses feel insignificant and overwhelming at the same time. *I've already been through so much. It's too much to lose anything else*, we think. *But this is nothing compared to what I've been through.*

Current losses usually activate pain from other losses. A friend took me on a tour of the building where she works. She heads an organization that helps people with HIV/AIDS. On the wall are pictures of people who died. Attending funerals is part of her job, she explains. "I don't get used to the death," she says. "Pain doesn't become routine. There's a room in my heart that holds the grief from all the people I've lost. When someone else dies, I find myself right back in that room. I feel the pain from all the other losses as well as the pain I'm feeling from the loss now."

How full is that room in your heart? Make a list of your losses now.

_____ Death of a child, spouse, or close family member

_____ Child, spouse, or loved one is in the process of dying

_____ Miscarriage

_____ Stillbirth

_____ Death of other loved ones (death significantly affects us)

_____ Death of someone (loss somewhat affects us)

_____ In the process of our own death (imminent, pending, know approximate death date)

_____ In the process of our own death and leaving minor children behind

_____ Abortion (we're the mother)

_____ Abortion (our child—we're the father)

_____ Unwanted child (we're the unwanted child)

_____ Unwanted pregnancy (us)

_____ Unwanted pregnancy (our child)

_____ Unwanted pregnancy (someone we love)

_____ Suicide (someone we love)

_____ Murder (someone we love)

_____ Suicide attempt, failed (us)

_____ Suicide attempt, failed (someone we love)

_____ Abduction/kidnapping (us)

_____ Abduction/kidnapping (someone we love)

_____ Missing child

_____ Missing adult

_____ Death of a pet

_____ Loss of a pet

_____ Placed a child for adoption

_____ Were placed for adoption

_____ Adopting a child who has unexpected mental or physical issues

_____ Inability to obtain and sustain adequate insurance

_____ Chronic illness (us)

_____ Chronic illness (someone we love)

_____ Living with the possibility of onset or recurrence of serious illness (Huntington's disease, cancer, etc., for us)

_____ Living with the possibility of onset or recurrence of serious illness (someone we love)

_____ Waiting for test results for serious illness (us)

_____ Waiting for test results for serious illness (someone we love)

_____ Unable to get proper medical diagnosis (us)

_____ Unable to get proper medical diagnosis (someone we love)

_____ Intractable pain (us)

_____ Intractable pain (someone we love)

_____ Unable to get proper treatment for intractable pain (us)

_____ Unable to get proper treatment for intractable pain (someone we love)

_____ Living with a potentially fatal or serious illness (us)

_____ Living with a potentially fatal or serious illness (someone we love)

_____ Permanent or long-term illness that impacts quality of life or ability to function (us)

_____ Permanent or long-term illness that impacts qualify of life or ability to function (someone we love)

_____ Ill spouse/partner who requires temporary caretaking

_____ Ill spouse/partner who requires long-term caretaking

_____ Ill family member who requires temporary caretaking

_____ Ill family member who requires long-term caretaking

_____ Illness as a child that affected our school or social participation

_____ Ill child with special needs (our child)

_____ Debilitating illness in ourselves that requires temporary caretaking

_____ Debilitating illness in ourselves that requires permanent or long-term caretaking

_____ Visually impaired (us)

_____ Visually impaired (someone we love or a child)

_____ Hearing impaired (us)

_____ Hearing impaired (someone we love or a child)

_____ Physically impaired temporarily (someone we love or a child)

_____ Physically impaired permanently (someone we love or a child)

_____ Surgery (someone we love or a child)

_____ Improper medical treatment that made injury or illness worse (us)

_____ Improper medical treatment that made injury or illness worse (someone we love)

_____ Accident (us)

_____ Accident (someone we love)

_____ Accident with long-term or permanent injury (us)

_____ Accident with long-term or permanent injury (someone we love)

_____ Loss of one or both breasts

_____ Loss of ability to bear children or to impregnate

_____ Loss of a limb or body part

_____ Loss of use of a limb temporarily

_____ Loss of use of a limb permanently

_____ Had an organ transplanted in us

_____ STD (have one)

_____ STD (spread one to someone else)

_____ Illness that carries perceived stigma (us)

_____ Illness that carries perceived stigma (someone we love)

_____ Illness that is contagious permanently (us)

_____ Illness that is contagious permanently (someone we love)

_____ Illness that is temporarily seriously contagious (us)

_____ Illness that is temporarily seriously contagious (someone we love)

_____ War (our country involved with war or we feel the impact of this war)

_____ Actively participating in war (us)

_____ Actively participating in war (someone we care about)

_____ War taking place in our country

_____ Natural disaster without personal losses (affects our community or those we care about; somehow we feel the impact although we didn't lose anything)

_____ Natural disaster with personal losses

_____ Terrorism that affects or threatens us

_____ Terrorism that directly affects or threatens someone we love

_____ Death of beloved leader or president

_____ Death of a hero, favorite figure, or entertainer

_____ Loss of irreplaceable possessions (photos, sentimental gifts)

_____ As a child, had adult household/family duties and responsibilities

_____ Adult with more than our share of household/family duties and responsibilities

_____ Single parent (by choice)

_____ Single parent (forced on us)

_____ Married or with partner, but partner doesn't hold up his or her share of responsibilities for child raising

_____ Married or with partner, but partner doesn't hold up his or her share of family/household responsibilities

_____ Victimized by business or charity scam

_____ Brainwashed or trapped by group or cult (us)

_____ Brainwashed or trapped by group or cult (someone we love)

_____ Abuse—physical, sexual, or emotional (us as child)

_____ Abuse—physical, sexual, or emotional (us as child by family member)

_____ Abuse—physical, sexual, or emotional (one or more of our children)

_____ Abuse—physical, sexual, or emotional (one or more of our children by a family member)

_____ Abuse—physical, sexual, or emotional (us as adult)

_____ Abuse—physical, sexual, or emotional (us as adult by family member)

_____ Abuse—physical, sexual, or emotional (our adult child)

_____ Abuse perpetrator (us as adult)

_____ Abuse perpetrator (us as child)

_____ Rape (our child)

_____ Rape (our child by family member)

_____ Rape (us as child)

_____ Rape (us as child by family member)

_____ Rape (our adult child)

_____ Rape (our adult child by family member)

_____ Rape (us as adult)

_____ Rape (us as adult by family member or friend)

_____ Rape or incest perpetrator (us as minor)

_____ Rape or incest perpetrator (us as adult)

_____ Assault (on us)

_____ Assault (on someone we love)

_____ Being stalked (we're the victim)

_____ Being stalked (someone we love is the victim)

_____ Stalking someone (we're the perpetrator)

_____ Stalking someone (someone we love is the perpetrator)

_____ Robbery (we're the victim)

_____ Burglary (we're the victim)

_____ Crime committed against us (by stranger)

_____ Crime committed against us (by someone we trusted or a friend)

_____ Criminal behavior, parole, probation, imprisonment, execution (by or of us)

_____ Criminal behavior, parole, probation, imprisonment, execution (by or of our child)

_____ Criminal behavior, parole, probation, imprisonment, execution (by or of someone we care about or love)

_____ Innocent but accused or convicted of a crime (us)

_____ Innocent but accused or convicted of a crime (our child)

_____ Innocent but accused or convicted of a crime (someone we love or a family member)

_____ Caused the death of another human being inadvertently, accidentally, in war, in self-defense, or as part of a job (for instance, law enforcement)

_____ Caused the death of another human being intentionally (not in a war or as part of a job)

_____ Caused serious harm to another human being inadvertently or accidentally, in war, in self-defense, or as part of a job

_____ Caused serious harm to another person deliberately

_____ Divorce (our own)

_____ Divorce (our parents)

_____ Divorce of a friend or relative (divorce affects our relationship with him or her)

_____ Became a stepparent

_____ Became a stepchild

_____ Loss of a stepparent

_____ Loss of a stepchild

_____ Loss of presence of one or both of our parents in our life (as a child)

_____ No contact with our family (as an adult)

_____ No contact with extended family (as a child, for instance, grandparents missing)

_____ No contact with extended family (as an adult)

_____ Loss of contact with a child (when child is a minor)

_____ Loss of contact with a child (when child is an adult)

_____ Loss of custody of a child

_____ Loss of foster child or child we've been caring for

_____ Severely dysfunctional relationship (with family member, friend, or loved one)

_____ Divorce (our grown child/children)

_____ Loss of relationship with son- or daughter-in-law who we treasured

_____ Loss of relationship with mother- or father-in-law who we treasured

_____ Divorce of grown child/children when our relationship with grandchildren is changed or severed

_____ Raising our grandchildren or a child we didn't plan to raise

_____ Adult child/children moved back into home after we had become used to them being gone

_____ Separation (our own)

_____ Separation (our parents)

_____ End of romantic relationship

_____ Broken engagement

_____ End of friendship

_____ Change in friendship (one person moves, gets married)

_____ Someone we love marries or dates someone we don't like

_____ Marrying or dating someone who someone we love dislikes

_____ Arguing, hostility with spouse

_____ Arguing, hostility with romantic relationship

_____ Arguing, hostility with family member or child

_____ Arguing, hostility with friend or neighbor

_____ Marriage dead but still in it

_____ Romantic relationship dead or ending but still in it

_____ Dissension with co-worker

_____ Major disappointment

_____ Move within same city

_____ Move to another city or state

_____ Move to another country

_____ Loss of home or living situation

_____ Inability to find appropriate living situation

_____ Having an affair (us)

_____ Having an affair (spouse or committed partner)

_____ Suspect partner or spouse of having an affair

_____ Spouse or partner suspects us of having an affair

_____ Having an emotional, not physical affair with someone (us)

_____ Having an emotional, not physical affair with someone (spouse or partner)

_____ Romantic partner or spouse left us for another person

_____ We left romantic partner or spouse for another person

_____ Bankruptcy

_____ Serious financial problems (still able to work, problems fixable)

_____ Serious financial problems (elderly or otherwise unable to work, problems difficult to resolve)

_____ Financially unstable (us)

_____ Financially unstable (a partner, someone we love, someone whose financial instability affects us)

_____ Loss of retirement funds, savings, or investments (us)

_____ Loss of retirement funds, savings, or investments (someone we love)

_____ Compulsively going into debt (us)

_____ Compulsively going into debt (someone we love or someone who's financial situation affects us)

_____ Problems with the IRS or any difficult tax situation

_____ Audit by the IRS

_____ Loss of credit

_____ No credit

_____ Loss of reputation

_____ Slander or libel (against us)

_____ Slander or libel (by us against someone)

_____ Identity theft

_____ Credit card theft or loss

_____ Wallet or purse loss

_____ Loss of valuable item

_____ Suing someone

_____ Someone suing us (legitimate claim)

_____ Someone suing us (fraudulent claim)

_____ Someone bringing false charges against us (criminal)

_____ Prosecuting someone else

_____ Bringing false charges against someone else

_____ Prejudice or discrimination (against us)

_____ Prejudice or discrimination (by us)

_____ Ashamed of something we did or that happened to us

_____ Ashamed of something family member or loved one did or that happened to him or her

_____ Loss of integrity

_____ Lying to someone

_____ Being lied to

_____ Manipulating someone

_____ Being manipulated

_____ Controlling someone

_____ Being or feeling controlled

_____ Deprived of ability to freely be who we are

_____ Deprived of freedom of self-expression

_____ Deprived of freedom of creative expression

_____ Deprived of ability to feel and express emotions

_____ Creatively stuck or blocked

_____ Deprived of ability to travel (health, marital, financial, or familial restrictions)

_____ Loss of joy (enraged, disappointed, or bitter)

_____ Loss of passion

_____ Loss of energy and vitality

_____ Loss of enthusiasm

_____ Loss of hope

_____ Loss of love (others for us)

_____ Loss of love (us for others)

_____ Loss of self-esteem

_____ Loss of self-confidence

_____ Loss of fun or pleasurable activities

_____ Loss of membership or participation in club or group

_____ Unable to furnish or fix living situation in pleasing way

_____ Loss of important recreational activity

_____ Restricted from important or valued activities (as a child)

_____ Restricted from important or valued activities (as an adult)

_____ Someone we love is restricted from valued activities and that affects us

_____ Feel like a failure

_____ Deprived of feeling blessed by God

_____ Loss of faith in God

_____ Significant change in religion, spirituality, or religious beliefs

_____ Loss of faith in ourselves

_____ Loss of innocence

_____ Living with guilt (us)

_____ Living with guilt (someone we love)

_____ Someone we love has lost innocence, faith, self-esteem, reputation, joy, or self-confidence

_____ Doing something that violates our ethics or standards

_____ Someone we love does something that violates our ethics or standards, and it affects us (e.g., friend is having an affair and we know friend's spouse)

_____ Stress (outer or inner—us)

_____ Stress (outer or inner—someone we love)

_____ Meanness, bitterness, or holding grudge (us)

_____ Meanness, bitterness, or holding grudge (someone we love)

_____ Someone has a grudge against us

_____ Someone is telling lies or spreading rumors about us

_____ Spreading rumors or lying about someone else

_____ Loss of quality of life due to deep and extended grief (us)

_____ Loss of quality of life due to deep and extended grief (someone we love)

_____ Contaminated environment, toxins (home, apartment, ground, neighborhood)

_____ Hurting someone's feelings intentionally

_____ Hurting someone's feelings accidentally

_____ Someone is hurting our feelings intentionally

_____ Someone is hurting our feelings accidentally

_____ Feeling denied or deprived of someone or something we really want

_____ Cannot read (us)

_____ Cannot read (someone we love of appropriate age)

_____ Cannot write (us)

_____ Cannot write (someone we love of appropriate age)

_____ Loss of purpose

_____ Loss of feeling needed

_____ Loss of job

_____ Loss of ability to work (due to age, health, or circumstances, including people in entertainment, in modeling, or with sports career)

_____ Loss of interest in career or vocation

_____ Fired from job (our fault)

_____ Fired from job (not our fault)

_____ Hour, salary, or benefit reduction at work

_____ Extensive necessary work travel (us)

_____ Extensive necessary work travel (someone we love)

_____ Working more hours than usual or desired (us)

_____ Working more hours than usual or desired (someone we love)

_____ Major change at job (policies, duties, role, leadership, business function, etc.)

_____ Cannot find job, career, or vocation we enjoy or like

_____ Bored with job, work, or career

_____ Cannot find work

_____ Business failed

_____ Business barely making it on ongoing basis, stressful

_____ Failed important test (school or work, e.g., bar exam, pilot or nurse licensure)

_____ Failed to make team (sports)

_____ Feeling trapped by family business or career expectations

_____ Trapping someone with business or career expectations

_____ Business outdated due to cultural evolution or corporate competition (family stores, etc.)

_____ Lost crops or products due to acts of nature or God

_____ Creative work failed or rejected

_____ Loss of important contract or job (if in business for ourselves)

_____ Loss of important, hard-to-replace documents, papers, etc.

_____ Someone we love lost important documents, papers, etc., and it affects us

_____ Uninsured loss (minor)

_____ Uninsured loss (catastrophic)

_____ Business failed due to competition

_____ Loss of lease on business premises or forced out of business due to rent increase or fire/flood/earthquake damage

_____ Deprived of wanted promotion

_____ Lost important award or victory

_____ Someone we love lost important award or victory

_____ Failure or blunder at work

_____ Failure at school

_____ Failure to graduate from high school

_____ Loss of favorite teacher, boss, or co-worker

_____ Loss of valued neighbor or employee at business we frequent

_____ Inability to get desired education due to finances or rejection from school

_____ Death of dreams

_____ Significant change or loss in financial situation

_____ Significant change or loss in partner's, spouse's, or roommate's financial situation

_____ Significant change in grown child's financial situation

_____ Significant change in friend or other family member's financial situation

_____ Learning disability (us)

_____ Learning disability (our child)

_____ Learning disability (someone we love)

_____ Alcoholism, addiction, eating disorder, gambling addiction, anger management problems (us)

_____ Alcoholism, addiction, eating disorder, gambling addiction, anger management problems (close family member or loved one)

_____ Alcoholism, addiction, eating disorder, gambling addiction, anger management problems (our child)

_____ Loss of childhood or ability to be a child

_____ Codependency (us)

_____ Codependency (someone we love)

_____ Phobia that restricts (us)

_____ Phobia that restricts (someone we love, and it affects us)

_____ Sabotaging or failure behaviors (us)

_____ Sabotaging or failure behaviors (someone we love)

_____ Living in a country and can't speak the language

_____ Living in a country and don't like or fit into the culture

_____ Mental illness (us)

_____ Mental illness (our child, young or adult)

_____ Mental illness (someone we love)

_____ Living with a person who is sloppy or unclean

_____ Living with our own messiness

_____ Living with someone else's uncontrollable clutter or pack-ratting

_____ Living with our own uncontrollable clutter or pack-ratting

_____ Living with a miserly or cheap person

_____ Living with our own stinginess or money fear

_____ Financially dependent on someone else

_____ Someone else is financially dependent on us (other than our minor children)

_____ Depression, anxiety, panic disorder, manic depression, OCD, (obsessive-compulsive disorder), ADD (attention deficit disorder), ADHD (attention-deficit/hyperactivity disorder) (us)

_____ Depression, anxiety, panic disorder, manic depression, OCD, ADD, ADHD (our child)

_____ Depression, anxiety, panic disorder, manic depression, OCD, ADD, ADHD (someone we love)

_____ Inability to get medications or medical care due to insurance restrictions, financial limitation, or limited resources (us)

_____ Inability to get medications or medical care due to insurance restrictions, financial limitation, or limited resources (someone we care about)

_____ Physical limitations due to aging

_____ Unwanted changes in appearance due to aging

_____ Unwanted gain or loss of weight

_____ Loss of hair

_____ Loss of continence

_____ Need long-term medication or medical treatment (us)

_____ Need long-term medication or medical treatment (someone we love)

_____ Need long-term rehabilitation or physical therapy (us)

_____ Need long-term rehabilitation or physical therapy (someone we love)

_____ Need to alter routine due to medical problems or restrictions (us)

_____ Need to alter routine due to medical problems or restrictions (someone we love)

_____ Living with serious side effects from medication or medical treatment (us)

_____ Living with serious side effects from medication or medical treatment (someone we love)

_____ Significant long-term or permanent change in appearance from accident, illness, or injury

_____ Loss of sexual activity in marriage or committed relationship (our ability or desire)

_____ Loss of sexual activity in marriage or committed relationship (partner or spouse's ability or desire)

_____ Loss of ability to be sexual (us)

_____ Loss of ability to be sexual (our partner or spouse)

_____ Loss of sexual appeal (us)

_____ Loss of sexual appeal (someone we love)

_____ Sexually inadequate or dysfunctional (us)

_____ Sexually inadequate or dysfunctional (someone we love)

_____ Deprived of intimacy with friends or family members

_____ Deprived of intimacy with spouse or romantic partner

_____ Deprived of sexual activity (cannot find appropriate partner)

_____ Loss of trust in a marriage (we lost trust)

_____ Loss of trust in a marriage (partner or spouse lost trust in us)

_____ Loss of trust in any close relationship, including child (we lost trust)

_____ Loss of trust in any close relationship, including child (other person lost trust in us)

_____ Deprived of personal time with romantic partner or spouse

_____ Deprived of personal time with child (minor or adult)

_____ Deprived of personal time with friend, family member, or other loved one

_____ Deprived of private time

_____ Deprived of privacy

_____ Depriving someone else of private time

_____ Depriving someone else of privacy

_____ Overisolating (us)

_____ Overisolating (someone we love)

_____ Bored (long-term) with spouse or romantic partner (us)

_____ Spouse or romantic partner is bored with us

_____ Not sharing interests or activities with spouse or partner, and it bothers us

_____ Not sharing interests or activities with spouse or partner, and it bothers him or her

_____ Feeling trapped in romantic relationship, marriage, or friendship

_____ Spouse, partner, or friend feels trapped with us

_____ Giving more than we're receiving in a marriage and feeling drained by it

_____ Giving more than we're receiving in a romantic relationship and feeling drained

_____ Giving more than we're receiving in a friendship and feeling drained

_____ Giving more than we're receiving at work and feeling drained

_____ Spouse or partner feels like he or she is giving more than he or she is receiving and feels drained by us

_____ Friend feels like he or she is giving more than he or she is receiving and feels drained by us

_____ Spouse, partner, child, or friend is extremely unhappy with life and his or her unhappiness affects us

_____ Power balance is off in marriage or romantic partnership—we have more power than the other person

_____ Power balance is off in marriage or romantic partnership—the other person has more power than us

_____ Power balance is off in friendship—we have more power than the friend

_____ Power balance is off in friendship—the friend has more power than us

_____ Power balance is off with our child—the child is controlling us (minor or adult child)

_____ Spouse's power balance is off with his or her child (the child is controlling him or her and it bothers us)

_____ Spouse is being controlled or used by his or her ex-partner (marital or romantic)

_____ Spouse's ex-partner (marital or romantic) is interfering in our relationship with spouse or partner now

_____ We earn more than our spouse or partner, and it bothers us

_____ We earn more than our spouse or partner, and it bothers him or her

_____ Spouse or partner earns more than us, and it bothers us

_____ Spouse or partner earns more than us, and it bothers him or her

_____ Friends envious of us

_____ We're envious of friends

_____ Spouse or romantic partner envious of us

_____ We're envious of spouse or romantic partner

_____ Child envious of us

_____ We're envious of our child

_____ Someone is behaving jealously with us

_____ We're behaving jealously with someone else

_____ We owe someone money and we're delaying paying it back (business)

_____ We owe someone money and we're delaying paying it back (friend)

_____ Friend owes us money and isn't paying us back on time

_____ Business or institution owes us money and isn't timely in paying us or is cheating us

_____ Being overcharged with no recourse (including interest rates)

_____ Overcharging someone and not giving him or her recourse

_____ Betrayal by someone we love

_____ Betraying someone we love

_____ Publicly embarrassed, humiliated, or shamed (us)

_____ Publicly embarrassed, humiliated, or shamed (someone we love)

_____ Desire romantic relationship but cannot find acceptable partner

_____ Loss of ability to participate in hobby or sport we enjoyed

_____ Loss of credit for work we actually did; someone else took credit for it

_____ We took credit for work but didn't do it

_____ Feeling trapped or overextended with volunteer activities (us)

_____ Feeling trapped or overextended with volunteer activities (someone we love)

_____ Deprived of contact with nature

_____ Deprived of sunshine

_____ Deprived of favorite foods or other substances (sugar, fried foods, tobacco, chewing snuff, etc.) due to diet, health, or lifestyle restrictions

_____ Sexual orientation not what we expected (us)

_____ Sexual orientation not what we expected (someone we love)

_____ Gender-identity issues (us)

_____ Gender-identity issues (someone we love)

_____ Sex change (us)

_____ Sex change (someone we love)

_____ Move into nursing home or special care facility (us)

_____ Move into nursing home or special care facility (someone we love)

_____ Deprived of social life

_____ Loss of political freedom or political expression

_____ Deprived of freedom of religious expression

_____ Loss of transportation

_____ Loss of ability to drive (age, physical, or legal restriction)

_____ Loss of ability to fly airplane, operate motorcycle, etc.

_____ Inadequate provisions for elderly years (us)

_____ Inadequate provisions for elderly years (someone we love)

_____ Confined to bed or housebound

_____ Need wheelchair or walker for mobility

_____ Need prosthesis for functioning

_____ Loss of teeth (permanent teeth)

_____ Loss of memory, mental acuity, and sharpness

_____ Loss of freedom for any reason

_____ Living alone (when used to living with people)

_____ Living with people (when used to living alone)

_____ Unwanted or extra house guests (spouse's family, etc.)

_____ Undesired family responsibilities (taking care of spouse's family, etc.)

_____ Loss of important person, such as hairdresser, doctor, therapist, minister, business associate, or employee

_____ Loss of favorite or important place, such as park, restaurant, theater, church, or business due to closure, moving, or circumstance

_____ Alternative lifestyle

_____ Expatriate

_____ Other:

Passages:

_____ Transition from infancy and childhood to attending school

_____ Change in schools

_____ Graduation from school and entering workforce

_____ Transition from childhood to adulthood

_____ Marriage

_____ Having children

_____ Maturing (age twenty-eight through thirty-two)

_____ Facing mortality

_____ Role reversal—we're taking care of our parents

_____ Changes in technology, industry, and jobs/workforce

_____ Fashion trend changes

_____ Menopause

_____ Empty nest

_____ Middle age

_____ Old age

_____ Retirement

_____ Death

_____ Cultural changes and cultural evolution that cause us to feel displaced

_____ Awakening or change in consciousness

Bibliography

Books

Ackerman, Diane. *A Slender Thread: Rediscovering Hope at the Heart of Crisis.* New York: Random House, 1997.

Acosta, Judith, and Judith Simon Prager. *The Worst Is Over: What to Say When Every Moment Counts; Verbal First Aid to Calm, Relieve Pain, Promote Healing and Save Lives.* San Diego: Jodere Group, 2002.

Akner, Lois F., with Catherine Whitney. *How to Survive the Loss of a Parent: A Guide for Adults.* New York: William Morrow, 1993.

Alcoholics Anonymous: The Big Book. 4th ed. New York: Alcoholics Anonymous World Services, 2001.

Anderson, George, and Andrew Barone. *Lessons from the Light: Extraordinary Messages of Comfort and Hope from the Other Side.* New York: Penguin Putnam, 1999.

———. *Walking in the Garden of Souls.* New York: Penguin Putnam, 2001.

Apollon, Susan Barbara. *Touched by the Extraordinary.* Yardley, PA: Matters of the Soul, 2005.

Appleton, William S. *The New Antidepressants and Antianxieties: What You Need to Know about Zoloft, Paxil, Wellbutrin, Effexor, Clonazepam, Ambien, and More.* New York: Plume, 1997.

Beattie, Melody. *Codependent No More: How to Stop Controlling Others and Start Caring for Yourself.* Center City, MN: Hazelden, 1987.

———. *Journey to the Heart.* San Francisco: HarperSanFrancisco, 1996.

———. *The Language of Letting Go.* Center City, MN: Hazelden, 1990.

———. *The Lessons of Love: Rediscovering Our Passion for Life When It All Seems Too Hard to Take.* San Francisco: HarperSanFrancisco, 1994.

Bernstein, Judith R. *When the Bough Breaks: Forever After the Death of a Son or Daughter.* Kansas City: Andrews McMeel, 1997.

Bloomfield, Harold H., Melba Colgrove, and Peter McWilliams. *How to Survive the Loss of a Love.* Allen Park, MI: Prelude Press, 1976.

Boss, Pauline. *Ambiguous Loss: Learning to Live with Unresolved Grief.* Cambridge, MA: Harvard University Press, 1999.

Breggin, Peter R., and Ginger Ross Breggin. *Talking Back to Prozac: What Doctors Aren't Telling You about Today's Most Controversial Drug.* New York: St. Martin's Press, 1994.

Breggin, Peter R., and David Cohen. *Your Drug May Be Your Problem: How and Why to Stop Taking Psychiatric Medications.* Cambridge, MA: Perseus Books, 1999.

Browne, Sylvia, and Nancy Dufresne. *A Journal of Love and Healing: Transcending Grief.* Carlsbad, CA: Hay House, 2001.

Caine, Lynn. *A Compassionate, Practical Guide to Being a Widow.* New York: Penguin Putnam, 1988.

Chodron, Pema. *The Places That Scare You: A Guide to Fearlessness in Difficult Times.* Boston: Shambhala, 2002.

Cockell, Jenny. *Across Time and Death: A Mother's Search for Her Past Life Children.* New York: Simon & Schuster, 1993.

Cooney, Denise. *A Plea from the Angels: Messages from Michael the Archangel.* Banbury, UK: Amethyst Books, 1996.

Copeland, Mary Ellen, and Maxine Harris. *Healing the Trauma of Abuse: A Women's Workbook.* Oakland, CA: New Harbinger, 2000.

The Dalai Lama and Victor Chan. *The Wisdom of Forgiveness: Intimate Conversations and Journeys.* New York: Penguin, 2004.

The Dalai Lama and Howard C. Cutler. *The Art of Happiness: A Handbook for Living.* New York: Penguin Putnam, 1998.

Das, Lama Surya. *Letting Go of the Person You Used to Be: Lessons on Change, Loss, and Spiritual Transformation.* New York: Broadway Books, 2003.

Day, Laura. *The Circle: How the Power of a Single Wish Can Change Your Life.* New York: Tarcher/Putnam, 2001.

Didion, Joan. *The Year of Magical Thinking.* New York: Knopf, 2005.

Donnelly, Katherine Fair. *Recovering from the Loss of a Child: Words of Comfort and Hope from Parents Who Have Survived Their Grief.* New York: Berkley Books, 1982.

Dunn, Paul H., and Richard M. Eyre. *The Birth That We Call Death.* Salt Lake City: Bookcraft, 1976.

Dunne, Edward J., John L. McIntosh, and Karen Dunne-Maxim, eds. *Suicide and Its Aftermath: Understanding and Counseling the Survivors.* New York: W. W. Norton, 1987.

Eicher, Peter. *Visions of Mary.* New York: Avon, 1996.

Eisenberg, Ronald L. *The JPS Guide to Jewish Traditions.* Philadelphia: Jewish Publications Society, 2004.

Epstein, Mark. *Thoughts Without a Thinker: Psychotherapy from a Buddhist Perspective.* New York: Basic Books, 1995.

Fine, Carla. *No Time to Say Goodbye: Surviving the Suicide of a Loved One.* New York: Broadway Books, 1997.

Fitzgerald, Helen. *The Grieving Child: A Parent's Guide.* New York: Simon & Schuster, 1992.

Fox, Emmet. *The Sermon on the Mount: The Key to Success in Life.* San Francisco: HarperSanFrancisco, 1934.

Fox, Matthew. *A Spirituality Named Compassion: Uniting Mystical Awareness with Social Justice.* San Francisco: HarperSanFrancisco, 1999.

Frankl, Viktor E. *Man's Search for Meaning: An Introduction to Logotherapy.* New York: Simon & Schuster, 1959.

———. *The Will to Meaning: Foundations and Applications of Logotherapy.* New York: Penguin, 1969.

Freyd, Jennifer J. *Betrayal Trauma: The Logic of Forgetting Childhood Abuse.* Cambridge, MA: Harvard University Press, 1996.

Furman, Joan, and David McNabb. *The Dying Time: Practical Wisdom for the Dying and Their Caregivers.* New York: Bell Tower, 1997.

Gawain, Shakti, with Laurel King. *Living in the Light: A Guide to Personal and Planetary Transformation.* Mill Valley, CA: Nataraj Publishing, 1986.

Gibran, Kahlil. *The Prophet.* New York: Knopf, 1923.

Giddens, Sandra, and Owen Giddens. *Coping with Grieving and Loss.* New York: Rosen Publishing Group, 2000.

Glenmullen, Joseph. *Prozac Backlash: Overcoming the Dangers of Prozac, Zoloft, Paxil, and Other Antidepressants with Safe, Effective Alternatives.* New York: Simon & Schuster, 2000.

Godman, David, ed. *Be As You Are: The Teachings of Sri Ramana Maharshi.* London: Penguin, 1985.

Goodman, Sandy. *Love Never Dies: A Mother's Journey from Loss to Love.* San Diego: Jodere Group, 2001.

Grollman, Earl A. *Living When a Loved One Has Died.* Boston: Beacon Press, 1977.

Haddock, Deborah Bray. *The Dissociative Identity Disorder Sourcebook.* Chicago: McGraw-Hill, 2001.

Haich, Elisabeth. *Initiation.* Redway, CA: Seed Center, 1965.

Hanh, Thich Nhat. *The Heart of the Buddha's Teaching: Transforming Suffering into Peace, Joy, and Liberation; The Four Noble Truths, The Noble Eightfold Path, and Other Basic Buddhist Teachings.* Berkeley: Parallax, 1998.

Harris, Maxine. *The Loss That Is Forever: The Lifelong Impact of the Early Death of a Mother or Father.* New York: Penguin, 1995.

Heindel, Max. *Ancient and Modern Initiation.* Oceanside, CA: The Rosicrucian Fellowship, 1931.

Heinemann, Faith M. *A Different Reality: An Alzheimer's Love Story.* Edited by Robert Estell. Malibu, CA: Faith Heinemann, 1999.

Herman, Judith. *Trauma and Recovery: The Aftermath of Violence—from Domestic Abuse to Political Terror.* New York: Basic Books, 1992.

Hill, Napoleon. *Think and Grow Rich,* rev. ed. New York: Random House, 1960.

Hoff, Benjamin. *The Tao of Pooh.* New York: Penguin, 1982.

James, John W., and Russell Friedman. *The Grief Recovery Handbook: The Action Program for Moving Beyond Death, Divorce, and Other Losses.* New York: HarperPerennial, 1998.

Katafiasz, Karen. *Grief Therapy.* St. Meinrad, IN: Abbey Press, 1993.

Kennedy, Alexandra. *Losing a Parent: Passage to a New Way of Living.* San Francisco: HarperSanFrancisco, 1991.

Kornfield, Jack. *The Art of Forgiveness, Lovingkindness, and Peace.* New York: Bantam, 2002.

Kübler-Ross, Elisabeth. *Death: The Final Stage of Growth.* New York: Simon & Schuster, 1975.

———. *On Death and Dying.* New York: Simon & Schuster, 1969.

———. *On Life After Death.* Berkeley: Celestial Arts, 1991.

Kübler-Ross, Elisabeth, and David Kessler. *Life Lessons: Two Experts on Death and Dying Teach Us about the Mysteries of Life and Living.* New York: Simon & Schuster, 2000.

Kushner, Harold S. *When Bad Things Happen to Good People.* New York: Avon, 1981.

Levine, Stephen, and Ondrea Levine. *Who Dies? An Investigation of Conscious Living and Conscious Dying.* New York: Anchor, 1982.

Lonely Planet: China. Melbourne: Lonely Planet Publications, 2000.

Luskin, Fred. *Forgive for Good: A Proven Prescription for Health and Happiness.* San Francisco: HarperSanFrancisco, 2002.

Marcus, Eric. *Why Suicide?* San Francisco: HarperSanFrancisco, 1996.

Martin, Joel, and Patricia Romanowski. *Our Children Forever: George Anderson's Messages from Children on the Other Side.* New York: Penguin Putnam, 1994.

———. *We Are Not Forgotten: George Anderson's Messages of Love and Hope from the Other Side.* New York: Penguin Putnam, 1992.

———. *We Don't Die: George Anderson's Conversations with the Other Side.* New York: Penguin Putnam, 1998.

McDonald, John. *The Message of a Master: A Classic Tale of Wealth, Wisdom, and the Secret of Success*. Novato, CA: New World Library, 1929.

Muhaiyaddeen, M. R. Bawa. *To Die Before Death: The Sufi Way of Life*. Philadelphia: Fellowship Press, 1997.

Murphy, James M. *Coping with Teen Suicide*. New York: Rosen Publishing Group, 1999.

Myers, David G. *Intuition: Its Powers and Perils*. New Haven, CT: Yale University Press, 2002.

Osho. *Intuition: Knowing Beyond Logic*. New York: St. Martin's Press, 2001.

Parkinson, Frank. *Post-Trauma Stress: A Personal Guide to Reduce the Long-Term Effects and Hidden Emotional Damage Caused by Violence and Disaster*. Cambridge, MA: Perseus Books, 1993.

Parnell, Laurel. *Transforming Trauma: EMDR®; The Revolutionary New Therapy for Freeing the Mind, Clearing the Body, and Opening the Heart*. New York: W. W. Norton, 1997.

Pelzer, Dave. *A Child Called "It": One Child's Courage to Survive*. Deerfield Beach, FL: Health Communications, 1995.

Prend, Ashley Davis. *Transcending Loss: Understanding the Lifelong Impact of Grief and How to Make It Meaningful*. New York: Berkley Books, 1997.

Rando, Therese A. *How to Go On Living When Someone You Love Dies*. New York: Bantam Books, 1988.

Reeve, Christopher. *Nothing Is Impossible: Reflections on a New Life*. New York: Ballantine Books, 2002.

———. *Still Me*. New York: Random House, 1998.

Rhodes, Leon. *Tunnel to Eternity: Beyond Near-Death*. West Chester, PA: Chrysalis Books, 1997.

Rich, Phil. *The Healing Journey through Grief: Your Journal for Reflection and Recovery*. New York: John Wiley & Sons, 1999.

Rinpoche, Sogyal. *The Tibetan Book of Living and Dying*. Edited by Patrick Gaffney and Andrew Harvey. San Francisco: HarperSanFrancisco, 1993.

Rosof, Barbara D. *The Worst Loss: How Families Heal from the Death of a Child.* New York: Henry Holt, 1994.

Rufus, Anneli. *The Farewell Chronicles: How We Really Respond to Death.* New York: Marlowe & Company, 2005.

Rutledge, Thom. *The Self-Forgiveness Handbook: A Practical and Empowering Guide.* Oakland, CA: New Harbinger, 1997.

Schiff, Harriet Sarnoff. *The Bereaved Parent.* New York: Penguin, 1977.

———. *Living Through Mourning, Finding Comfort and Hope When a Loved One Has Died.* New York: Penguin, 1986.

Schiraldi, Glenn R., and Melissa Hallmark Kerr. *The Anger Management Sourcebook.* Chicago: McGraw-Hill, 2002.

Schreiber, Flora Rheta. *Sybil.* New York: Warner Books, 1973.

Seligman, Martin E. P. *Authentic Happiness: Using the New Positive Psychology to Realize Your Potential for Lasting Fulfillment.* New York: Simon & Schuster, 2002.

Sheehy, Gail. *New Passages: Mapping Your Life Across Time.* New York: Random House, 1995.

Tavris, Carol. *Anger: The Misunderstood Emotion.* New York: Simon & Schuster, 1982.

Teresa, of Avila, Saint. *The Life of Teresa of Jesus: The Autobiography of Teresa of Avila.* New York: Doubleday, 1944.

The Tibetan Book of the Dead. Translated by Robert A. F. Thurman. New York: Bantam, 1994.

Tolle, Eckhart. *The Power of Now: A Guide to Spiritual Enlightenment.* Novato, CA: Namaste Publishing and New World Library, 1999.

Ueshiba, Morihei. *The Art of Peace.* Translated and edited by John Stevens. Boston: Shambhala, 2002.

Van Praagh, James. *Talking to Heaven: A Medium's Message of Life After Death.* New York: Penguin, 1997.

Wiitala, Geri Colozzi. *Heather's Return: The Amazing Story of a Child's Communications from Beyond the Grave.* Virginia Beach, VA: A.R.E. Press, 1996.

Wilkinson, Bruce, with David Kopp. *The Prayer of Jabez Devotional: Thirty-One Days to Experiencing More of the Blessed Life.* Sisters, OR: Multnomah Publishers, 2001.

Williams, Margery. *The Velveteen Rabbit.* New York: Doubleday Dell, 1922.

Wolfson, Ron. *A Time to Mourn, a Time to Comfort: A Guide to Jewish Bereavement.* Woodstock, VT: Jewish Lights Publishing, 1993.

Wright, Lloyd. *Hepatitis C Free: Alternative Medicine vs. the Drug Industry; The People Speak.* Malibu, CA: Lloyd Wright, 2002.

———.*Triumph Over Hepatitis C: An Alternative Medicine Solution.* Malibu, CA: Lloyd Wright, 2001.

Wright, Machaelle Small. *Behaving as if the God in All Life Mattered,* 3rd ed. Warrenton, VA: Perelandra, 1997.

Yogananda, Paramahansa. *Where There Is Light: Insight and Inspiration for Meeting Life's Challenges.* Los Angeles: Self Realization Fellowship, 1988.

Individuals

Egleston, Scott (original guru story)

Koukkari, Sharon, M.S.L.P.

New, Marcie

Quick, Bradley, The Cool Change Foundation, Inc., www.BradleyQuick.com

Ray, Sonja (ancestral forgiveness work)

Wills, Howard (forgiveness prayer), www.howardwills.org

Studies

Carter, Michael. "No Sexual Transmission of HCV Seen in Repeat HIV Testers in San Francisco." January 14, 2004.

Department of Health and Human Services, Centers for Disease Control and Prevention.

Hammer, G. P., et al. "Low Incidence and Prevalence of Hepatitis C Virus Infection among Sexually Active Non-intravenous Drug-Using Adults." *Sexually Transmitted Diseases* 30 (2004): 919–924.

Mayo Clinic. "Milk Thistle (Silybum marianum)." Evidence-based monograph prepared by Natural Standard Research Collaboration (2006).

U.S. Census Bureau. "The Effects of Government Taxes and Transfers on Income and Poverty." (2004). Robert Bernstein, Public Information Office.

Vandelli, Carmen, et al. "Lack of Evidence of Sexual Transmission of Hepatitis C among Monogamous Couples: Results of a 10-Year Prospective Follow-Up Study." *American Journal of Gastroenterology* 99 (6): 855–859.

Newspaper Articles

Brody, Jane E. "Personal Health: Let's Get Serious About Relieving Chronic Pain." *New York Times,* January 10, 2006.

Brown, Patricia Leigh. "Growing Old Together, in New Kind of Commune." *New York Times,* February 27, 2006.

Butler, Katy. "Beyond Rivalry, a Hidden World of Sibling Violence." *New York Times,* February 28, 2006.

"Disc Patient Becomes Advocate." Excerpted from *OrthoKnow* (June 2004), ©2004 by Knowledge Enterprises, Inc.

Gross, Jane. "Aging at Home: For a Lucky Few, a Wish Come True." *New York Times,* February 9, 2006.

Harris, Gardiner. "Medical Marketing—Treatment by Incentive: As Doctor Writes Prescription, Drug Company Writes a Check." *New York Times,* June 27, 2004.

La Franiere, Sharon. "Nightmare for African Women: Birthing Injury and Little Help." *New York Times,* September 28, 2005.

Leonhardt, David. "Why Doctors So Often Get It Wrong." *New York Times,* February 22, 2006.

McGeehan, Patrick, et al. "The Plastic Trap: Soaring Interest Compounds Credit Card Pain for Millions." *New York Times,* November 21, 2004.

Moss, Michael. "Erase Debt Now (Lose Your House Later)." *New York Times,* October 10, 2004.

Null, Gary, Carolyn Dean, Martin Feldman, Debora Rasio, and
 Dorothy Smith. "The American Medical System Is the
 Leading Cause of Death and Injury in the United States."
 www.ourcivilisation.com/medicine/usamed.

O'Connor, Anahad. "Sick of Work: Cracking Under the Pressure? It's
 Just the Opposite, for Some." *New York Times,* September 10,
 2004.

Potyk, Darryl. "Treatments for Alzheimer Disease." *Southern Medical
 Journal* 98, no. 6: 628–635.

"Raining Money." Editorial. *New York Times,* January 4, 2004.

Spiegel, Alix. "More and More, Favored Psychotherapy Lets Bygones
 be Bygones." *New York Times,* February 14, 2006.

Movies

Just Ask My Children, directed by Arvin Brown, 2001.

Pulp Fiction, directed and written by Quentin Tarantino, 1994.

About the Author

Melody Beattie is the author of numerous best-selling books, including *Codependent No More* and *The Language of Letting Go*. Readers may visit her Web site at www.melodybeattie.com. She lives in Malibu, California.

Other titles by Melody Beattie that may interest you:

Codependent No More
How to Stop Controlling Others and Start Caring for Yourself
Is someone else's problem your problem? If so, you may be codependent—
and you may find yourself in this book. This modern classic holds the key to
understanding codependency and charts a path to a lifetime of healing, hope,
and happiness. Softcover, 264 pp.
Order No. 5014

The Language of Letting Go
Melody Beattie integrates her own life experiences and fundamental recovery
reflections in this unique daily meditation book, inspiring readers to understand their own recovery process. Softcover, 408 pp.
Order No. 5076

More Language of Letting Go
These daily meditations distill Melody Beattie's compassionate insights on
how best to nurture spiritual and emotional health. She touches on questions
of honesty and surrender, defensiveness and drama addiction, healthy communication and unhealthy tendencies. Softcover, 432 pp.
Order No. 1976

52 Weeks of Conscious Contact
Meditations for Connecting with God, Self, and Others
This week-by-week guidebook will get you thinking about—and acting on—
ways to bring more balance into your life by nurturing inner peace, reaching
out to others, carrying through on good intentions, making time for fun, and
cultivating a deeper prayer life. Softcover, 280 pp.
Order No. 1984

Hazelden books are available at fine bookstores everywhere. To order directly
from Hazelden, call 1-800-328-9000 or visit www.hazelden.org/bookstore.